FOREX TRADING SECRETS

TRADING STRATEGIES FOR THE FOREX MARKET

JAMES DICKS

New York   Chicago   San Francisco   Lisbon   London
Madrid   Mexico City   Milan   New Delhi   San Juan
Seoul   Singapore   Sydney   Toronto

The **McGraw·Hill** Companies

Copyright © 2010 by The McGraw-Hill Companies, Inc. All rights reserved. Printed in the United States of America. Except as permitted under the United States Copyright Act of 1976, no part of this publication may be reproduced or distributed in any form or by any means, or stored in a database or retrieval system, without the prior written permission of the publisher.

1 2 3 4 5 6 7 8 9 0   DOC/DOC   1 0 9 8 7 6 5 4 3 2 1 0

ISBN   978-0-07-166422-6
MHID   0-07-166422-X

This publication is designed to provide accurate and authoritative information in regard to the subject matter covered. It is sold with the understanding that neither the author nor the publisher is engaged in rendering legal, accounting, or other professional service. If legal advice or other expert assistance is required, the services of a competent professional person should be sought.

—*From a Declaration of Principles jointly adopted by a Committee of the American Bar Association and a Committee of Publishers.*

McGraw-Hill books are available at special quantity discounts to use as premiums and sales promotions, or for use in corporate training programs. To contact a representative please e-mail us at bulksales@mcgraw-hill.com.

To be successful you have to have a mentor. Someone who can inspire you, someone that will listen to you, someone that will give you sound advice whether you want to hear it or not. If you don't have a mentor, that someone to help you get to the top, then keep looking. For me it's My Uncle Jack. I know there were many times that he felt I was not listening but I always was. Thanks for everything you do, this book is dedicated you.

Contents

Preface   xi

Acknowledgments   xiii

Disclaimer   xv

Introduction   xvii

Part 1   The Basics   1

1   What You Must Know to Get Started   3
     Back to the Basics: A History of the FOREX   3
     FOREX versus Stocks   7
     FOREX versus Futures   9

2   Major Currencies and Pairs   11
     The U.S. Dollar   11
     The Euro   12
     The Australian Dollar   12
     The Canadian Dollar   13
     The British Pound   13
     The Swiss Franc   14
     The Japanese Yen   14
     The New Zealand Dollar   15
     The Dollar Index   15
     The Dow Jones Industrial Average (DJIA)   16
     Gold CFDs   16
     Crude Oil   17
     Cross-Rate Currency Pairs   17
     Exotic Currency Pairs   18
     Chinese Yuan or Renminbi   18
     Swedish Krona   18
     Norwegian Krone   19
     The Iraqi Dinar   19

3 Anyone Can Learn the FOREX   21
FOREX 101   21
Opening a Position   21
Trading on Margin   23
Managing a Position   23
Closing a Position   24
Pips and Lots   24
The Lot   27
Order Types   27
Where Is the Market Going?   29
Stops and Targets   32
Spreads and Swaps   33
Technical versus Fundamental   34

4 Preparing Yourself Adequately before Jumping
    into the Market   37
FOREX Trading Accounts   37
Choosing a Broker   38
Tools   47
Who Trades the FOREX?   49
What Kind of Trader Am I?   50
Trading Techniques   51
The Trader's Levels of Ascension   55

Part 2   Money Management   59

5 The Secret to Making Money   61
Are You Really Fit to Trade in the FOREX Market?   61
Trading Plans   62
Rules and Discipline   67
How the Market Works   73
Rules for Working with the Market   74
Paper Trading   77

6 How to Keep Your Profits   81
Money Management   81
Managing Risk   86
Leverage and True Leverage   87
Overtrading and Overconfidence   89
Overleveraging   91
Trade Expectations   92

Part 3   Trading Psychology   93

7   Mastering Emotions   95
Trading Psychology   95
Emotions of Trading   99
How to Get Out of a Bad Trade   105
Become a Pro   110

8   Mind over Matter for Huge Profits   113
Affirmations   113
Power of Networking   117

Part 4   Fundamental Analysis   121

9   Economics   123
What Does Economic Release Mean?   123
Fundamental Analysis   123
Dow Theory   125
Fundamental Indicators   127
Japan's Monetary Policy   137
FOREX Currency Carry Trade   139
Interventions   140
Gross Domestic Product (GDP)   142
Trading the News   143
What Are Contrarian Indicators?   145

Part 5   Technical Analysis   147

10   Technical Indicators   149
Technical Analysis   149
Types of Charts Showing Price Action   150
Trend Indicators   162
Market and Volatility Indicators   168
Understanding Oscillators   173
A Unique Indicator: Ichimoku Kinko Hyo   176
Divergences   177

11   Technical Patterns   181
Candlesticks   181
Chartism Patterns   185
Reversal Patterns   186
Continuation Patterns   192

Elliott Waves   203
Harmonic Price Patterns   208
Fractals   214
Trading Naked (Only Price Action)   215

12   Support and Resistance   217
Support   217
Resistance   218
Trendlines   219
Moving Averages   219
Other Indicators   220
Entering Positions   221
Exiting Positions   222
Pivot Points: Do They Work?   222
Psychological Levels   226
Using Multiple Time Frames   228
Trend Is Your Friend   231

13   Automated Trading   233
Expert Advisors and Automatic Programming
    Interfaces (APIs)   233
Advanced Robots: Neural Networks in the FOREX   235

Part 6   Building Your Portfolio   239

14   Secrets to FOREX Diversification   241
FOREX Options   241
Spot FOREX Options   246
FOREX Futures   247
FOREX Exchange-Traded Funds (ETFs)   248
Contracts for Difference (CFDs)   249
Commodities   250
Indices (Securities)   251

15   My Favorite Ways to Trade   253
Breakouts   253
Channeling   258
Hedging   261
Basic Oscillator-Based Strategy   262
Basic Moving-Average Crosses   263
Trading Gaps   264
Daily High-Low   265

CONCLUSION   269
APPENDIX   273
GLOSSARY   289
BIBLIOGRAPHY   299
INDEX   301

Preface

There are many books on the market that cover the subject of FOREX trading. But I believe that until now, there has never been a book on this unique topic that has so vividly described the subject of the FOREX—a universe completely of its own. The FOREX market is an anonymous entity that bears many faces, and each individual who participates in it leaves a footprint that just might change the course of their personal circumstances based on their individual hopes and dreams for success.

This book was written with several purposes in mind. First of all, this book is designed to inform and educate the potential FOREX trader about a field that is growing exponentially around the world and is reaching millions of individuals from all walks of life. It is a market that was reserved for a select few just a decade ago but now is in the hands of anyone, even those without a formal financial education. For this reason, it is very important to include a qualified point of view from a real trader's perspective, a trader who has already traveled through all the steps and experienced numerous pitfalls but now wants to share this information with you to help you avoid or, at the very least, minimize any potential negative impact through education and solid money management techniques.

This book also is intended to provide an overview of all the fundamentals involved in the FOREX and of the trading process so that any new trader can easily obtain all the tools needed to ensure a quick start. It is also aimed at the intermediate trader who has already started the process but could use some guidance and additional tools, with an emphasis on the importance of a solid money management program and the right mind-set to develop a successful trading career.

Written from the insider's perspective of an experienced FOREX trader who has gone through every step until reaching a stable and consistent success, this book is focused on pointing out the potential hazards that every trader will encounter at some point. In the beginning, it will offer solutions to help you understand how to mitigate many of the risks involved by centering on dedicated attention to the preliminary preparation, education, and training needed to become a true professional in this field.

The overview includes a history of the FOREX and its basics, as well as a thorough description of all the fundamental, technical, and psychological aspects and how they merge and interact in the market's behavior.

Finally, some of the preferred trading systems are described in detail and discussed as additional elements to help you practice and build your trading toolbox.

I hope that you will enjoy this book and its concepts. May it bring you a step closer to becoming a consistent winner and an educated and confident FOREX trader.

Acknowledgments

As you so often read on the acknowledgments page, the author takes a few brief lines to say thanks. A page of appreciation is in nearly every book and this one is no different; primarily because a project like this is just impossible to successfully complete without the combined effort of an entire team. For me I must give thanks first.

I can do everything through Him who gives me strength. — Philippians 4:13

We cannot do it on our own. It is the strength that comes through Jesus Christ that allows us to master the difficult situations of life and to succeed where all human wisdom sees only failure.

I was reading through my first book's acknowledgments (*FOREX Made Easy: Six Ways to Trade the Dollar*) and noticed that some of my same team is still with me and assisted on this project, so thanks to all. I also noticed that my family is now even bigger; I would not have been able to complete this book if it were not for my absolute significant other, my beautiful wife of more than 10 years. Thanks, Deb, for all the trust and confidence you gave me each and every day. In my last book, I was able to get my son James' name in the book, so I better add my daughter Jacqueline to this one; I love you both dearly.

I, of course, will simply not be able to thank everyone individually for their help, but for the handful of constant contributors I will try.

When working to get a book such as this completed it takes lots of reading by lots of people. Jack Lott has been there every step of the way. Thanks Jack for being such a great friend and team member. I know you have read through this book a few hundred times and everyone reading it will appreciate your effort, as I do. I am already looking forward to the next project. Michael Thomas has done his fair share of reading of this book and his specific attention to the FOREX strategies will have the reader's appreciation and understanding. Thanks for all your help and friendship. I would like to give a special thanks to Caroline for her help in getting this project moving and off the ground.

Finally and certainly not least, thanks to my publisher McGraw-Hill and the entire team for their dedication of getting this book to you.

Disclaimer

The information in this book is for educational purposes only. I am not giving advice or specific financial recommendations. You must seek guidance from your personal advisors before acting on this information. Trading can result in losses. I accept no responsibility for any losses you may incur. *Do not invest more than you can afford to lose.*

NFA- AND CFTC-REQUIRED DISCLAIMERS

Trading in the Foreign Exchange (FOREX) market is a challenging opportunity where above-average returns are available for educated and experienced investors who are willing to take above-average risk. However, before deciding to participate in FOREX trading, you should carefully consider your investment objectives, level of experience, and risk appetite. *Do not invest money you cannot afford to lose.*

FOREX futures and options trading have large potential rewards but also large potential risk. You must be aware of the individual risks and be willing to accept them to invest in FOREX futures and options markets. *Don't trade with money you can't afford to lose.* This book is neither a solicitation nor an offer to buy/sell FOREX futures or options. No representation is being made that any account will or is likely to achieve profits or losses similar to those discussed in this book. The past performance of any trading system or methodology is not necessarily indicative of future results.

There is considerable exposure to risk in any foreign exchange transaction. Any transaction involving currencies involves risks, including, but not limited to, the potential for changing political and/or economic conditions that may substantially affect the price or liquidity of a currency.

Moreover, the leveraged nature of foreign exchange trading means that any market movement will have an equally proportional effect on your deposited funds. This may work against you as well as for you. The possibility exists that you could sustain a total loss of your initial margin funds and be required to deposit additional funds to maintain your position. If you fail to meet any margin call within the time prescribed, your position will be liquidated, and you will be responsible for any resulting losses. Investors may lower their exposure to risk by employing risk-reducing strategies such as stop-loss and limit orders.

CFTC RULE 4.41

Hypothetical or simulated performance results have certain limitations. Unlike an actual performance record, simulated results do not represent actual trading. Also, since the trades have not been executed, the results may have under- or overcompensated for the impact, if any, of certain market factors, such as lack of liquidity. Simulated trading programs in general are also subject to the fact that they are designed with the benefit of hindsight. No representation is being made that any account will or is likely to achieve profit or losses similar to those shown.

Introduction

What is FOREX? FOREX (also known as FX) is the contracted name of FOReign EXchange, an international trading market where banks, businesses, and public and private investors of all the countries in the world can obtain and exchange their respective currencies so as to perform commercial transactions or simply speculate. This market functions in a different way from the stock market; the stock exchange has a fixed daily schedule for opening and closing, whereas the FOREX is open 24 hours a day, five days a week nonstop. FOREX activities start on Sunday afternoon at 5 p.m. Eastern Time (ET) and close on Friday at 4 p.m. ET. This continuous activity is possible because there are always open markets around the world, and today there is no need for the traders to be physically present at the exchange location because the funds can be traded electronically from any country.

The main markets involved in the FOREX are New Zealand, Sydney, Tokyo, China, Frankfurt, London, Zurich, and New York. The FOREX market is the largest in the world, where more than \$3.2 trillion is being transacted every day (traditional daily turnover was reported to be over US \$3.2 trillion in April 2007 by the Bank for International Settlements. *Source:* Triennial Central Bank Survey, BIS, December 2007), which is many times larger than the combined volume of all U.S. equities and futures markets, and thus the FOREX is also the market that possesses the greatest liquidity. Late in 2008, with all the uncertainty in the equities markets, the FOREX daily turnover surpassed US \$6.5 trillion in a day. This market will continue to attract more and more investors.

Currency trading used to be an exclusive activity reserved to government central banks and commercial and investment banks. In recent years, the market has opened up and become available to smaller investors and speculators, thanks to computers and the Internet.

There is a broad electronic network that allows central banks from all over the world to share their quotes and actual currency rates. This is known as the *Interbank*. In this way, central banks are able to exchange and convert their currencies one into another in real time. The currencies that are traded most commonly are the U.S. dollar, the Japanese yen, the euro, the British pound, the Swiss franc, the Canadian dollar, and the Australian dollar. The Interbank's activity being continuous, and thanks to decentralization from any physical location or exchange, access to real quotes and the speed at which transactions can be performed are greatly increased.

When you are transacting on the FOREX market, you are simultaneously buying one currency and selling another. Currencies are always traded in pairs, for example, pound sterling/U.S. dollar (GBP/USD) or U.S. dollar/Canadian dollar (USD/CAD).

You would be executing a trade when there is an expectation that the currency you are buying increases in respect to the one you are selling. If the value of the currency you have bought effectively increases, you then would sell the position and take a profit. Currency pairs are composed of a *base currency,* which is the first on the quote, and a *counter currency* (also called the *quote* or *payment currency*), which appears as second on the quote. When the U.S. dollar is the base currency, quotes are given in $1 USD per counter currency, for example USD/CAD or USD/JPY.

The role of the FOREX in the world economy is very important because there is always an increasing need of currency exchange owing to the development of technology, communications, and general international commerce. Countries need the FOREX market to be able to sell their products to other countries and receive payment in their own currency or pay for their imported goods to the foreign producer in its own currency.

In addition to commercial turnover, though, plenty of money is used for speculation, and thus the great liquidity of the FOREX allows traders to profit at any moment, provided they are using the right techniques and strategies.

Over the last few years, the FOREX market has gained significant ground in the U.S. retail marketplace. Through my many Web sites, such as the James Dicks FOREX Network (*www.JamesDicks.com*), educational tools and services, I have introduced millions of individual investors to the retail FOREX marketplace.

The CNBC "Million-Dollar Portfolio Challenge" is well known among retail investors. To see firsthand how exciting, how popular, and how big the FOREX market is getting, just check out the results of the past challenges. The winner and top investors all dominated the challenge, trading the FOREX.

P A R T

1

THE BASICS

1

WHAT YOU MUST KNOW TO GET STARTED

BACK TO THE BASICS: A HISTORY OF THE FOREX

The FOREX (i.e., FOReign EXchange) market is an international market where the money (currency) of every country is sold and bought freely. It was launched in the 1970s at the moment of introduction of free exchange rates, and the price of one currency against another that occurs from supply and demand is determined only by market participants.

There is no external control, and competition is free because all the participants can decide to transact or not. In this respect, the FOREX is a perfect market because it can't be controlled or monopolized by any of its participants. The enormous number of transactions executed day after day in a continuous activity make it the biggest liquid financial market. According to various assessments, money masses in the market constitute up to US $4.5 trillion a day.

This market has seen recent turnover as high as US $6 trillion in a day, and the average most recently has been hovering at around US $3 trillion a day. The exact figure can't be determined because the transactions are not centralized on a single exchange.

Trading is conducted all over the world through telecommunications and electronic networks 24 hours a day, 5 days a week starting from 00:00

Greenwich Mean Time (GMT) on Monday (some starting a little earlier) to 10:00 p.m. GMT on Friday (some closing a little later). There are dealers quoting currencies in every time zone through the main central markets: Frankfurt, London, New York, Tokyo, Hong Kong, Australia, New Zealand, etc.

To get a better understanding of FOREX quotes, you just have to know that one unit of the base currency is equivalent to the exchange rate in the quote currency. For example, if EUR/USD is trading at 1.2762, the price of 1 euro (base currency) in dollars (quote currency) will be 1.2762 dollars.

FOREX trading is conducted through individual contracts. The standard contract size (also called a *lot*) is usually 100,000 units. This means that for every standard contract you acquire, you are controlling 100,000 units of the base currency. For this contract size, each *pip* (the smallest price increment) is worth $10. Many companies offer mini accounts in which you can trade units of 10,000, where the pip value is $1 or even smaller.

In comparison with other markets, trading the FOREX market allows very low margin requirements because of leverage. In FOREX, you don't need to obligatorily buy a currency first in order to sell it later. It is possible to open positions for buying and selling any currency without actually having it at hand: For a standard account size, usually Internet brokers establish a minimum deposit such as $2000 for trading in the FOREX market and grant a leverage of 1:100. That is, opening the position at $100,000, a trader invests $1000 and receives $99,000 as a credit.

For those wishing to get started at a smaller investment size, many brokers offer a mini account. The FOREX mini account offers smaller contract sizes controlling $10,000 units. The usual account minimum to start a mini account is about $250.

With a mini account, you only need $50 as a margin deposit requirement per every $10,000 lot traded. The leverage is usually 200:1 (10,000 ÷ 50 = 200), and in some cases it can rise to 400 or 500:1 (you then would need even less margin to operate). Thus, with $250, you could trade a maximum of 5 minilots; with $500, a maximum of 10; with $1000, a maximum of 20; etc.

This leverage is 50 times greater than for stocks (stock day trading provides a 4:1 intraday leverage for traders who have $25,000 or more in an account by U.S. law). Using a high degree of leverage is not always appropriate because it can be very risky, but it provides the trader with a higher degree of flexibility for the execution of different trading strategies.

Even further, now some brokers are offering a micro account. I personally would not recommend these because the leverage is really high, but a micro account may be a good way to get your feet wet, so to speak, by trading real money before moving on to a more standard size account. Micro accounts require as little as $25 to open and be able to control $1000 units. The pip values, on average, are about $0.10 (10 cents).

You can always go to *www.JamesDicks.com* to see what brokers I use.

The FOREX is able to maintain its objectivity and avoid being controlled or manipulated by one or few of its participants because the volume transacted is so high that if any of them would want to do so, by changing prices at will, they would have to operate with tens of billions of dollars. This is the reason why the FOREX can't be influenced by any single participant, and even though there are situations where a huge transaction can seem to take control of the market for a few moments, the balance is established again almost immediately because of the great liquidity involved. This also allows traders to get a profit by opening and closing positions within a few seconds.

The FOREX market is always moving. You can chose to maintain a position for a very short time or for longer periods, even years; it will depend only on your own trading strategies.

In the FOREX, it is possible to perform speculative activities without the need for a real money supply. This is referred to as *marginal trading.* The amount required as a guarantee for the transaction is low, thus providing an opportunity to open positions with a small account in U.S. dollars (some local brokers also accept some of the main currencies, such as the euro, pound sterling, Japanese yen, etc.) and buy or sell a lot of other different currencies.

Transactions can be conducted very quickly and yield a profit while the exchange rates go up or down. Marginal trading implies operating with borrowed capital, where you need only a small percentage of the total sum of the transaction.

For example, you have analyzed the situation in the market and have come to the conclusion that the euro will go up against the dollar. You open 1 lot for buying the euro (EUR) with a margin of 1 percent (1:100 leverage) at the price of 1.2750 dollars per euro (the margin needed will be $1275) and wait for the exchange rate to go up. Sometime later, you see that your analysis was right. You close the position at 1.2827 and earn 77 pips ($770).

Most currencies have a daily range of fluctuation of about 100 to 150 pips on average, some even more. This gives FOREX traders the opportunity to make money on these changes.

There are several tools that allow the trader to be able to understand and make decisions on the market, grouped basically under *fundamental* or *technical analysis.* There is a constant exchange of political and economic information going on, and it is important to be informed on this because this will have an impact on the overall behavior of the market and will show market reaction as price changes. This is called *fundamental analysis,* an overview on all this information and how it affects a particular country and currency value. Fundamental analysis takes account of rumors, political events, and the local and international economy, such as, for example, the rates of inflation and unemployment, taxes, and interest rates. The political stability of a particular country and unexpected events also have great influence on the fluctuations of that country's currency.

Sometimes, especially in the case of economic forecasts, this information can become a self-fulfilling prophecy in that a certain outcome is expected, so the market reacts *before the fact,* thus starting a movement in prices that can be seen as an early move, and if the forecast is confirmed, the prices suddenly can start going in the opposite direction from the real move because the predicted result has already occurred, and traders are now closing their positions. This can lead to market reactions that seem completely opposite to what the economic releases are implying for the currency, although there are also many details that could be modifying the outcome because all the currencies are moving in unison, and their respective interaction will affect all the others. Thus the fundamental details sometimes can be too big to grasp completely. Only the big banks and financial institutions, which employ professional economic analysts, can have access to a more precise and wide array of information with timely accuracy.

Technical analysis affirms, on the contrary, that all this information is already priced in and that the resulting reactions are visible on charts. It is based essentially on prices, time, and volume: What are the lowest and highest prices that a currency has reached in how much time or during what period, and how many transactions were performed?

Technical analysis also assumes the repetitiveness of the market, which it most probably will perform again in the future as it has already performed in the past. It analyzes past quotes and predicts the prices to come based on statistical and mathematical calculations.

Both technical and fundamental analyses complement each other. A professional trader should consider both sides at any moment because some of the elements of each type of analysis will be present in the other. For example, a fundamental trader will have to consider resistance and supports, and a technical trader must be aware of the news that will have an impact on price changes.

FOREX VERSUS STOCKS

What are the differences between trading in the FOREX and operating in the stock market?

The FOREX market is always open. Like some supermarkets that are open 24 hours, the FOREX is a "supermarket" of currencies, open 24 hours a day, 5 days a week. The FOREX opens in most of the brokers on Sunday at 3 to 5 p.m. Eastern Time (ET) and stays open until Friday at 4 p.m. EST (it must be borne in mind that the opening and closing—Sunday and Friday—may vary from broker to broker). In this way, traders have the ability to operate either in the American, Asian, or European markets, which gives them the advantage of being able to react to certain events or news that is bound to emerge and also gives them the opportunity to decide their schedules.

No commission is charged. Most brokers do not charge additional fees or commissions to buy or sell currencies, whether online or by telephone. This is so because of the use of a fixed spread that is consistent and transparent. The cost of a buy/sell in the FOREX market is much lower than in any other market (e.g., stock, futures, etc.). A side note to this is that because of the competition for narrower spreads and faster executions, some brokers are providing very tight spreads and extremely fast execution with little latency. In order for them to do this, however, they are now starting to charge commissions. The commissions vary, and with a little due diligence, you will be able to find just the right broker.

Orders are executed instantly. In normal market conditions, the execution of orders at a given price is done instantly. The trader places the order at the quoted price, which is being updated in real time. There is no difference between the price shown by the broker and the price at which the purchase order is executed. There are special conditions, though, in which market volatility is such that orders can be delayed or requoted, but under normal conditions, there are no such delays.

There are no restrictions on short selling. Unlike the stock market, the FOREX has no restrictions to open sell positions (short). In the FOREX, there is a chance to buy or sell regardless of whether the market is bullish or bearish. Owing to the fact that in the FOREX there is always someone buying a currency and selling another at the same time, there is no structural bias in the market. A trader can operate both upward and downward in the market.

What, then, is the relationship between the stock market and the FOREX? The stock market serves as a key indicator for the FOREX market. Technology has facilitated the possibility of investing in markets other than the local market/country, no matter their geographic location. Therefore, it has forged a relationship between the stock market and the currency of the country like this: If the stock market is going upward, it increases the investment in dollars, but in a market that is on the downside, investors tend to sell shares of companies in that country, attempting to recover capital and investing in another country.

Here's a table showing the main advantages of the FOREX versus stocks:

Advantage	FOREX	Stocks
24-Hour market	Yes	No
No commissions	Yes*	No
Instant execution	Yes	No
Short selling	Yes	No

*Some exceptions.

There are no intermediaries. Stock markets that tend to be centralized have advantages for the operator. But a problem with this is the need for an intermediary between the stock market and the trader. However, FOREX intermediaries do not exist, and thus the trader may buy or sell in the FOREX market without physical intermediaries that can buy or sell a particular pair at the time that they wish or think is appropriate. In the absence of an intermediary, the trader gets higher profits at lower costs.

The market is not controlled for buys or sells. The stock market is more susceptible to speculation based primarily on rumors of buying or selling by other companies. I can see this when a big company buys another relatively smaller company, and the value of the company's shares increase. But the stock market is also likely to go down when you think that a company has been making profits and that investors tend to take profits by selling the shares.

The analysts and firms are less influenced. The stock market is more influenced by rumors of one company being bought by another. This is why sometimes the firms or analysts can recommend a purchase of a particular share when in fact such share will fall based on rumors of a takeover of one company by another.

In the FOREX market, analysts just base their studies on the market and are not influenced by rumors of purchase. This is a market that generates billions of dollars a day for banks and certainly is necessary for the success of global markets.

Four currencies against thousands of shares. In the FOREX market, there are six major pairs, whereas in the stock market, there are thousands of companies. So analyzing four key pairs is much easier than analyzing thousands of companies. In the FOREX, obviously there are more than a hundred pairs, but those that are the most subject to transactions include only six major pairs.

FOREX VERSUS FUTURES

Is there a significant difference between trading futures and FOREX?

The FOREX operates at a higher volume, thus offering better liquidity. As I have said, the FOREX is the market with more volume, which already operates daily with highs peaking close to US $6 trillion in turn over a day and an average near US $3 trillion a day in turn over. This market can absorb the volume of that daily operation. The futures market, on the other hand, operates with approximately US $30 billion a day. This is nothing compared with US$3 trillion. This is why the futures market has limited liquidity, whereas the FOREX market always has complete liquidity, which tells us that sales or purchases can be settled at any time or stop losses can jump without affecting the market in volatile conditions. It must be said that the FOREX is more than 45 times bigger than all the combined futures markets.

The FOREX is a 24-hour market. This is precisely the major disadvantage of the futures market. The FOREX is a 24-hour nonstop market, but the futures market is open only for 7 hours. Therefore, FOREX traders have the ability to react to news that arises elsewhere, whereas futures traders have to wait for the opening of the daily meeting.

No commissions are involved. In the FOREX, the broker earns money from the spreads that the broker provides. The intermediary is eliminated, and the transactions are being done online through the platform provided by the broker or by telephone. Logically, the broker assumes the spread, which is the difference between the bid and ask prices. In the futures market, on the other hand, a certain commission has to be paid to the broker. Some brokers in the FOREX are starting to charge commissions so that they can provide the tightest spreads possible. It really is a preference, but the bottom line is that the broker will make money somehow. After all, that is why they are in the business.

The price is known, and the execution is instantaneous. In a FOREX transaction, the price that the trader sees at the moment is the price that he or she will get; orders are executed instantaneously under normal market conditions. On the other hand, in the futures market, the order is not executed immediately. Sometimes the price does not reflect the current market price, but the price of the final purchase price will not necessarily be the one at which the trader is buying.

There is a guarantee of limited risk. In the FOREX, traders can limit their risk of losses. The risk is minimized by the platform, which automatically generates a margin call if the margin required exceeds the available capital in your account. Futures losses are always a possibility; a position can be closed with losses, and therefore, you may have a deficit in your account and incur a debt. Keep in mind that there is always a potential to lose money trading. All the futures commission merchants (FCMs) will provide you with disclaimers, which they are required by law to provide. I have been trading in the FOREX for many years, and I have never had or seen a negative account in the spot FOREX owing to a margin call.

The main advantages of the FOREX versus futures include the following:

Advantage	FOREX	Futures
24-Hour market	Yes	No
No commissions	Yes*	No
Instant execution	Yes	No
Leverage to 400:1	Yes	No
Known price	Yes	No
Limited risk	Yes	No

*Some exceptions.

2

MAJOR CURRENCIES
AND PAIRS

THE U.S. DOLLAR

The U.S. dollar (USD) is the base or quote currency with the following FOREX major currency pairs: USD/JPY, USD/CAD, USD/CHF, EUR/USD, GBP/USD, AUD/USD, and NZD/USD. Additionally, the USD is the base currency and is paired with the following currencies: NOK, SEK, SGD, DKK, CNY, MXN, BRL, ZAR, and other exotic currencies depending on each broker's availability.

The USD (also abbreviated $) is the official currency used in the United States of America. It is considered the standard currency unit that is used in commodity markets across the globe (especially gold and crude oil markets). It also is currently the most employed reserve currency in the world. This allows the country to hold trade deficits with other countries without experiencing depreciation.

The volatility of the currency is usually low to medium. The economy of the United States has the strongest influence on the rest of the world, especially in the computer technology, medical, aerospace, and military fields. It is principally market-oriented; thus corporations and private businesses lead in decision making.

THE EURO

The euro (or EUR) is the base or quote currency with the following FOREX major and crossed-rate currency pairs: EUR/USD, EUR/JPY, EUR/GBP, EUR/CHF, EUR/AUD, EUR/CAD, and EUR/NZD. Additionally, the EUR is the base currency and is paired with the following currencies: NOK, SEK, SGD, DKK, CNY, MXN, BRL, ZAR, and other exotic currencies depending on each broker's availability.

The euro is the currency that is actually used in most member countries of the European Union. It was created in 1999 and implemented in 2002 and represents the result of the most important monetary reform on the entire continent. It was designed with the intent of rendering free trade easier between the members of the Euro zone, aiming at the same time for a political integration. The EUR/USD currency pair is nicknamed "fiber," and this is said to come from the fact that the Euro zone comprises the greatest optical fiber network in the world. Its market volatility used to be low, but it has been seen to increase to medium in the recent months.

The European Central Bank (ECB) and the other central banks of every member country manage the currency through the European System of Central Banks (ESCB). The ECB is the only authority that has the power to set monetary policy, whereas the issuing and distribution of notes and coins are done by the other members of the ESCB. All the decisions and procedures among the members of the European Union are based on agreements between its member countries. Adoption of the euro has allowed the Euro zone to become the largest economy in the world. This actually makes it a stronger currency than the U.S. dollar.

THE AUSTRALIAN DOLLAR

The Australian dollar (AUD) is the base or quote currency with the following FOREX major and crossed-rate currency pairs: AUD/USD, AUD/JPY, AUD/CHF, AUD/NZD, EUR/AUD, GBP/AUD, and AUD/CAD. It is also the base currency in some exotic pairs.

The AUD is the official currency of the Commonwealth of Australia. It is also familiarly called the "Aussie," which nickname also extends to the AUD/USD currency pair. It is the sixth most traded currency in the FOREX market and accounts for about 5 percent of worldwide foreign exchange transactions. Its popularity stems from the almost inexistent intervention of Australia's government in the FOREX market, with the add benefit of

Australia's political and economic stability. The volatility it shows in the markets is low.

Australia's economy is based on domestic industrial production (particularly of machinery and transportation equipment) and export of raw materials (mostly from its huge mining activity) and products from its agricultural sector.

THE CANADIAN DOLLAR

The Canadian dollar (CAD) is the base or quote currency with the following FOREX major and crossed-rate currency pairs: USD/CAD, CAD/JPY, CAD/CHF, AUD/CAD, EUR/CAD, GBP/CAD, and NZD/CAD.

The CAD is the official currency of Canada. Coin and bill denominations are similar to those of the U.S. dollar. It is familiarly called the "loonie" because of the image of a loon that appears on one of the faces of the coins, and traders also use this nickname to designate the USD/CAD currency pair. The volatility of the Canadian dollar in the FOREX market is low, although it is heavily related to fluctuations in oil prices.

The economy of Canada is quite similar to that of the United States, being market- and production-oriented, having evolved from a mostly rural economy (before World War II), and now being principally urban and industrial, with the increase in manufacturing, mining, and service sectors. Its principal trading partner is the United States.

THE BRITISH POUND

The British pound sterling (GBP) is the base or quote currency with the following FOREX major and crossed-rate currency pairs: GBP/USD, GBP/JPY, EUR/GBP, GBP/CHF, GBP/AUD, GBP/CAD, and GBP/NZD. Additionally, the GBP is the base currency paired with the following currencies: NOK, SEK, SGD, DKK, CNY, MXN, BRL, ZAR, and other exotic currencies depending on each broker's availability.

The GBP is the official currency used in the United Kingdom (Great Britain). It is one of the world's most widely traded currencies, along with the U.S. dollar, the Japanese yen, the euro, and the Swiss franc. Additionally, it is the currency unit with the highest value among the "majors." The GBP/USD currency pair is familiarly called the "cable" in traders' slang because the rates originally were transmitted via a trans-Atlantic telegraph cable. The market volatility of this currency is low to medium.

The economy of the United Kingdom is one of the largest in the world, with a strong agriculture and mining industry. The services sector represents the main percentage of the gross domestic product, and tourism has been developing strongly in recent years.

THE SWISS FRANC

The Swiss franc (CHF) is the base or quote currency with the following FOREX major and crossed-rate currency pairs: USD/CHF, CHF/JPY, GBP/CHF, EUR/CHF, CAD/CHF, AUD/CHF, and NZD/CHF.

The CHF is the official currency of Switzerland and Liechtenstein. The currency is used by the Central Bank of Switzerland. The letters CHF stand for "Confederatio Helvetica Franc." The USD/CHF currency pair is familiarly referred to as the "Swissie" among FOREX traders. The volatility of the Swiss franc in the FOREX market is usually low to moderate.

The CHF is a fairly stable currency, especially in its relationship to the euro, with which it maintains a strong correlation. This causes the EUR/USD and USD/CHF currency pairs to be the highest negatively correlated pairs, with a factor of more than 90 percent. Thanks to Switzerland's strong political and economic stability, the currency is used mostly as a reserve currency by financial institutions and wealthy private individuals throughout the world.

THE JAPANESE YEN

The Japanese yen (JPY) is the base or quote currency with the following FOREX major and crossed-rate currency pairs: USD/JPY, EUR/JPY, GBP/JPY, CHF/JPY, CAD/JPY, AUD/JPY, and NZD/JPY.

The JPY is the official national currency of Japan. Originally pegged to the USD after World War II, the yen switched to a system of floating exchange rates after 1971. The volatility of the JPY in the FOREX market is usually low to medium.

Japan's economy is predominantly based on its manufacturing industry. The JPY traditionally has been a weak currency because its circulation is limited to domestic business, thus hindering Japan's position with regard to foreign trade. Additionally, the country depends completely on oil imports and exclusively on its export of manufactured goods; this renders the JPY very sensitive to rises in crude oil prices and overall energy costs.

The weakness of the currency has been maintained over the years as a protection for the local manufacturing and export industries; however, the JPY has been experiencing a rising trend that has diverted some foreign investments to other countries, where much lower costs still can be found. The most important index of Japan's economy is the industrial production index, which is strongly correlated with the export index.

THE NEW ZEALAND DOLLAR

The New Zealand dollar (NZD) is the base or quote currency with the following FOREX major and crossed-rate currency pairs: NZD/USD, NZD/JPY, GBP/NZD, EUR/NZD, NZD/CHF, and NZD/CAD.

The NZD is the official currency of New Zealand and some of the islands on the Pacific Ocean. The currency is informally called the "kiwi" because of the image of a kiwi bird that appears on its $1 coin, and the term also designates most particularly the NZD/USD pair. The volatility of the NZD in the FOREX market is low to medium.

Similar to what happened in Australia, the economy of New Zealand has been transformed from an agricultural-based market limited to British concessionaries into a free and industrialized market now competing on the global scene. This has greatly helped the development of technology; however, New Zealand's exports still depend mostly on agricultural products.

THE DOLLAR INDEX

The U.S. Dollar Index (USDX) measures the global value of the USD relative to a basket of foreign currencies (e.g., Euro, Japanese yen, Pound sterling, Canadian dollar, Swedish krona, and Swiss franc) through a geometric progression weighted-average calculation. It was started in March 1973 with a value of 100, when the leading trade nations agreed to freely quote their currencies one against the other. After reaching a peak of 165, the USDX has been trading lower over the recent years, dropping almost to 70 in March 2008. The USDX is listed on the New York Board of Trade, and its value is updated continuously 365 days a year. Its volatility can be compared with that of stock index futures because of its amplitude and variability.

THE DOW JONES INDUSTRIAL AVERAGE (DJIA)

DOW THEORY

In 1884, Charles H. Dow, who was editor of the *Wall Street Journal,* created two averages or sectorial indices for the New York stock market, one called the *Dow Jones Industrial Average* (DJIA, or Index of the Industrial Sector) and the other called the *Dow Jones Transport Average* (DJTA, or Index of the Transportation Sector). In this way, Dow tried to establish an indicator of economic activity, using for it an average of the evolution of certain sectors in the stock market.

Dow thought that a rise in economic activity implied greater industrial production. Thus, when economic activity was increasing, companies would see increased demand for their stocks, and therefore, the quotations for these companies on the indices would rise.

As a result, the other sectors would be affected, and their businesses would benefit and, consequently, the prices of their shares would rise. Based on these indexes, Charles Dow formulated his theory that is today the basis of modern technical analysis and therefore of *chartism* (analytical study based on graphs of the evolution of price for a particular company).

DOW JONES INDEX

The Dow Jones Industrial Average (quoted as DJI on the New York Stock Exchange, also quoted as DJIA and informally named "the Dow") is the second-oldest market index in the United States, after the Dow Jones Transportation Average (DJTA) from the same creator. This index shows how certain stocks have been trading. It was developed to evaluate performance within the most important sectors of the American stock market. It is calculated by computing the stock prices of 30 public American companies that represent the wider range of shares held in the market.

It is possible to invest in the DJI through a series of exchange-traded funds (ETFs) and options tied to those ETFs (see Appendix table "Dow Jones Industrial Average").

GOLD CFDS

Metals, and most particularly gold, are usually traded through the futures market or gold exploration stocks. More recently, introduction into the markets of *contracts for difference* (CFDs) has allowed traders to have easier access to market transactions involving metals. The market quoted by the CFD provider is a two-way market, as with FOREX currency pairs, and thus the provider obtains a profit by means of the spread, charging no commissions on transactions.

A gold CFD is a financial derivative that represents a theoretical order to buy or sell at least 10 ounces of gold, which is the minimum required to open a gold transaction. The margin required is quite low on gold CFDs, usually representing 2 to 3 percent of the value of the transaction. You can take the contract on the spot price or the futures price, with standard contracts providing the equivalent of US $100 per $1 movement in the gold price and mini contracts providing one-tenth that size.

There is also another type of CFD used for gold, called the *binary CFD,* that is based solely on the daily rise or fall in the price of gold, with value taken at the daily close. If gold rises, the binary CFD will close at 100, and if gold falls, it will close at 0 at the end of the day. The investor's profit or loss is determined by the difference between the effective opening and closing prices.

CRUDE OIL

The price of crude oil is influenced directly by OPEC (Organization of the Petroleum Exporting Countries), which is made up of 12 nations whose economies depend on oil export revenues. The fluctuation in prices is related to production quotas that are imposed by this organization. The final prices that consumers pay for oil products are determined by several components: supply and demand, effective production, refinery costs, and taxes on oil, which can vary greatly depending on country.

Crude oil is traded on the market as a commodity through futures and spot markets as well as CFDs.

CROSS-RATE CURRENCY PAIRS

The currency pairs that derive their respective rates from their individual relationships with a third FOREX currency rate are called *crosses* or *cross-rate pairs.* All currency pairs that do not include the U.S. dollar fall into this group: EUR/GBP, EUR/CHF, EUR/AUD, GBP/CHF, CHF/JPY, CAD/JPY, EUR/JPY, and GBP/JPY. They are usually very volatile owing to a lesser liquidity, and this causes the spread between bid and ask prices to be much wider than on most majors, for example, the most liquid pairs, such as EUR/USD and USD/JPY. This can be a disadvantage because it increases the trading risks, but some of them can represent a very interesting option, such as the GBP/JPY pair, precisely because of its high volatility.

EXOTIC CURRENCY PAIRS

Some of the secondary foreign currencies that are yet somehow traded heavily in the FOREX market are the *exotic currency pairs* and a few European but non-euro-based denominations. They are usually traded as quote currency and paired with some of the most prominent majors (e.g., USD, EUR, GBP, and AUD), but they also can become the base currency between each other.

CHINESE YUAN OR RENMINBI

The Chinese yuan (CNY) is the official currency of China. CNY is the official International Organization for Standardizations (ISO) code for the renminbi (RMB), issued by the People's Bank of China. The currency displays a low to medium volatility in the FOREX market. In July 2005, China revalued the yuan (which was pegged to the USD) to allow it to fluctuate versus a basket of currencies and protect it from large swings owing to its ties with the American currency. China's economy has become increasingly market-oriented and open to foreign trade and investments since 1978, which represent a strong element in its overall growth.

SWEDISH KRONA

The Swedish krona (SEK) is the official currency of Sweden. Its volatility is evaluated as medium to high mostly owing to the wide extent of foreign trade, where it constantly depends on the economic status of other currencies. Sweden is a member of the European Union, but it didn't adopt the euro and instead maintains its local currency as official. The country shows a low and stable inflation rate, and its economy is mostly based on exports, especially in the areas of information technology and telecommunications.

NORWEGIAN KRONE

The Norwegian krone (NOK) is the official currency of Norway. The country is one of the largest exporters of oil, and increases in the demand for oil have injected a great deal of money into its economy, making it very dependent on fluctuations in oil prices, however. The volatility of the currency itself is low.

The economy of Norway is more service-oriented, and the country is involved in a great number of offshore activities. It is a small country with a small population, but it is one of the wealthiest countries in Europe.

Other exotic currencies you can find are the Danish krone (DKK) and The Singapore dollar (SGD) with low volatility, the Mexican peso (MXN) and the Brazilian real (BRL) with low to medium volatility, and the South African rand (ZAR) with medium volatility.

THE IRAQI DINAR

Although not yet traded on the FOREX, the Iraqi dinar has been highly promoted as a good investment in recent years since Central Bank of Iraq started issuing a new and stable currency that experienced a great revaluation, rising approximately four times its original value (from about 4000 dinars per dollar as its lower low to 980 dinars per dollar as its highest high, actually trading at around 1200 dinars per dollar). This boom had started a series of wild speculations and the spread of a huge promotion, especially on the Internet, as well as scams associated with that promotion, where unusually higher rates of exchange and thus extraordinary returns were promised in the hope that enough speculators would be attracted, thus making the exchange rate explode much higher as soon as the currency enters the market.

However, the rates for the currency vary over a wide range, and there is a huge difference between the official fixed rate of 1449 dinars for $1 set up by the International Monetary Fund (IMF) for the Central Bank of Iraq and retail quotes from dealers and trading companies, which offer quotes between 1050 and 1350 dinars per $1. Additionally, this is a currency with practically no liquidity, mostly because of the discrepancies in price and the fact that the banks do not trade the dinar openly with the public. In addition, dealers will sell dinars to the market but not always buy back the dinars, so there are few counterparts for transactions, making it difficult for the investors to cash out of the currency.

Finally, the overextended negotiations on the Internet, with inexperienced investors trapped and blinded by the fabulous promotion, allow dealers to mix old dinars, bought at a much cheaper price, and new dinars, thus lowering the value of the original amount purchased, which puts the investor immediately at a loss. Some other dealers offer just a blatant scam, taking the money of the investor and disappearing, never delivering the currency. It is extremely important to be well informed before risking funds into any currency investment, especially when the offers are "too good to be true."

ANYONE CAN LEARN THE FOREX

FOREX 101

You've probably heard or read about bid and ask or bid and offer. What are those? Price quotes for a currency pair are double, one for buying and the other for selling. The difference between the two prices is called the *spread,* which will be discussed later on.

As a side note, the opposite is meant when using the same word in a news release. For example, when there is a considerable number of pending orders awaiting for the price to reach a lower value to buy, it is said that there are many *bids* on the market, but when sellers have pending orders at a certain price higher, it is said that there are many *offers* sitting at that price.

This happens because the *bid* price is actually the end-value price of a *long* position, which is purchased at the *ask* price to allow for the spread to be paid. The same occurs in the inverse situation; the end-value price of a *short* position is the actual *offer* price, and it is purchased at the *bid* price, so the spread is paid at the moment the particular position is closed.

OPENING A POSITION

The reason for trading the FOREX market is to make money and to diversify your current portfolio. You do this through the positions you take by means of buying and selling a different set of currencies. When a currency rises in value after you have bought it at a lower price, you realize a profit when you close the position at a higher price. At the moment you close the working order, you are selling back the base currency and buying its counterpart currency. This operation implies a relationship of relative worth because the value of one of the components of the currency pair will be compared with the value of the other one; thus any currency will only have value as a result of its comparison with another currency of a different country.

The *position,* or *order,* represents the net amount of exposure in a particular currency and in its counterpart currency because they always work in pairs. The position is said to be *flat* when there is no exposure, *long* if more currency has been bought than sold, and *short* if more currency has been sold than bought. When you perform currency trading, you are in fact exchanging one currency for another, expecting that the currency that you buy will see its value rise in comparison with the currency you sell in the operation. In the FOREX market, currencies always trade in pairs. We are constantly and simultaneously buying one currency (the base currency, mentioned first in the pair quote) and selling the other (the quote currency, mentioned second in the pair quote). If we decide to realize the profit, then we need to sell back the currency that we bought earlier at the higher current price. If we decide to hold and do not realize the profit for a while, the amount of a particular currency bought or sold is not being sold to or bought back from the market and thus is said to be an *open position.*

Purchasing a particular currency pair, where you are also acquiring a certain amount of the base currency and selling the same amount of the quote currency, is also called *going long* or *longing the market.* If we go long 10,000 units, for example, in the EUR/USD pair, we are purchasing 10,000 units of the euro, which is the base currency, and selling the equivalent sum in U.S. dollars, which is the quote currency, which at a rate of 1.40 for EUR/USD would represent 14,000 units of U.S. dollars. The selling of USD units guarantees the buying of the EUR counterpart.

The same rules apply in the inverse position, where we are then *shorting the market* or *going short* in a particular base currency, when you see that its value is decreasing with respect to the quote currency. Now we would be selling, for example, the 10,000 euro units and buying back the 14,000 units of U.S. dollars because we expect the euro value to decrease, and we would buy it back at a lower dollar price thereafter to realize the profit.

One is said to be *long* in one currency when we buy it and *short* in that currency when we sell it. Long, or buy, positions use the offer or ask price of the quotes. For example, if you acquire one lot of GBP/USD at a rate of 1.4722 bid/1.4727 ask, this means that you'll be buying 100,000 GBP units at 1.4727 USD. Short, or sell, positions use the bid price of the quotes. Thus, in the preceding situation, we would be selling 100,000 GBP units at 1.4722 USD.

Trading currency pairs is simultaneous and symmetrical; this implies that we will always be long in one currency and short in another at the same time. In the previous example, if we exchange those 100,000 GBP units at 1.47220 USD, we will be short in pounds sterling and long in U.S. dollars.

A position that is running and active will be called an *open* position. Its value will change depending on fluctuations in market rates. Profits and losses will be influence the margin account but will not be official until the position has been closed.

TRADING ON MARGIN

Trading on margin is equivalent to borrowing money from a bank or a broker to purchase a particular security or currency pair. The margin needed depends on the leverage offered by the financial institution and represents the guarantee needed to control a certain quantity of units.

For example, when using a 100:1 leverage, the trader controls a $100,000 lot with only $1000 on margin in the account. Smaller lot sizes of $10,000 may be controlled with only $100 on margin.

Higher-leveraged accounts may allow control of greater amounts of money in the market with less margin, but this also can be dangerous when losses are experienced. A lower margin requirement can induce the trader to risk more than is wise. I will discuss leverage and true leverage in detail in Chapter 6.

MANAGING A POSITION

The position can be set up from the start of the trade, with its individual stop-loss and target-profit levels, or it can be managed as it develops. Setting and trailing the stops, balancing partial profits, and shifting entry prices in pending stop or limit orders are other ways of managing your trades.

CLOSING A POSITION

A position will be closed automatically when it reaches either the target-profit or stop-loss set price resulting in a loss. Positions also can be closed manually through specific controls on the platform or by calling the broker directly. When you close a position manually, you are subject to the same conditions as when opening at market price, such as requotes if the prices have changed.

Positions also can be closed by opening a matching and opposite trade in the same currency pair (a limit order, a stop-loss order, or simply a market order can be used). For example, if you have gone long in one lot of GBP/USD at the offer price, you may close out that position by going short in one GBP/USD lot at the actual bid price. However, this is not possible with brokers that permit *hedging* through opening long and short positions on the same currency pair. Hedging has been halted in the United States in the FOREX by recent rule changes enacted with the farm bill in October 2008. You still can use hedging strategies via different accounts and different futures commission merchants (FCMs), although not quite with the same affect. You also can open an offshore account, which some FCMs in the United States will allow you to do so that you can still hedge your FOREX trades.

PIPS AND LOTS

The *pip* or *point* (percentage in point) is the minimum unit of movement of a currency. It symbolizes a 0.0001 variation in four-decimal-based currency pairs, and a 0.01 increase or a decrease in two-decimal-based pairs. In this way, assuming that the previous price is, for example, 1.2750 on the EUR/USD and it rises to 1.2799, you will have a difference of 49 pips.

Each pair can have a different pip value, which is based on the relationship between the varying currency rates. It would not be calculated by the same method for pairs where USD is the base currency as for pairs where USD is the quote currency. This is also true in the case of crossed-rate currency pairs.

A currency's price moves are usually measured by the number of pips. Every pip a currency moves will equal a specific amount of profit or loss in real USD on every trade. Often the value of a pip changes based on which currency pair is being traded. Only if currency pair includes USD as the quote currency, listed second in the pair, will the value of a pip consistently stay the same. This happens because it is how much of the base currency you can buy or sell for the USD that fluctuates.

To determine the amount of loss or gain on a particular trade, you first should set up the value of a pip and then multiply it by the number of pips the currency has changed for or against your position since the trade began. If the base currency is increasing in relation to the quote currency, each pip above the price at which you purchased it will be counted as profit. And vice versa, every pip that is lower than the price at which you purchased it would increase your loss.

It's extremely important to remember that if the countercurrency is USD (e.g., the pair is EUR/USD), the value always remains 1 pip = $0.0001 USD (1/100 of a cent) for every dollar traded. This is a value of US $10 per pip for every usual lot amount of US $100,000 traded and is US $1 for mini lots of US $10,000. Most other currency pairs will have a pip value that changes constantly between US $0.00006 and US $0.00009 per pip depending on the current rate of exchange. This is US $6 to US $9 per pip for every US $100,000 lot traded or US $0.60 to US $0.90 per pip for every US $10,000 lot traded.

Here are some more examples of the calculations to be made depending on which are the base and quote currencies:

Currency Pairs with USD as the Base Currency

USD/CHF, USD/JPY, USD/CAD

Examples:

USD/CHF
Currency value = 1.1718
Pip value = 0.0001/1.1718 = 0.0000853388

On one standard lot, the pip value would be

$$0.0000853388 \times 100{,}000 = \$8.53$$

USD/JPY
Currency value = 92.29
Pip value = 0.01/92.29 = 0.000108354

With one standard lot, the pip value would be

$$0.000108354 \times 100{,}000 = \$10.83$$

Currency Pairs with USD as the Quote Currency

EUR/USD, GBP/USD, AUD/USD, NZD/USD

Example:

EUR/USD
Currency value = 1.2658
Pip value in euros = 0.0001/1.2658 = 0.000079

Additional formula rate to USD:

Pip value = 0.000079 × 1.2658 = 0.0001

On one standard lot, the pip value would be

0.0001 × 100,000 = $10

The same calculations apply to any other currency pairs with USD as the quote currency: pound sterling, Australian dollar, New Zealand dollar—where the final pip value will consistently be $10.

Crosses (Currency Pairs Where USD Is Not Present as Either the Base or the Quote Currency)

EUR/GBP
Currency value = 0.8913
Pip value in euros = 0.0001/1.2658 = 0.000112196

Additional formula rate to USD:

Pip value = 0.000079 × 1.4194 (GBP/USD rate) = 0.000159251

On one standard lot, the pip value would be

0.000159251 × 100,000 = $15.93

The same calculations will apply to any of the other cross-currency pairs: GBP/JPY, EUR/JPY, EUR/CHF, etc.

The pip values in these examples are calculated to show a result in U.S. dollars because this is the main currency used in most trading accounts. However, many brokers permit traders to open and retain their accounts in local and foreign principal currencies, such as euros, pounds sterling, Japanese yen, Swiss francs, etc. In these cases, the calculations must be made taking the different rates into account with respect to the deposit currency.

The following table of equivalences illustrates the pip value for each type of contract, from standard lot to nanolot, based on the preceding examples and rates.

Currency Pair	Standard	Mini	Micro	Nano
Units	100,000	10,000	1000	100
EUR/USD	$10.00	$1.00	$0.10	$0.01
USD/CHF	$8.53	$0.85	$0.085	$0.0085
USD/JPY	$10.83	$1.083	$0.108	$0.0108
EUR/GBP	$15.93	$1.59	$0.159	$0.0159

THE LOT

The contract amount that a bank or brokerage firm allows a currency to be traded in is called a *lot*. Usually, brokerages recommend two different kinds of accounts: standard and mini. A standard lot size is $100,000, and a mini account lot size is $10,000. There are also smaller retail institutions than offer micro account and nano account lots, equivalent to $1000 and $100, respectively.

ORDER TYPES

BUY/SELL MARKET ORDERS

A *market order* is an order to buy or sell at the current market price and can be used to enter or exit a trade. Market orders should be used carefully because in fast-moving markets there may be a difference between the price seen at the time a market order is given and the actual price of the transaction. This is due to *slippage*—the amount the market moves in the few seconds between issuing an order and having it executed. Slippage potentially could result in the loss or gain of several pips.

Online trading platforms may differ a little in the manner in which they initiate a trade, but a trade normally is accomplished through a form that shows the current bid and ask prices. Some platforms ask for a confirmation of the order; others have a direct one-click order capability. Usually execution of the order is instantaneous or, at the very most, it takes just a few seconds to appear as executed.

Sometimes market orders also can be placed over the telephone at the broker's dealing desk. The etiquette to follow this procedure should be verified with your broker.

BUY/SELL LIMIT ORDERS

A *limit order* is an order to buy or sell at a certain limit. It can be used to buy a currency below the market price or sell a currency above the market price. When buying, your order is executed when the market falls to your set limit-order price. When selling, your order is executed when the market rises to your set limit-order price. Normally, there is no slippage with limit orders. The order essentially contains two variables, price and duration. The trader identifies the price to buy/sell a certain currency pair and also specifies the amount of time the order should remain active.

A common use of limit orders is when a trader anticipates the price to bounce back from a given resistance or support area after a rally or fall. This is especially true when the currency pair has been trending.

BUY/SELL STOP-LOSS ORDERS

A *stop-loss order* is an order to buy above the market value or to sell below the market value. This type order is used most commonly as stop-loss orders to limit losses if the market moves opposite that which the trader expected. A stop-loss order will sell the currency if the market falls below the point set by the trader. The order contains the same two variables, price and duration. The main difference between a limit order and a stop-loss order is that stop-loss orders are used frequently to limit loss potential on a transaction, whereas limit orders are used to enter the market, add to a pre-existing position, and/or engage in profit taking.

A trader uses a stop-loss order when he or she expects a price breakout to happen and wants to seize the opportunity to "ride" the breakout on any side if it develops.

OCO (ONE CANCELS THE OTHER) ORDERS

This type of order is used when placing a limit order and a stop-loss order simultaneously. If either order is executed, the other is canceled, which allows the trader to make a transaction without monitoring the market. If the market falls, the stop-loss order will be executed, but if the market increases to the level of the limit order, the currency is sold at a profit. This is used in a straddle when trading news, a type of trading strategy used. An OCO order is a mixture of two limit and/or stop-loss orders. Two orders with price and duration variables are placed above and below the current price. When one of the orders is executed, the other order is canceled.

IFD (IF DONE) ORDERS

Using an IFD order allows a trader to program particular strategies in which there can be a sequence of trades. These trades will not be executed until the first one is accomplished.

TIMED ORDERS

GTC (Good Till Canceled) Orders

A GTC order will remain active in the market until the trader decides to cancel it. It will not be terminated by the dealer. For this reason, it is very important to remember open pending orders after a strategy is executed because any of them can become a market order at any moment when the market price matches the order price.

GFD (Good for the Day) Orders

A GFD order remains active in the market until the end of the trading day. This will have some deviations depending on the server time of your broker.

Good until Date/Time Orders

This is another timed order in which the trader can specify the exact time of the day and the date on which he or she desires to keep the order active.

WHERE IS THE MARKET GOING?

This depends on a number of factors. The market is always in a perfect equilibrium, which it succeeds in holding thanks to the periodic variations related to interactions between the elements of which it is composed (currencies, people, events, traders, etc.).

If you monitor using a very big time frame, you will notice something very interesting: In *almost all* cases, the currency pairs move upwards or, at least, relatively sideways.

Many long-term operators, namely, hedge funds and large capital investors, don't constantly open and close positions, but they use a strategy with several elements that allows them to achieve a constant growth, slow but safe, and almost as important, with nominal risk. However, if you look at intraday or intraweek trading, a very diverse and opposing scenario is seen. If you fail to match them up and understand them from their individual perspectives, they will bring you to a tremendous amount of confusion because it will seem to you that the market isn't going up or down. When you see the market rising and you decide to open a position, that could be the precise moment the market goes against you, and you end up dazed and frustrated.

It has been said that it is appropriate to use at least two time frames. However, to combine them is not the same as mixing them. You should use one longer time frame and one shorter time frame. This is the safest way to work because you will find more precise entry and exit points for every trade you make. In this way, you can better assure yourself of entering a trade on time and exiting it without leaving too much on the table.

You might object that this method of combining two or more time frames. Many people believe that this can distract the trader's focus on what is being done because at a certain point during the trade the shorter period will go in an opposite direction from the longer time frame. However, when applying this approach in real time, you may observe that the shorter period doesn't impede the longer one when the trade is in progress; instead, the smaller time frame allows you to better pinpoint a suitable exit. You should use a combination with which you feel comfortable, but there are particular combinations that I find more harmonic:

Two time frames (the longer one for watching the trend and following the position, the smaller one for entries and exits):

- 5 minutes and 1 hour
- 15 minutes and 4 hours
- 1 hour and daily
- 4 hours and weekly

Three time frames (trading the intermediate time frame and using the longer one for the trend and the smaller for entries and exits)

- 1 minute, 5 minutes, and 30 minutes (for extreme scalping; not recommended for starters)
- 15 minutes, 1 hour, and 4 hours (intraday operation)
- 1 hour, 4 hours, and daily (intraweek or swing trading)
- 4 hours, daily, and weekly (longer term or position trading)

Something that increases the confusion when you are analyzing and observing market movements is the overcrowding of charts with trendlines and indicators that later overlap each other if you change the time frame. It would be more efficient to use a single chart for each time frame and then choose one that will be used only to perform the actual analysis.

Another confusion arises when you try to trade in a shorter time frame (5 or 15 minutes) but you pretend with this to make a 100- or even 200-pip-long run (and in a few hours, too). This is not impossible, but this is what usually happens: The risk management is proportional. Let's say that, on average, the relationship is 2:1 (reward to risk) or, ideally, 3:1. More often than not, it is 1:1 (or less) if the entries haven't been studied with precision.

There is an average time/trade relationship that is about four or five times greater than the time frame incrementally. For example, a position opened on a five-minute chart, if it has potential, shouldn't last much more than half an hour or up to an hour if there is not much volatility. For a position opened on the 15-minute chart, one or two hours is a maximum. If, after the time has elapsed, there are no results, it would be better to close the position and wait for the next breakout. On the other hand, a position opened on a four-hour chart can last for the entire day or even two days, and a position opened on a daily chart can last up to a week.

Another very important issue to take into account when switching time frames is the size of the stops. You can use a fairly dependable tool, the *average true range* (ATR), to measure the actual volatility and potential scope in that time frame. Features of the ATR will be discussed in detail under "Technical versus Fundamental" below.

You can't afford to open a medium-term position with targets that call for the trade to "breathe," that is, perform its logical wave fluctuation inside the particular range of each pair, with a 7- or 10-pip stop loss that will close the position much earlier than desired; maybe after half an hour or a few hours later, unless you get extremely lucky and are able to pick the top or bottom of the price.

The ATR offers the exact measure for an adequate stop loss (you should add the spread and, if your risk level allows it, some additional pips to achieve increased safety). Based on this, you could expect double or triple the ATR value as a target profit if the position is successful and more so if it happens to be the bottom or top of a longer run and is followed up with trailing stops, especially if you are trading in the same direction as the higher-time-frame trend.

For a 15-pip stop loss, a target profit of 45 pips is fine (risk-reward ratio 1:3). It's not wise to place a stop loss much higher than the target you expect unless your strategy will give you a 90 percent record of winning trades, which is possible but probably won't last for very long because the markets change and change quite a bit. The best option is not to go lower than 1:2 or at a minimum 1:1.5 (stop loss: 15 pips; target profit: 22 pips, or 30/45, etc.). A 1:1 ratio also works if the performance of the strategy is above 50 percent.

STOPS AND TARGETS

HOW TO SET A STOP LOSS

I have already mentioned ATR-based stop-loss sizing. There are other ways to define the level at which keeping a specific position open is no longer useful.

Support/Resistance-Based Stops

These are stops that are usually set at the most recent swing high or low or at a specific price that the market has bounced off of repeatedly. It is recommended to set the stops a couple of pips higher or lower than the area to allow for more safety.

The parabolic stop and reverse (SAR) is another technical indicator that can help you set and trail a relatively safe stop loss, especially when the currency pair is trending. Be advised that this is not recommended in choppy or sideways markets.

Trailing Stops

There are two kinds of trailing stops. One is set automatically at a given distance from the price and is initiated at a set level, increasing thereafter every time the price advances in the direction set. The other way of using a trailing stop loss is manually, changing its price level as the trade develops. Automatic trailing stops can be set on the server side of the platform, which is the better option in case of a connection failure, or on the client side.

A stop loss order is always used to exit a trade while at the same time limiting the eventual amount of loss. Some traders use them all the time as a regular exit strategy, whereas others will have "emergency stops" only, to be used in the event that something unpredictable occurs. A normal or regular stop usually is close to the price, depending on the time frame, and represents the maximum amount of loss the trader will allow himself or herself to lose on a single trade just in case it goes the wrong way.

Backup and emergency stops are set up much farther out because the trader doesn't expect them to be filled. They are set only to mitigate that unplanned power outage or connection issue that could harm the account financially and are seen as a last resort.

A stop-loss order always should be used because it allows a quick and automatic exit on bad trades, even if it the trader is not actively watching the trade. Some traders do not use stops because they fear that if their orders are visible in the market, they are more prone to be swept away by "stop hunting" or that they might get caught by unusual price spikes in moments of high volatility before the trade continues in the appropriate direction.

Scalpers often trade without stop-loss orders because trades might be held for only a few seconds. However, there is still potential for trouble, and at least an emergency stop should be set up to avoid ending up with a margin call.

TARGETS

Targets (or *take-profit levels*) are represented by the number of points or pips a trader believes a currency pair will rise or fall depending on his or her strategy and time frame. Calculations can be made using several tools, supports and resistance, or the ATR and depend heavily on the time frame being traded. A higher time frame will allow the setting of wider targets, but this also will require a wider stop loss.

SPREADS AND SWAPS

SPREAD

The *spread* is the difference between the bid and ask prices and typically constitutes the broker's or financial institution's profit on a transaction. The size of the spread is normally a measure of the volatility of a given market, but some brokers also offer fixed spreads. Most often spreads are widened at the moment of a news release, when higher volatility is expected.

For example, if you want to exchange euros into dollars (selling euros and buying dollars), you will receive $1.2825 for each euro sold. Inversely, when you buy euros, you will have to pay $1.2827 each, assuming that the value of the spread at that moment is 2 points.

SWAP

The *swap,* also called the *overnight* or *rollover interest,* is the fee that is charged by the banks at the end of a 24-hour trading day on open positions and is calculated according to the respective interest rates of the currencies involved. In the FOREX, banks have determined that all trades must be set-tled within two business days. Traders who desire to keep their positions open must "close" the positions before 5 p.m. Eastern Time (ET) on the settlement day and reopen them at the start of the next trading day. This rolls over the settlement by another two trading days. This strategy is created through a swap agreement, and depending on the position's direction and the interest rates of the currencies; it will generate a positive or negative amount.

The trader is in fact borrowing money to sell one currency and purchasing the other, so the trader pays interest on the borrowed currency and earns on the purchased currency, the rollover interest being the net result of the different rate calculations.

Although the interest rate for each currency is identical, swap rates may vary from broker to broker. Some have fixed rates on long and short positions until a rate change issued by the central banks, whereas others may vary the rates every day depending on the liquidity and volume of transactions.

To be able to calculate a swap for a given currency pair, you need the short-term interest rates of both currencies, the actual price or exchange rate of the currency pair, and the amount of lots purchased. For example, let's assume that a trader has an open position of 10,000 units long of EUR/USD. This is the number of euro units that he or she owns. The actual exchange rate is 1.2825 bid/1.2827 ask, the short-term interest rate paid on the euro purchase (base currency) is 2.35 percent, and the interest rate on the U.S. dollar short (the quoted currency) is 0.15 percent. In this case, the rollover interest earned would be $[10,000 \times (2.35\% - 0.15\%)]/(365 \times 1.2825) = \$0.47$.

On an inverse position (i.e., short EUR/USD), the interest paid with a short-term interest rate on short EUR of 1.85 percent and a short-term interest rate on long USD of 1.25 percent would be $[10,000 \times (1.25\% - 1.85\%)]/(365 \times 1.2827) = -\$0.13$.

The interest is earned on the currency that is owned (long side) and paid on the currency that is being borrowed (short side).

TECHNICAL VERSUS FUNDAMENTAL

There are two types of analysis that can be applied to FOREX trading—fundamental and technical—and traditionally they are thought of as "opposed" views. There has always been a controversy about which one is better or which one is the "truest" one. The truth is that both are an important gauge and a reflection of the markets. Each one has its own methodology and rules.

I will be discussing each one in detail in Parts 4 and 5 of this book, but I want to give you a summary here that will help you to integrate both views into your basic trading skills.

FUNDAMENTAL ANALYSIS

Fundamental analysis helps you to understand the macroeconomic indicators and political decisions of every government. It provides you with an indication of the economic situation in a given country that results from political decisions that quite possibly have an effect on currency value. When a trader studies the global economic environment and the political situation of the day, he or she will be able to develop a perception of the world situation and its influence on the various markets involved. Unlike technical analysis, fundamental analysis focuses on the *cause* and not the *effect*.

TECHNICAL ANALYSIS

Technical analysis is used to interpret price charts. You can see what is happening in real time and react instantly. You also can study past prices and volumes and, based on that information, make projections of the probable levels to be attained.

With several technical analysis tools, you can identify trends and patterns that reflect the buy and sell operations being made by all market participants at any given moment. Those trends and patterns can be seen on short, medium, and longer time frames, allowing the study of recurring patterns or particular conditions that are related to specific economic situations.

You must be able to understand and apply both types of analysis because the best-studied technical strategy based on past action can go horribly wrong if fundamental events are not part of the equation.

PREPARING YOURSELF ADEQUATELY BEFORE JUMPING INTO THE MARKET

FOREX TRADING ACCOUNTS

Most brokers offer a wide array of trading accounts and different platforms. In almost every one of them, you will find a demo or practice account that will allow you to get acquainted with their platform's particular characteristics and implement your strategies in a safe environment without the risk of losing any of your funds until you are totally confident about the mechanics involved.

Real-money accounts are diversified to allow traders of any skill level and capitalization to start their trading career in the measure of their capabilities. The smallest trading accounts you can find are the micro- or mini accounts, where the starting capital required is usually very small (ranging from $25 to $500) and where there are certain limitations as to the number of lots traded. Almost all brokers offer a very high leverage on those starter accounts, which ranges from 100:1 to as much as 500:1.

In mini- or micro accounts, you can trade mini lots, which represent as little as 1/10 of a standard lot ($10,000) or 0.1 lot, with a small margin requirement, yielding $1 per pip. Some brokers even allow trading of microlots, which are 1/100 of a standard lot or 0.01 lot, at a value of 10 cents per pip or nanolots ($100), which represent a value of approximately 1 cent per pip.

Among standard accounts, some brokers allow only regular full standard lots ($100,000), whereas others add the option of trading fractional or mini lots. The initial capital requirement for standard or professional accounts is much higher, ranging from $2000 to $50,000 and more, with different levels in between, as well as added benefits or limitations, particularly with respect to leverage, which is usually not higher than 100:1.

CHOOSING A BROKER

Finding the most appropriate broker is a task that shouldn't be overlooked because it can make all the difference between your success or failure in the FOREX market. Speed of execution is paramount, but also honesty and transparency have to be considered. Demo accounts are good for practicing and acquiring trading skills, but they won't allow you to gauge their performance and attitude in real life. The actual features come onto the scene only after you open a real-money account.

I always say paper trade, paper trade, paper trade. You simply have to be getting consistent results with your paper trading (demo trading) before you can start using real money. Most investors, especially first-time traders ("newbies"), tend to trade well on a demo and then lose it when they shift over to a real or live account. Why is this? Simple. I have heard it all too many times: "James, I made 20 plus trades without a looser. When I shifted to a real account, I felt like every trade I made went against me." Then I follow by saying, "Aren't you doing the same thing" I usually hear: "Well, I couldn't do the exact same thing. It is *real* money." Therein lies the difference in results. Paper trading is part of the learning process. Once you have mastered it, then you can move on to a real account.

Some traders will pick this up faster than others; it could take you a few weeks, months, or even years. That's right, it could take you some time before you are ready to trade real money. If you want to see the true success of the FOREX market, you have to put some time in.

With the advent of the micro account, I have found that opening an account with $25 to $150 is actually better than demo trading because you are now learning with real money, and you are developing good trading habits. Regardless of what you do, make sure that you practice your trading plan prior to trading any large accounts with real money.

Not every broker is suited for every trading strategy. Thus it is quite difficult to choose the best FOREX broker for you. Some strategies, such as scalping, will require extremely low spreads and swiftness of execution; for other, longer-term strategies that involve overnight interest, swap will be a major concern. Evaluation of the trading-platform software before making a decision is important because there are significant differences among them, and some might perform better than others, as well as offering different features, such as hedging capabilities on some of them and one-cancels-the-other (OCO) orders and if-then options on others. However, this is only the means to access the broker's services, which in reality is the most important part and what has to be assessed in detail before you trust any broker with your hard-earned money.

With the most recent FOREX oversight initiatives enacted within the farm bill, changes are coming. As of this writing, not all the anticipated changes have been implemented across the board. I would suggest that you stay informed. The best way that I can help to keep you informed is to provide real-time updates and valuable FOREX information at your fingertips through my Web site, *www.JamesDicks.com.*

It is easy to check a broker's reputation over the Internet and, more particularly, to see if the broker is regulated or not at least in its country of origin. A good broker should comply with a few minimum basic requirements.

REGULATION, REPUTATION, AND SIZE

Although the FOREX market is not regulated, because there is no central exchange, individual brokers have to operate under a set of regulations defined by every country's own financial regulatory bodies. For example, in the United States, a broker should appear as registered with the Commodity Futures Trading Commission (CFTC) as a futures commission merchant (FCM) and as a member of the National Futures Association (NFA). The status of a broker can be verified directly with those organizations; additionally, a broker should be showing a clean record with them. Some brokers, especially offshore brokers, don't possess any kind of financial regulation, so they represent a risk in dealing with your money because they could disappear and leave you with no legal recourse. Brokers in the United Kingdom are regulated by the Financial Services Authority (FSA).

You should check carefully the kinds of regulatory bodies with which the broker claims to be registered and verify if indeed it is a real financial regulatory institution or simply a business generic registration.

Currently, several U.S. FCMs allow you to choose if you would like to open an account in the United States or overseas, most specifically in the United Kingdom, which has good oversight as well.

The reason for doing this is that with the most recent changes, some traders are electing to go overseas so that they can continue to trade the way they want. One example of this is that in the United States, you can no longer hedge your trades in the same account. Thus traders who like to use hedging—a strategy that requires you to go long one currency and go short the same currency at the same time—now will have to use multiple accounts or go offshore.

If your broker is affiliated with any of the important exchanges, this adds a significant qualification because it implies that the broker is larger in size and thus has more representation on the markets, and it vouches for longer-term expectations for its business life. Check, for example, for any membership at the Chicago Board of Trade, the London Metal Exchange, the New York Mercantile Exchange, or other commodity exchanges. Size and years in business are extremely important because they further guarantee that there will be less of a chance that the broker falls into bankruptcy, unlike a broker that is new and barely starting its activities. Having a large number of customers and a bigger capitalization testifies to the broker's level of responsibility and commitment.

The reputation of a FOREX broker can be easily checked on Internet by adding the word *review, scam,* or *problems* to the broker's name in your favorite search engine. Read the opinions of other traders on forums and trading communities; do thorough research before entrusting your money to any broker. You must have a great deal of confidence in your broker, and this confidence has to be backed up by real facts, not just the advertising hype (smoke and mirrors). Use a practice account for a while, prepare some basic questions, and ask the broker's customer-support team to gauge the broker's credibility and responsiveness.

I highly recommend that you deal only with certified brokerage firms. Check the possible connection to banks or financial institutions. Although there are not many brokers who will disclose the names of all their liquidity providers, investigate these relationships further. FOREX transactions are mostly based on credit, and therefore, this is a very important element in your research.

GUARANTEE OF PRICES AND FILLS

Quotes on currency pairs should be guaranteed, as well as the fills on your stop-loss and limit orders. This is usually expressed as a "no slippage" policy, where the price offered should be the same as that at which your market or pending order will be transacted on entry as well as on exit. If there are no clear rules on this subject, keep searching further. A good broker should have enough financial strength to meet these requirements and guarantee the quoted prices, at least in normal market conditions.

HONESTY

How does your broker control prices? Are there blatant differences with other price feeds in the industry? A dishonest broker can take advantage by delaying entries and manipulating the price feed, showing a different price or constantly requoting, slipping, and spiking prices.

LOCATION

Where is your broker located? If it is an offshore FOREX broker, is there any kind of regulatory institution where it is duly registered and acknowledged? If not, how can you obtain a guarantee on your funds should the broker file for bankruptcy? You might obtain some advantages with an offshore business with respect to taxes, but check first to see if it is really worth the risk.

MINIMUM INITIAL DEPOSIT

It is usually safer to go with a broker that asks a low deposit for starter accounts. Asking for higher amounts from the start, especially in the case of retail brokers, can be a red flag. You should look for a broker that asks for a small initial requirement, usually around $200 to $500, which is designed for new traders to test the markets with a real account without putting too much money on the line.

INTRODUCING BROKERS

As you start looking around for brokers, you will find numerous (actually, lots) of *introducing brokers* (IBs). Most of an FCM's business comes from referrals, IBs spreading the word and introducing the customer to an FCM. With the farm bill of October 2008, more oversight has been placed on these IBs. Now, IBs must be registered with the NFA and have sufficient net capital as set forth by the NFA. This adds a level of protection to the consumer.

It is perfectly okay to use an IB; just do your due diligence. My registered IB is *www.XpressFX.com*. One of the benefits I have always discussed with my customers is that when using an IB, make sure that it is able to assist in all your FOREX needs. For example, I have introduced more traders to the retail FOREX market than any other person in the United States. Because of this fact, I am able to assist my customers with much more authority and resolve than any of my fellow IBs. When a customer calls me, I can get the FCM on the phone right then and there and help my customer get a resolution. The reason for this is that I simply have so many customers that the FCM must listen to me. My goal is the longevity of my customer, and I know that I will not remain in business if I can't provide the service my customers deserve. Thus, when you are searching for a broker, an FCM, or an IB, just be on the lookout for that personal touch that is so hard to find these days.

CUSTOMER SERVICE
Good customer service is very important, especially when problems arise. A broker should treat all its customers with the same level of professionalism and courtesy and be swift at providing orientation on complicated matters and questions that could arise when markets are very volatile or should a technical problem occur with the price feeds or connection to the platform's server. Since FOREX trading hours are continuous from Sunday to Friday afternoon, the broker's customer service should be available during the same time span, 24 hours a day, 5 days a week. IBs often will piggyback the customer service of their FCMs when it comes to specific trade questions. If you have any question about your closed or stopped-out orders, you need to be able to receive a fast response independent of the time of the day.

Some brokers offer an online chat support service; others have only a phone-based support desk. Make a list of sensible questions, and take note of the attitude and knowledge the support staff show when they answer. They always should be courteous and eager to help and have appropriate knowledge of common matters that arise in day-to-day transactions and events. If you don't feel totally comfortable with their answers or perceive any doubtful behavior, keep looking elsewhere.

SPREADS AND SWAPS
FOREX overnight swap rates should be publicly available, either on the broker's Web site or via the trading platform. Some have fixed swaps;

others vary slightly every day depending on price fluctuations and number of transactions. Check for any excessive difference with regard to the usual calculation of overnight interest.

The *spread* is the amount of money a broker makes on every transaction its customers perform. If the difference between the bid and offer prices is low, the broker's service is cheaper, and the profit value will be higher. It is always better to choose a broker with lower spreads.

I always like to say that you get what you pay for. Keep in mind that just because you get the tightest lowest spreads in the industry doesn't that mean you are not paying somewhere else. IBs and FCMs are in business to make money—profit is not a dirty word—*but* everyone has to make money or it is not a good opportunity. You will just have to use good due diligence or a referral to find the best place to trade. I go to great lengths to make sure that the FCMs to which I refer customers from *www.XpressFX.com* are the best.

Also keep in mind that some brokers, in order to provide the tightest spreads, are now charging commissions—a fee to get in and a fee to get out—similar to the equities markets. IBs are usually paid a fee for the customers they introduce to the FCM. This will have no impact on you as a trader unless otherwise stated. IBs get paid out of the spread, so if you use an FCM that has a too-wide spread on the EUR/USD, that spread is too wide whether you use an IB or not; you just get an extra layer of customer support for the same 2-pip spread. Again, in some cases (which have to be disclosed), an FCM actually may increase the spread to compensate the IB for its referral. I do not allow this to be part of my IB; just check the spreads yourself or ask.

MARGIN-REQUIREMENT RULES
Examine your broker's margin requirements and margin-call rules carefully. At what level will your position be liquidated should the price take a plunge or rise against your direction' Some brokers will close all positions without warning, whereas others will issue some notification that the account is near the limit they have set.

LEVERAGE LEVEL
The leverage levels can vary a lot from one broker to another, but they are usually in a range from 50:1 to 500:1. A higher leverage can be somewhat risky but can give you more opportunities to obtain a bigger profit. A small initial capital investment will require a higher leverage. (Take note that

with leverage comes risk, but with risk comes reward and, of course, the potential for loss.)

TRADING PLATFORM

You can find a wide array of trading software among brokers, from simple Web-based platforms to more complex applications that have to be downloaded. You also will find mobile platforms that give you the opportunity to trade or monitor your positions while you are on the go. Practically all brokers offer practice accounts that are an exact replica of the live trading platform so that you can familiarize yourself with the interface and test its features.

The platform should be professional-looking and easy to understand and operate. Not all of them have the same tools available, but a good FOREX broker should have at least charts that update in real time, technical analysis tools, and alerting capability. Some of them also include news feeds.

When I first started trading, I used one of the most complicated trading platforms known to humankind, or so I thought. I set out to develop an easy-to-use trading platform based on simple-to-use technical indicators with color-coded graphics. Today, the platform has many variations and includes advanced charting capabilities. I refer to it more as a learning environment than as a software platform because it has education and training integrated into it. The platform will take a beginning trader and walk him or her right through the various steps to becoming a professional currency trader. There are numerous FCMs out there that are currently using my technology, and there are more every day. You can find out more or download a free trial at *www.JamesDicks.com*.

CURRENCY PAIRS

A good broker will offer a good variety of instruments to choose from and will provide the currency pairs that interest you the most. A good broker also will have other types of instruments, such as metals, indexes, or commodities, as well as certain exotic currency pairs, which will allow you to widen your options and build a more diversified portfolio.

AUTOMATION CAPABILITIES

Some trading platforms allow users to run automated trading strategies through an external application programming interface (API) or with its functions integrated directly from inside the software. If you are interested in this trading style, you should look for a broker that offers automation capabilities that are easy to implement.

In addition to the basic requirements that you will have to go through and examine, you also need to know that there are two major types of FOREX brokers: the retail brokers or market makers and the electronic communications networks (ECNs).

I have developed a code premiere advisor language (PAL); this allows me to integrate automated trading strategies into my trading platform, including the ability of the customer to write his or her own automatic strategy or transfer one that may have been running on another system. The wave of the future surely will be automated/program trading. The big institutors have used this type of trading for many years, and now you have the same capabilities. You can find all sorts of trade robots out there, but I haven't found any with adequate support yet.

MARKET MAKERS

Market makers have a dealing desk. The broker usually acts as a counterpart for almost every transaction made by traders. Brokers hedge their own risk by opening trades in the opposite direction for the same amount. Very few orders are sent to their liquidity providers because most of the trades they handle are under the minimum standard lot requirement from the banks. Bigger positions can be hedged in-house, transferred to another associated market maker, or transacted directly with the liquidity provider through pooling of funds and opening a position directly with the bank. Orders are matched or covered one with another; for example, if one trader is selling and another is buying the same currency pair, any difference in quantities is assumed by the broker. This often leads to conflicts of interest: When the trader wins, the broker can lose, and vice versa. To protect themselves, some brokers widen the spreads, use slippage, or even 'disconnect' the trading server during heavy volatility caused by economic news.

Because of program trading and more retail customers in the FOREX market, most FCMs have found it difficult at best to trade against their customers. What they know, and what you are seeing, is that if a customer sees his or her FCM playing any of these sorts of games (i.e., wide spreads, off quotes, etc.), he or she simply will leave and go to a new FCM. Thus the FCMs are off-laying their trades directly to the Interbank, the source of the trillions of dollars of turnover. This allows the FCM to focus on proving the best possible trading environment, one with a lot fewer conflicts of interest. The Interbank market is so big that it is less likely to be concerned with the average retail trader making money because the amount is so insignificant in the face of total daily turnover.

You still will have FCMs managing their books as I mentioned earlier. If you and I took opposite positions on the EUR/USD, the FCM would have a balanced book, and one of us would lose and one of us would make money. The broker makes the spread on both sides. This is an ideal situation for the broker and certainly an acceptable business practice. However, what happens if we both go long the EUR? Then the broker has a unbalanced book. Three things will happen: Either the broker will hold the trade and thus trade against the customer, or it will go out into the marketplace to offset the position either in full or at a percentage to minimize its risk, or it simply will offload the transaction directly to the Interbank. The goal is to have as many customers as possible so that the broker has a better chance of having a balance book and making the spread on both sides. There is nothing wrong with the FCM making money as long as you understand the process and don't get manipulated along the way. Education and knowledge are the keys to success. I am happy that you are reading this book and have put your trust in me to help fill that FOREX knowledge you need to achieve success as a FOREX trader.

ECNS

ECN-type brokers do not have a dealing desk. The broker serves as an intermediary to connect traders with the banks but does not take the trades itself. Such brokers usually charge a commission on every transaction because they do not profit from hidden charges on the spreads. They also do not manipulate spreads and prices, those being the quotes received directly through the Interbank. The spreads are usually lower than those of market makers, and this is an advantage for scalping strategies. However, the spreads are not fixed and can experience huge variations during volatile conditions. An ECN environment is conducted according to real market prices, and such prices can be moving very fast based on the availability of buyers and sellers. There is no price guarantee. However, you have the advantage of being able to see the real market with total transparency and actual quotes and volume of transactions being made. ECN operation is most like the banks at Level II, but the ECN is still functioning as an intermediary. Additionally, you probably will need a higher capitalization for ECN trading because most ECNs allow only full-lot transactions and offer a lower leverage than retail brokers.

On the NASDAQ, when a trader places an order to buy or sell stock they are placed through many different market makers and other market participants. Level II is a more detailed look into who has what interest in a particular stock. Level II will show you the best bid and ask prices giving you detailed insight into the price action of the stock. For day traders knowing exactly who has an interest in a stock can be extremely useful.

TOOLS

SAFETY REQUIREMENTS FOR ELECTRONIC TRADING

Although it is possible to deal in the FOREX through a dial-up connection, it is recommended that you have a fast digital subscriber line (DSL) or cable setup, especially if the platform you will be using requires continuous reception and update of data feed. If you are a long-term trader who checks the charts only occasionally and who operates mostly with pending limit or stop orders, this will not be a high priority, but a scalper, for example, will need a stable Internet flow and a fairly huge bandwidth, which will allow a fast connection to and from the broker's server. The computer itself doesn't have to possess the ultimate high-tech gadgets, but it should be in optimal condition and properly maintained periodically.

A second alternative connection should be considered in case the main one fails. It is good practice to have more than one avenue with which to access your open positions in the eventuality of an Internet failure or even a power outage, especially if your broker doesn't offer phone access. Mobile access is a good option, although not every company offers that possibility yet. You could combine your DSL connection with a dial-up, wireless, cable, or mobile backup. Having a power generator or uninterruptible power supplies (UPS) is a must if you live in an area where there are frequent electricity outages.

Finally, all the usual safety requirements concerning protection of your data, such as virus protection, anti–key loggers, firewalls, etc., should be set up before installing the software and logging on to your real-money account.

USING MULTIPLE MONITORS

Is it really necessary to use more than one monitor to become a successful trader? This will depend on your own trading style and other professional needs.

Having multiple monitors (at least two) seems to be a must in today's busy computer world, where multitasking is pretty much a common practice—one screen for the main program with which you are working and another one for miscellaneous activities such as chatting, watching videos, listening to music, or accomplishing any other task you need or desire to perform simultaneously.

In FOREX trading, having multiple monitors can be very useful in that you can watch several currency pairs at the same time or maybe just several time frames of the same currency pair without having to minimize the charts so that they all fit on the screens, watch the news, follow up your favorite trading group seminar or live trading conference, or simply use your other programs and Web browser. However, you should carefully decide whether multiple monitors really represent a positive addition or if, instead, the avalanche of available information is a distraction that hinders your ability to focus completely on what you intend to do.

The use of multiple trading terminals, for a very active trader, can justify the acquisition of an additional screen, especially when the trading platform on which you place your trades is different from your charting application. Having two or even three monitors allows you to see the charts in a more comfortable way with less eye strain. But how many is too many?

Professional traders usually recommend focusing on one or at best two currency pairs. It is really useful to you to be permanently scanning each and every market available in the expectation of the perfect setup? Most often one of the reasons some traders need more monitors is because the charts the use are overcrowded with too many indicators, so they have to watch them full screen to see all the details. Does a bigger size make the charts more readable, though? Before you run to the store and buy an additional screen for your equipment, you really should determine if all the indicators that you intend to use are absolutely essential to your strategy and trading style. Do you manage several accounts at the same time?

I use a laptop just about everywhere I go; at home, it is the only thing I use. I actually place trades and follow numerous currency pairs from my laptop. In addition, I have paid subscribers to my FOREX alert service, and I both monitor multiple currency pairs and delivery timely trade alerts from my laptop. So you don't need a lot of monitors or equipment to trade the FOREX. However, on the other side, at my office, my FOREX strategist and FOREX traders use lots of screens. In fact, I think one of them has at least 12 or more screens just for himself. This is a little overboard, if you ask me, but whatever works, I say. I do like using a multiple-monitor system when I am at the office because it allows me to see a lot of things going on at one time, but it is *not* a requirement to be successful in the FOREX market.

THE APPROPRIATE TRADING ENVIRONMENT
FOREX is a business, and it should be treated as such when you are choosing the location from which you will be opening and monitoring your

positions. Although working from home may be more comfortable and allow more freedom, it also makes it a little more difficult to separate normal family activities from your business, and this could lead to unfortunate interruptions that could damage your trading results.

Your home office should be laid out carefully and professionally because you probably will spend several hours a day in it. Thus the furniture and layout have to be practical and, above all, comfortable. Take the time to build your perfect workspace; it will have a direct and positive influence on your overall mood and attitude at the moment you decide to step into the FOREX market.

WHO TRADES THE FOREX?

The market nowadays has changed from what it was in earlier years, with technological development and the ability to conduct transactions overseas with more ease; other financial/nonfinancial institutions are able to participate in the FOREX market as well as individual investors and traders.

More than 80 percent of the FOREX market's overall daily activity comes from speculation, where transactions occur in a wide range from commercial banks to individual traders. The main players that take part in the FOREX market are central banks, individual banks, commercial companies, individual investors, brokers, and traders who jointly interact in the FOREX market to profit from price fluctuations in exchange rates of currencies by means of buying and selling currency pairs as a speculative activity. Another reason to enter the FOREX market is to hedge other investments, such as the trading of goods and services. Finally, a few traders look to profit on the overnight rollover amounts that are generated by differences in each currency's interest rates.

Commercial banks perform large transactions daily for their own benefit and also act as intermediaries for their customers. Central banks participate as controllers of the money supply of the respective country, with the aim to help the economy achieve its goals. For example, central banks can operate in the markets to restore the price stability of the exchange rate, protect certain price levels, or when specific economic goals need to be achieved, such as the control of inflation or growth.

Some of the most important central banks are the U.S. central bank (the Federal Reserve, the Fed), the Bank of Japan, the Bank of England, the Bank of Canada, the Swiss National Bank, the European Central Bank, and the Reserve Bank of Australia.

Commercial companies can participate in the FOREX market for speculation; to address the need to exchange foreign currencies in their export, import, and touristic activities; and also to be able to hedge their exposure if the home currency is seen as depreciating, avoiding in this way the effects that price fluctuations could have on company stability.

Specific types of commercial companies are represented by investment funds or hedge funds, which include all kinds of retirement, arbitrage, and mutual funds, as well as international investments. These firms hedge and protect one investment with another and have been entering more and more into the FOREX scene.

Brokers are intermediaries who allow buyers and sellers of foreign currency to interact. They obtain their profits through the spread between the bid and ask prices. As discussed earlier, there are two types of brokers: market makers and ECNs.

Finally, traders can be individuals or small groups that perform speculative and investment operations for their own account or as money managers for third persons.

WHAT KIND OF TRADER AM I?

Before starting to put your own real money at risk, it is a good idea to observe yourself and your usual living conditions, as well as your personality, and try several different trading techniques to see which of them will suit you the most. Do you have a lot of free time to dedicate to your trades, or instead, do you already have a busy schedule, maybe a full-time job or career studies? How much risk capital, which you do not need for a living, can you afford to set apart for your FOREX activities? Ask yourself: Am I a patient or impatient person? Can I perform under stress, or do I have a short attention span?

Another area to consider is your trading strategy itself. Are you more inclined toward fundamentals and economics? Or, on the contrary, is technical analysis more appealing to your mind structure? Would you prefer to use a mechanical system or a discretionary approach?

With all this in mind, you can develop a preliminary idea that will allow you to start by choosing a few strategies among the hundreds of systems that already exist and testing the waters on a practice account, comparing the different time frames and how you feel in each and every circumstance, besides checking the system's own performance and results. Maybe then you will want to develop a system of your own with the skills that you have acquired through observation of the markets from several points of view.

TRADING TECHNIQUES

Trading techniques can be divided in two general groups: long term and short term. Below I will provide a summary of some of the advantages and disadvantages of those two basic groups before I give a more detailed description of each of the components they include.

In *long-term trading,* traders base their analysis on end-of-day data and look to hold trades for a few weeks or even up to many months. They usually follow the trend. The advantages of long-term trading are that there is no need to watch the markets intraday and that traders perform much fewer transactions, thus lowering any commission costs. In addition, there is no need for using fancy equipment or software because the time spent analyzing and watching the markets is very short.

However, long-term traders will need to set much larger stops and will experience large equity swings. Thus they will need to be well capitalized and prepared for this eventuality. Trades are very few, and exceptional trades are fewer. Much patience is needed to wait for a trend to develop to its full potential. Losing months can be frequent.

In *short-term trading* traders will depend on the analysis of intraday data and aim to hold their positions for a few days or up to one or two weeks. Short-term traders usually perform swing trading. A shorter-term trading approach is referred to as *day trading,* where trader try to take small profits from intraday swings, exiting all positions before or at the daily market close. The advantages of short-term trading are that there are much more opportunities for trades, thus also less chance of experience losing months, and that traders do not have to rely on one or two trades a year to make money. With day trading in particular, since positions are closed daily, there is absolutely no overnight risk.

On the negative side, the cost of their transactions will be higher in short-term trading (traders will be paying more spread). Swing traders also incur in overnight risk. Day traders have to confront more difficulties psychologically because of the frequency of trading and having to monitor the markets constantly. The need to exit positions at the end of the day will limit their profits.

SCALPING

The main idea behind the scalping strategy in FOREX trading is to take very small profits very quickly from very small movements of price, such as 2 to 10 pips. The trades normally are entered and exited within minutes or even seconds. Small profits add up because the number of daily trades can be very high, ranging from 20 to 100 trades on average.

Scalping is considered to be a risky trading style. However, this will depend on which times of the day and which types of markets are used. Although it is possible to scalp successfully in trending conditions, the best trading times are when the market is ranging inside consolidation patterns. Most of the time, this is so; thus there are plenty of times to choose from to implement this strategy. High volatility or news releases are not recommended because of a higher risk involved.

The strategy has to be very well determined in advance, as for any trading system, especially in terms of risk management. A fast reaction and decision time is paramount, getting out of bad trades as soon as possible with low pip losses. Since the trader will be taking many more trades throughout the session, it is better to take profits as they present themselves, small pips here and there, not aiming for more because the strategy is to sum up the overall quantity of trades. Scalping is usually performed on very short time frames; thus the average range available is also very small, and one shouldn't expect more than 5 to 10 pips on average.

INTRADAY TRADING

Intraday or day trading is a technique that requires all positions to be closed at the end of each day. The number of trades is much lower than in scalping, and although very short time frames can be used to pinpoint better entries, trades are usually analyzed and performed over short- and medium-term time frames, such as 1-hour or 30-minute charts, with 5 or 15 minutes for entries. Traders can use a variety of technical analysis tools and wait for the appropriate signal or opportunity to open a position. If there is no good opportunity, they can stay on the sidelines and wait for a better chance the next day.

POSITION TRADING

The position- trading technique is a strategy in which you increase your position size incrementally as the trade evolves, maintaining the same initial level of risk. It is also called *averaging into a position;* the trader adds a new position of the same size and in the same direction every time the risk of the previous one can be covered.

For example, you could buy 0.1 lot of EUR/USD at 1.2550 and set the stop loss at 1.2500. Your risk would be of $50. When the price goes up, you buy a second mini lot at 1.2600 with a stop loss at 1.2550, setting the stop of the first position at breakeven (1.2550). You now will have two mini lots while maintaining your overall risk at $50. If the price keeps on rising, you can buy a third 0.1 position at 1.2650, setting the stop loss at

1.2600, and trail the stop of the first two positions equally to 1.2600. Should you be stopped out, all three mini lot trade are now at breakeven! Should the price continue rising, you can buy a fourth mini lot at 1.2700, setting all the stops for the positions at 1.2650, which will protect your profits. You then buy a fifth mini lot at 1.2750, setting all the stops as previously, and your protected profit amounts to $250 ($150 + $100 + $50, with the fourth mini lot at breakeven and $50 risk on the last position). In this way, you can limit your risk and exposure, which will remain the same in the whole process, and can accumulate great benefits. This style of trading allows you to stay in the trend and is ideal to use in longer time frames such as daily or weekly charts.

Another option that can be used is to convert a profitable day-trading position into a long-term sequential trade as soon as enough positive points are covered. You can go on adding to the position in the same way explained earlier and reap the profits later on with minimal risk.

Position trading should be attempted with small position sizes and no more than 1 or 2 percent capital risk. The advantage of this trading style is that you do not need to monitor the market all day, only check from time to time to adjust the stops and protect the profits already made. This strategy is much less stressful, and you can earn more profit with very small potential losses.

SWING TRADING

Price fluctuations in large moves are also called *swings*. The price goes up for a while, and then it goes back down. Swing trading is the strategy employed by traders who ride those swings and obtain profits from them. Swing trades usually are kept open for a few days, as long as the swing or trend is continuing. As soon as the price seems to be reaching a top or a bottom, the trader will enter short or long the market to profit from the expected move.

Markets usually range most of the time around 70 to 80 percent of the market activity being done sideways. However, those are "trends within trends" because each side of a sideways move is a small trend in itself and can yield many profits because the time frames used are higher than in scalping. A swing trade usually can give around 100 or more pips per trade.

This strategy is somewhat risky, though, because picking tops and bottoms is not so simple to do. Sometimes, what is seen as a reversal is only a small retracement, and the price continues rising or falling a short time after, which will cause huge losses if it is not estimated carefully. The accuracy in determining if the market has reached a peak or a trough will benefit the trader's use of several technical analysis tools and in evaluating the ranges that the market usually develops in the time frame used.

A solution to this is to ride the middle of the swing, without trying to enter at the very top or bottom. The swing will start going in one direction and then will retrace a little, and this is the best moment for an entry.

NEWS TRADING: STRADDLE

A *straddle* is the action of placing both a buy and a sell pending stop order above and below the current price. No direction is expected, and the trader prepares for the eventuality of a move either way. Straddles are used commonly in news trading and are implemented before the outcome of a news release kicks in. All the usual elements of trading are set up in the straddle, such as stop losses and target prices. OCO orders, where available, can be used so that whenever one of the trades gets triggered, the other one is automatically canceled.

This technique can be used on breakout expectations and in various other ways, such as, for example, based on the cross of either side of a particular moving average. Straddling involves some maintenance because orders that haven't been triggered yet need to be updated periodically as prices and conditions evolve. Besides, it is important not to leave active pending orders behind that are not needed any more. This is a mechanical approach that doesn't need a great deal of analysis; the market will move either way, and the trade will be managed accordingly when triggered. Orders are placed in the same way and at the same time by the rules of the chosen system, and the trader will only have to wait until any of the options gets effectively on the market.

Straddle trading is very useful during undecided market conditions, after long periods of consolidation, and of course, before fundamental announcements. It is often used to trade the news because of the difficulty of predicting such a move and also because entering in a highly volatile market sometimes can be totally impossible, whereas a stop order usually should be filled at the price chosen. However, straddles also are very risky because both sides could be stopped out in a big swing reaction, so the stops and targets have to be planned very carefully and set at precise levels.

Straddle-based trading systems can be very appealing to traders who don't have much time to spend at their computers.

THE TRADER'S LEVELS OF ASCENSION

In the process of becoming a professional FOREX trader, there are five levels through which it has been proved that practically everyone will have to evolve. Sometimes you might think that you have reached a higher level, just to find yourself again at level one or two. I like to use the following as a way to help determine where you are at a certain point in your evolution as trader. Assume that you are on your way to my office building to work with me as a professional currency trader. When you get to the lobby, you find out that all the professional traders in my office are on the fifth floor. The problem is that there is only one way to get to the fifth floor, and that is to work your way up. Obviously, you have made your mind up that trading currency is something you want to do, and you have committed to by investing in this book. So you decide to take the journey and start off on the first floor.

FIRST FLOOR: YOU DON'T KNOW THAT YOU DON'T KNOW

What is the first thought that attracts people to FOREX trading? The magic promise of making money fast and easy and being able to live a life of luxury. Maybe it is only the desire to quit a boring and demanding full-time job or to earn a little more in order to pay off all one's debts and thereafter retire in a more comfortable financial situation.

Prices go up, and then they go down. It seems easy. Besides, there are a lot of success stories, real or not so real, of millionaires who got their fortunes through currency speculation. All the glamour and hype built around the financial world are amazing!

Then you open your first account, probably test the waters a little on a demo account, but what you really want is real money. Practice accounts are most often left aside and seen as boring and useless for your immediate purposes. You don't even bother to understand what all those "technical indicators" on the trading platform are for. You just need to know where to click for buying and selling—that's all.

So there you are, clicking away on your path to total financial freedom! You take trade after trade, risk after risk. You probably don't even use a stop loss! You become overconfident and start risking greater amounts of money to accelerate its multiplication. So simple it is! The price goes up, you buy; the price goes down, you sell. What could go wrong? If you fail to plan, then you have planned to fail. With this attitude and mind-set, you will guarantee yourself failure, not just in trading the FOREX but also in life. The good news is that all you need is a little knowledge, and with that knowledge, you can begin to see what all the fuss is about, for then you will graduate and move up to the next floor.

SECOND FLOOR: YOU KNOW THAT YOU DON'T KNOW

You start opening your eyes and look around for answers that will explain to you the reasons for your recent failures. You become aware that you need more training and education. After all, you want to make this a full-time professional and stop working that endless low-paying job or retire and control your own financial destiny, one that will allow you to produce a constant profit. You start surfing the Internet or the local book store, looking for trading formulas. You want to know more about each and every indicator that is available on your platform, trying them all at once, transforming your charts in a Picasso-like spaghetti mix.

Your quest for the FOREX Holy Grail has just begun! You subscribe to a FOREX forum and jump from thread to thread, looking for the best system that makes the greatest number of pips. If you have enough money to spend, you believe every snake-oil peddler and buy every automated pip machine that is advertised on the Web in the hope that next month your account will finally be approaching the five- or six-figure mark!

Every day you happen to find a new "perfect system" that will only last until you try the next "Can't lose! Guaranteed!" one. You don't have the patience or discipline to find out if they really work because you expect them to start producing pips per minute, and because they don't, you keep on your endless search. Every new indicator is "the one."

Every new system is the Aladdin's lamp that you will rub and rub away in the hope that cash will start flowing like a river into your bank account. You will chase the market, pick tops and bottoms, and draw channels, trendlines, and Fibonacci retracements until price can't be distinguished any more on your charts.

Trying and failing one system after the other, frustration will accumulate, and anger will come into the picture. You will ask for advice but will not listen to it because "you know better." Overtrading, overleveraging, and overconfidence will make you risk much more than what prudence dictates. Then you'll seek again for more signals, automated systems, and other traders' calls until you end up exhausted and totally confused because nothing seems to work. You will start thinking that maybe the FOREX is not for you, and maybe you give up and quit. But don't despair, the FOREX is an exciting market, and many traders profit beyond their dreams. You simply have to take the bull by the horns and get the education you need to move up to the next floor.

THIRD FLOOR: AWARENESS

All of a sudden, you start realizing that the issue might not be the system, but you. You understand that each and every trader who is successful may have different strategies and styles, but there must be something that connects them and represents a common denominator. You can see now that there just may be a reason all those traders on the fifth floor are driving fancy cars and living the life they have always wanted. Now it's your turn.

You start immersing yourself much deeper into money management and investigate more about trading psychology, identifying the traits that are slowly producing a global understanding of the whole picture. You become aware that it is not possible to predict market price moves. You stop looking outside for the answers and start finding them on the inside.

You begin developing your own personalized system and integrate all that you have learned before, adapting your trading style to your own personality, time, and needs. You start getting positive results with the change. Your greater accuracy in money management allows you to have a happier attitude about losses because now you are confident that it is only a part of the trading business.

If you get into a bad trade, you will close it and move on. You have tested your system, and it has proven to work. You know it well, and you stick to your plan with discipline.

It's really on the third floor that traders figure it out. I teach lots of classes all over the country, and my most successful traders are the ones who travel to my offices to take their classes. Why? Because they have made it to the third floor. They realize that it is time to invest in their FOREX trading future. It's not just a good trading platform; it is the education, training, and support; it is the network of other traders with whom you can discuss training ideas; and it's the team that gets it.

Think for a moment: How long does a doctor, lawyer, or engineer have to go to school to learn his or her trade? And that is just to be an entry-level person. Think about how long a doctor has to go to school: four years for college, four years for medical school, a few more years for specific specialty, and then, what, two years of residency, then and only then to be a full-fledged doctor earning decent money. Well, what happens when the doctor goes on vacation? Nothing; they don't get paid. A currency trader controls his or her own future; a trader can work from anywhere. Traders can be in a trade making money while at the beach or on a golf course, fishing, whatever. *But* you will only get out of this what you put into it. You will have to find a mentor and start learning. Some of you will pick it up faster than others, but in the end, you can make it to the next floor.

FOURTH FLOOR: KNOWING THAT YOU KNOW

Now you're on cruise speed. You follow your system and rules, you have developed a trading plan, and you take losses and wins without letting emotions run over you. You will get to break even most of the time, having winning periods and then losing periods, but in general, most of your trades will be good, and you will not be losing money. Gradually, your win-loss ratio will increase consistently. You put your time in and now have a decision to make. Are you ready to quit your boring job, maybe retire early, and take on the status of FOREX trader? You are confident that you can make the money. The next step is yours. See you on the fifth floor.

FIFTH FLOOR: BEING A PROFESSIONAL

You made it—the secret society of professional FOREX traders. You look around, and it is not so unfamiliar to you. You have seen some of these same people walking around before. They are people you have passed in the hallways of life, people who have made the same decision you have, people who have decided to take charge of their financial lifestyles and do something about it. They didn't give up on floors one and two. They kept going.

Now you find that your skills are totally integrated, and you follow your trading routine every day on an unconscious level. You watch the charts, and thanks to the endless hours of screen time, you now "know" and understand how the market moves.

You start making more profitable trades, and the daily outcome doesn't take you out of control, whether you lose or win. Your account starts growing, your emotions are reasonably under your command, and above all, you are at peace and can trade without stress.

You keep on refining your own trading system so that it evolves with every market change. You keep an eye on risk and reinforce discipline. Trading is now just like any other job, sometimes maybe a little boring, but you have mastered all that it takes to get the profits you have planned on.

You can make money in the FOREX, and you can lose money in the FOREX. It is not an ATM machine for which someone will send you a PIN number so that it will start spitting cash out at you. You have to work at it. I have traders who have been with me for many years who are very successful. Ninety-nine percent of the traders I've seen who have lost money did so because of poor discipline, no patience, and just plain greed, and they didn't listen to all the education, training, and support they were getting or that was available at their fingertips. You have to go out and build your FOREX knowledge—if not from me, then from someone else—but this is a real market, and it is wide open for you to make of it what you will.

MONEY MANAGEMENT

CHAPTER 5

THE SECRET TO
MAKING MONEY

ARE YOU REALLY FIT TO TRADE IN THE FOREX MARKET?

FOREX trading is becoming more and more popular among individuals of all walks of life. In the thoughts of many, it would seem from the outside that it is an easy option to get easy money, quit your daily job, and start your path to the rich and famous gallery.

However, this is not true. Although you now can start trading with a very small amount of money, you also need to possess some basic elements of personality and character that are paramount for a successful career as a FOREX trader. FOREX trading should be treated as a business. It is an investment venture. Unfortunately, most people who throw themselves in the market without any previous preparation tend to treat it as a lucky gamble and end up with an unpleasant experience.

Before attempting to start trading, especially on a live account with real money, you should evaluate your motives and capabilities:

- Are you willing to apply yourself, and do you have some spare time to learn and prepare yourself thoroughly?
- Are you just looking for easy money, thinking that you'll get rich quick?
- Are you capable of following rules and discipline, leaving emotions out of your decision-making processes?
- Are you clear about how much money you will allow yourself to invest and how much you can afford to lose?

TRADING PLANS

What is a trading plan? A *trading plan* is a complete set of rules that have to be defined before starting to operate in the market. It should cover every aspect of your trading in detail.

Building a trading plan, however, is not an absolute guarantee that you will succeed, but it has all the elements necessary to prevent things from going wrong or bring a solution when they do, providing you with the tools to react in the best possible way to any possible outcome.

Markets can't be controlled, but you *can* control yourself. With a trading plan, you are establishing control of the most important part of your trading—the trader. The number one reason FOREX traders do not succeed is the fact that they did not build a trading plan.

One of the benefits of a trading plan is that it simplifies your trading because you will have a defined sequence of rules to follow one after the other before opening a trade. You will be able to control yourself and establish a discipline, which, in turn, will help you to leave emotions out of the picture, making it easier to monitor your trades and detect any mistakes much faster. You can review your plan at any time should it bring about unexpected results, and you can check to see if you are indeed following the plan based on the rules or if any of the elements of the plan have to be redesigned.

BUILDING THE PLAN

You should adapt your trading plan to your trading style, personality, skill level, and availability of resources. It is important to be totally honest when you are defining the plan, including most especially your emotional and psychological issues.

THE COMPONENTS OF A COMPLETE SYSTEM

A complete trading system covers each of the decisions necessary for successful trading:

Markets: What do you want to buy or sell?

Position sizing: How much do you want to buy or sell?

Risk management: How much can you afford to lose if things go wrong?

Entries: When do you want to buy or sell? (This would include market hours and possible news releases.)

Stops: When do you want to get out of a losing position?

Exits: When do you want to get out of a winning position?

Strategy: How do you want to buy or sell?

Time frames: How much can you expect to win from a particular entry?

In addition to the general plan, you also should elaborate a more detailed checklist to ensure that all these elements are being taken into account.

Here is an example of a trading checklist that you can use before entering a trade: Before entering a *long* or a *short* position:

What is the market (e.g., EUR/USD, GBP/JPY, or gold)?

Strategy: What are the main indicators and secondary indicators?

Risk areas: Are there bars or candlesticks that show risks for your position?

Breakeven price: Where would your trade be at breakeven, with no gain and no loss?

1. Identify the actual market position in relationship to previous activity by checking higher time frames (daily chart).
    a. Prices are not near a long-term resistance or support.
    b. Prices are not in congestion.
    c. Prices are not overextended.
    d. Prices are not near the high or the low of the previous day.
    e. Check the news and economic reports.
    f. Check possible gaps on weekends and holidays.
2. Identify the candlestick or bar in which you will be entering the trade so that you can confirm a potential future direction of the trend.
    Alternatives:
    a. *Long* = Main trend is rising up with a downward swing on the main indicator greater than the two previous downswings.

        Short = Main trend is falling down with an upward swing on the main indicator greater than the two previous upswings.
    b. *Long* = The secondary trend is going down and comes back up in the same direction as the main trend.

        Short = The secondary trend is going up and comes back down in the same direction as the main trend.
    c. *Long* = The secondary trend is going down and comes back up in the same direction as the slope of the moving average.

        Short = The secondary trend is going up and comes back down in the same direction as the slope of the moving average.

Risk management:

3. *Buy entry price:*

   Buy when the prices are above the high of the signal bar plus 1 tick.

   Sell entry price:

   Sell when the prices are below the low of the signal bar minus 1 tick.

4. *Initial risk price:*

   Long = Risk set to the swing low (minus 1 tick) of the signal bar or of the last three or four bars depending on the time frame.

   Short = Risk set to the swing high (plus 1 tick) of the signal bar or of the last three or four bars depending on the time frame.

   Long = Set stop to breakeven (entry price) after a range of four bars above the entry price.

   Short = Set stop to breakeven (entry price) after a range of four bars below the entry price.

5. *Never* let a positive trade become negative!

6. *Exit strategy:* Take profit.

   Alternatives:

   a. Using one lot (or mini- or microlot) = Take profit at about 60 percent of the average price range.

   b. Using two lots = Take full profit in one of the lots. Trail the stops using last short-term supports as a guide.

   c. Using three lots = Take full profit in one of the lots. Trail the stops using last short-term supports as a guide. Keep the remaining positions open until a reversal signal shows up or the end of the trading session.

How many of you really plan your trades by writing all your rules on paper with so much precision? You have to define *what* (entries and exits) you are going to do, *when* (the signals of your strategy or system) to do it, and *how* (risk management rules and other details). If you don't plan carefully and follow your own fixed rules strictly, the trades you'll initiate will be wrong even if their outcomes are positive, and paradoxically, if you follow your rules, they will be correct even if they bring about a loss because you will have been sticking to your plan.

Another important part of a trading plan is to keep a detailed record of all your trades (winners *and* losers): entry price, exit price, date, time, stops and targets, indicators that you used, signals taken, etc. Why did you take the trade? What was your emotional state at that moment? What were the environmental conditions at that moment, positive or negative? (Also include interruptions, time of the day, physical condition, etc.)

In this way, you can easily determine the weak spots and correct them later on, as well as reinforce the strong elements so that they can represent a greater asset as you go further in your trading career. If you don't do this, you will be swinging in the hands of luck, which is the same as saying that you will be just gambling blindly.

Before taking a trade, evaluate your skills. Have you tested your system, and are you confident about its results? Are the signals easy to understand and follow?

Prepare yourself psychologically. How are you feeling? Did you eat and sleep well? Are you ready to trade?

If you are not totally focused and ready to confront the daily challenge of the market, it is better not to trade because you will be prone to make huge mistakes.

If you feel tired or sick or are angry, worried, or distracted by other personal issues, you will be unable to focus and follow your discipline rule by rule.

Define your risk level. How much money can you risk on a particular trade? You shouldn't risk more than 1 to 3 percent of your equity on each single trade depending on the situation. Is the trade riskier than average, or does it have great potential to create greater risk? When should you stop? What is the total daily maximum risk you can allow? How many losses will you take before you stop trading for the day?

Define your goals. Establish a realistic ratio between risk and reward, based on your strategy and risk appetite. Clearly state which is the highest risk and smallest reward your strategy allows after evaluating your usual win-loss ratio. Carefully check what the potential profit expectations are based on the time frame you will be using and the minimum stop loss required for optimal safety. The risk should be lower than the reward expected, although this will depend heavily on your particular system. For example, a scalping strategy with a 90:10 win-loss ratio will allow up to a 3:1 risk ratio and still be very profitable (winning trades being one-third of losers), whereas a system that yields fewer winners but a potential for much longer runs would need the ratio to be inverted (usually a 1:1.5 risk ratio is the smallest that should be allowed).

Investigate the win-loss percentage that you need to break even, and base your calculations accordingly.

Set your goal in points and also in money to be made (or profit percentages on your equity) daily, weekly, monthly, and annually.

Evaluate the economic situation that's going on. Check the financial news, and be alert about economic news releases. How are the markets doing? Check also stocks and indexes that offer a good perspective on market mood. Wait for news release figures before placing a trade because they usually affect the market, causing random and contradictory moves. You should wait at least a half hour after every market open and not trade a half hour before any market close, as well as at least an hour later than a significant economic release.

Prevent technical issues. Check that your Internet connection and computer are working properly. Perform routine maintenance daily, clearing memory and temporary folders. Be sure to have in place the utmost security software (i.e., antivirus, antispyware and anti–key loggers) to protect your account data. Prepare your trading charts and indicators so that all the signals and support/resistance levels are seen clearly, and check that the sound volume is appropriate if you use sound alerts.

Make sure that you will not be interrupted or distracted during your trading activity either by other people (turn off the phone, TV, or radio if needed, and close the door of your trading space) or by other activities you could attempt to do simultaneously (no Web surfing, chatting, or even reading FOREX forums while you are trading).

Have a clear set of rules for entries and exits. Except in the case of scalping, where entering a trade also has to be very precise, exit rules are more important than entry rules.

Set the appropriate fixed stops, or get out at the level you have planned if you happen to be using mental stops. Don't make the mistake of letting losses run in the hope that the market will come back. If a trade is wrong, take the loss, and move on. You will still be making profits if you limit losses without looking back and manage your risk conservatively, even if your winning trades are less than your losing ones.

Mental stops have to be written down even if you don't place them physically on the platform. You can set a line on the chart at that level to help you react at the proper moment.

The same goes for target profits. You should know where to lock the benefits and set a written target price, either on the platform or as a first goal when using several contracts or trailing the stops thereafter. When you get there, take a partial profit on your position, move the stops to break even in the rest, and trail the stops using your preferred method (automated or manual).

Know your signals and system well. Your strategy should be simple so that you can make a fast decision and not struggle with a series of conflicting signals. Too many conditions to be met will lead to trade paralysis.

When conditions are met, you enter the trade without any doubt or hesitation. Since you have already tested your system and know its potential, it doesn't matter if the trade is going to be right or wrong because you rely on the probabilities of the strategy and thus are confident about the overall outcome.

Track your performance. Record your winning and losing trades with the same detail and care. Go back over past trades, and review what made them right or wrong. Good decisions will be reinforced, bad decisions will be analyzed, and the lessons learned will prevent you from making the same mistakes again.

Try to write down all the details of your trades, along with any comments about what led you to open those specific positions, your mood, the time of day, other circumstances, and general prevailing conditions.

Keep track of the drawdown (not only the net drawdown, which is the sum of all lost positions, but also the ongoing floating drawdown while your trades are still open). Keep a trading journal in which you reference all those details for further study.

Professional traders treat their trading activity as a business. This is paramount if you really want to trade full time and be successful at trading in the currency markets. You also need to know and accept that you can't always win, that losing trades are a necessary part of the picture in the FOREX. It is important to let your profits run and cut your losses short, and the accuracy of your own money management is what will bring about success in the end.

RULES AND DISCIPLINE

You might think that it is only necessary to have a winning system in place to succeed in the FOREX market. But are you able to follow the rules of your system exactly, trade after trade?

A good system certainly is a positive edge in ensuring your success, but there is another, more important element that has to be present: your discipline and steadiness in executing the rules by the book without adding, changing, or omitting parts of the strategy. Tested and proven winning systems include a series of rules as well as a series of losing and winning trades that have to be brought to completion. Not everyone is prepared to assume such a discipline because it requires changing some of your ingrained habits.

ATTITUDE TOWARD LOSING

In the everyday life, losing is seen as a bad thing. In the FOREX market, losing is part of the equation that leads to a successful result. The FOREX is a zero-sum game, where no additional resources are created and where someone's loss is another trader's win.

GROUP MENTALITY

Don't let others influence you. In the FOREX, you are on your own and can't depend on the decisions of others or other people's points of view. You need to develop your own system, which will be based on successive experiences, trial and error, until you are satisfied with the potential results. You are the one watching the charts and feeling the market.

Don't confuse this with being part of a network of like-minded investors. The James Dicks FOREX Network (*www.JDFN.com*) is just that—individual investors sharing ideas, strategies, and stories on the market, individual currency pairs, etc. In the end, the trade decision is yours, but what I have found is that discussing trades that may be setting up can provide an added benefit when it ultimately comes time to place the trade.

Make sure that you don't talk yourself out of a trade. Nine of 10 times if you follow your plan and go with your gut, you will be right, even if the trade goes against you. Moreover, you don't have to be right all the time. In fact, with good money management, you can be right just 34 percent of the time and still make money in the FOREX. This is better than a coin flip. Focus on your own opinion. Of course, you can compare different approaches to the same situation, but in the end, you are the one who will make the decision and the only one responsible for your trading.

RESPONSIBILITY

Be your own leader; make your own the rules! FOREX markets are a force made of orderly chaos, a powerful mix of human emotions, economic circumstances, and strong financial interests. The market is always right because it moves as it wants and when it wants and has no fixed rules by itself. The only stable data on which to depend are your system and you, the trader, and your ability to make the rules and to change them as many times as necessary to adapt to ever-changing market conditions.

WORKING HARD VERSUS WORKING EFFICIENTLY

The more you work will not make a difference in your results. Unlike most working situations, in the FOREX what counts is how efficient you can be, not how many hours you spend in front of your charts.

LETTING PROFITS RUN

Holding to a trend can be difficult if, based on the previously mentioned attitude of expecting results proportional to the effort made, you think that it is too easy and can't accept huge profits. Most traders "hit and run" and don't have enough discipline to wait patiently for a trend to develop. Instead, they cut their profits as soon as they appear in fear that they might go away. I have seen this many times, and I too am guilty of. It is a difficult attitude to overcome, but stay focused, and you will. Traders often find themselves in a trade that is going against them and completely forget about their trading plan. They let their emotions get the best of them, saying such things as, "It will come back," "I have a feeling about this," and "I will cost-average down or double my position so that I can make money when it comes back." This is *not* good; it is the wrong state of mind. What ends up happening is that you have a huge loss, and then, when you place your next trade and are up a few dollars, you start saying, "I've got to take money off the table now," and thus put yourself in an upside-down money management position, willing to risk hundreds of dollars to gain only a few.

There are some basic rules that never should be broken. First of all, you need to have a clear objective and know what you really want to achieve. Without a goal, it is much more difficult to obtain a result because your efforts will lack direction and focus. Stating your goals and milestones clearly will help you greatly in achieving success, one step at a time.

Most traders start with the sole purpose of just "making money"—as much and as soon as possible. However, the other side of the coin has to be planned as well, and risk has to be defined even more carefully because it will make or break your final results. Goals also have to be realistic. Your rules should be measurable and achievable in terms of potential returns and time and resources available.

This is not to say that you can't aim big, but don't expect either to become a millionaire by the end of the month if your available equity is only $10,000. Aiming above your real capacities will only lead you to frustration and failure.

I often ask my students, "How much return would you like to make on your investment" I then follow up by saying, "Let's be realistic. Before there was the FOREX, what would you have been happy making on your money in the stock market" You would be surprised; 5 to 12 percent is the usual reply. That's right, not an unrealistic goal. Think of it this way: The rule of 72 says to take 72 and divide by the rate of return you would like to earn. Thus 72 divided by 20 percent = 3.6. This is the number of years it would take to double your investment—3.6 years. This is a number I like to

strive for because doubling my portfolio every 3.6 years is certainly something I can live with.

With that said, people make huge returns in the FOREX. I see it every
day. In fact, I live it as well. But be realistic. A 20 percent return means that
it takes 3.6 years to double your investment. Thus a 40 percent return means
that in 1.8 years you will double your money. What happens if you make
40 percent in one year? I would suggest that you may want to be even more
conservative with your trading for the rest of the year. If you end the year at
40 percent, you should be very happy. In fact, if you end the year up 20 percent, you also should be happy. Keep that in mind when you are placing
trades and developing that realistic goal you are shooting for in terms of
return on investment, don't get carried away trying to make 1 percent a day
or more because with risk comes reward, but so does the potential for loss.
Just think smart, and stick to your plan.

NOW YOU NEED A SYSTEM

Whether you adopt an already defined trading strategy or choose to
develop one yourself with the various technical tools at hand, you will have
to follow its rules and make sure that all the needed steps are included—
when to enter, when to exit, and what targets and stops it allows. This is
why having a mentor, someone who has already paved the way, a leader in
the field, is important. I am confident that after reading this book, you will
want to learn more, and I know I can help you by sharing with you my
FOREX journey. If not me, then make sure that you get someone to help
you along the way.

You have to be confident in your system, know all its details perfectly,
and have practiced with it enough to be certain of its probable results. The
rules have to be simple and clear, and you should have the discipline to follow them to the letter. Trading impulsively and randomly, led by the flow of
your emotions, and without a precise plan will only lead to negative results.

Your system should include a solution for every situation that you
might encounter in your trading. In this way, the results you obtain from
your testing will be accurate, thus adding to your confidence and ensuring
that you will be trading with consistency in any situation that might arise.

In addition, you should have answers that address all the possible sce-
narios that can develop and have a precise action plan prepared for each of
them. If all the possible circumstances that can arise are not anticipated and
planned for, an unexpected event could cause you a huge loss. Everything
should be predictable, even the situations that you couldn't even think
might happen.

Here's a list of some of the most basic rules:

Stay with the trend. Identify as soon as possible the main trend and its subsequent intermediary cycles to minimize the risk for losses. As is often said, the trend is your friend. If you are going with the trend, any minor retracement will not affect the final result when it comes back in your direction. If you are counter-trending, be careful because the price can move against you and possibly never recover as it picks up with the long-term trend. In a bullish market, go long. In a bearish market, go short. In a sideways market, it is better to stay on the sidelines and wait for a better opportunity.

Buy strong, sell weak. Identify which currencies are showing more strength and which ones are weak, and try to pair them up.

Buy low, sell high. Always try to get the best possible price both when buying and selling. Never sell into a support level nor buy at a resistance point.

Let your profits run, and cut your losses short. Control your fear of losing when you are in a winning trade, and learn to develop patience so that a trade can evolve to its full potential. Conversely, as soon as a trade has proven to be wrong, don't hesitate for a second in closing it according to the rules you have defined for your risk level. Don't fall into the temptation of widening your stops because last time you were stopped out the trade went back in your direction.

Past performance is not a guarantee of future performance. Your system might have been performing very well, and suddenly there is a change in the market behavior. Be aware of the signs of such a change, and adjust your system accordingly. Markets could have been trending for a long time, and they now are consolidating sideways. Be sure to have several strategies ready to use in each different market condition.

Have an alternate power supply and supplementary Internet connection, as well as the phone number of your broker's dealing desk, ready at hand in case you experience an unexpected power outage, server disconnect, or general Internet failure. There are now several options through mobile communications that allow traders to open or close positions that could be at risk in such an event.

*Know exactly what to do in case you are unable to trade, if you
happen to lose a certain percentage of your account, or if the
markets are closed and you need to get out of your current
positions.*

Develop your patience. Not having a position is also a position. There
will be moments when the best trading approach is to stay on the
sidelines and wait patiently for a setup to develop. Never jump
into a nonplanned trade out of impatience or boredom. Wait for
pullbacks to enter if you have missed the initial entry. The market
moves in waves, and by waiting for the correction, you will have
the odds in your favor as to the necessary stops. Reaching that
rate-of-return goal does not have to be done over night. In the
FOREX, it could be reached quickly, allowing you to sit on the
sidelines the rest of the year if you choose to. Have patience.

Let your trade breathe and develop fully to its complete potential.
Inversely, be impatient and eager to close any trade that is proving
itself wrong from the beginning. Capital preservation is a must.

Don't count and cry over missed pips. Missed money is better than
lost money. There always will be a better opportunity to enter the
market.

Add to your winning trades; never add to your losing positions.
Averaging down is down is a very risky practice that could make
you lose much more than you planned initially. Inversely, when a
trend is developing successfully, consider adding to your trade
after each small correction.

*Never risk more than 5 to 10 percent of your equity total and not more
than 1 to 2 percent on a single trade.* In this way, if you happen to
hit a losing streak, you still will have more than enough capital
left to take losses back to breakeven.

Avoid trading at news time and when markets open or close. Too
much random volatility can kill your account very fast. Wait for
the market sentiment to settle down, and go with the flow as
soon as the direction is clear. Trade only when conditions are at
their best.

*Periodically review your past performance, and redefine your plan if
needed.* Adjust your money management and position size
according to your profits or losses on equity. Evaluate your
results, and compare them with your goals. Readjust your goals if
necessary.

If you experience a heavy loss, take some time off to reevaluate the situation and clear your mind. Stop trading for a few days. Absolutely do not trade for revenge! You shouldn't allow yourself to fall into the need of getting your money back as soon as possible. Instead, examine the reasons that caused the loss, recheck all your rules and trading plan, and take some rest to be able to come back refreshed and with a clear focus.

Match your position properly to your account size. Risking more than the recommended percentage can increase your gains tremendously, and you could be tempted to do so because the high leverages and small margin requirements of some brokers allow you to exceed your capabilities. Remember that it works the other way around as well: Losses can become unmanageable very soon. Think and plan for a long-term career.

Learn to read chart patterns and price action. Draw trendlines, and study and analyze the market's past behavior and present trends. Watch carefully how price reacts on supports and resistances. Try to understand what happened at every point of the price wave.

Consider scaling out of your position when it is profitable, if its size allows. In this way, you take some profit at an appropriate moment and still remain in the market for the long run, should it happen. If the trade then goes against you, at least you took some profit at a good point.

When being extremely successful, proceed with extra caution. Reinforce the discipline or, better, take a day off from the market. Overconfidence can occur insidiously and you could lose in a few hours what took you several days to build. Keep your profits, and stay alert!

HOW THE MARKET WORKS

A market is a situation where there is an imbalance in supply and demand between its participants that results in continuous and unpredictable fluctuations in the exchange rates. What causes the market to be so unpredictable?

- Different traders interpret the same fundamental factors differently.
- The intents of various market participants are different, as well as their reasons and purposes for conducting a transaction. Reasons may include hedging, purchase of currency with the purposes of

financing an international commercial project, or a bargain for a speculative profit.

- Since the market is simultaneously influenced by the various fundamentals and contradictory forces, the final reaction can vary, causing fluctuations in the market, and not comply with the expected reaction to some fundamental event or process.

In addition, even powerful financial institutions can make mistakes because institutional traders are just people like you and me. This also adds to the randomness of the whole picture.

RULES FOR WORKING WITH THE MARKET

Try to have no particular bias about the market's future behavior. Follow your own system and rules, and react to the signals the market is giving you (trade what you see, not what you think). Examine the signals given carefully, and be aware of those that go against your point of view instead of looking for signals that confirm your point of view.

Never try to predict. Listen to what the market is really telling you, here and now. Forecasts (especially long-term ones) are useless in an unpredictable and changing situation such as the FOREX market. Be here and now, and trade what you see. The need to be right is a waste of energy and time, which you should invest instead in focusing on real-time conditions. Moreover, if your predictions turn out to be wrong, this would add unnecessary stress to your emotions.

There are no guarantees of success independent of your own past performance in this or any other professional activity. Logic and common sense will not work; for example, the same results in fundamental news can bring about completely opposite reactions in different time spans because there are too many details in between that exert an influence on market sentiment. Markets will react based on their interpretations of fundamentals more than to any specific figure itself.

Most FOREX transactions are done as a result of international business and commerce. The FOREX is used much less as an investment vehicle, although there is much room also left for speculation. Commercial participants at the international level only want to produce and sell their products. They are seldom interested in all the details about exchange rates. Banks initially only provided the exchange rate between currencies. They bought the foreign currency at one rate, added a commission for their services (the spread), and sold the currency to the customers at a higher rate.

Thereafter, based on the growing volume of all those commercial transactions, bank traders started to speculate on future currency rates. They then could give a quote at a certain rate and hold the transaction until another one came by at a better price. Given these practices, the banks were able to expand their profits. On the other hand, though, the liquidity redistribution made some transactions impossible to complete.

For this reason, the market was opened to nonbank and noncommercial participants. More orders started to flow into the market from less experienced participants, from which banks could make an additional profit, providing a better liquidity distribution for their international orders.

The largest proportion of transactions in the FOREX market is performed by the largest central banks from major countries through a series of communication agreements. This is also known as the *Interbank,* which has no physical location. All of the central banks are independent of each other unless the need arises to execute a transaction (i.e., the exchange of each country's currency), and then they interact.

Since it would be difficult for each other to keep track properly of all the transactions made and resources available, the electronic broking service (EBS) was created as a central server that allows interconnection between all the computers of the banking network. Through this service, the banks can show each other the prices at which they are willing to sell or buy any other currency and their own, creating in effect the Interbank market. In itself, the Interbank is not a market, nor is it a market maker. Rather, it is an application that is used to see the various bid and offer prices from all the banks involved.

The EBS—the Interbank—is the first component of the currency markets. The next component is every bank in itself because any one of them can buy or sell currency to any individual, institution, or business that needs to exchange one currency into another.

The third component is the sum of all the retail brokers (i.e., market makers) and electronic communications networks (ECNs). A market maker is usually associated with a bank from the second level, which will provide liquidity for all its transactions. Since these are retail institutions, it is not easy to know how many liquidity providers with whom they are associated. Very often, small transactions are kept in house and never reach the Interbank market. Orders are matched and resolved internally, and if needed (depending on the number of lots required), they can be transferred to another market maker or placed directly with the liquidity provider.

This structure allows the market makers to accept negotiations with smaller amounts, such as mini and microlots. On the Interbank market, the smallest amount is the standard lot (minimum $100,000). A market maker is the counterpart of almost all its customers' transactions.

ECNs, on their side, are automated brokers that route your orders to the best price on the platform from multiple liquidity providers. These liquidity providers may be banks or other traders connected to the platform. The deals are performed directly on the Interbank without any intermediary dealing desk.

FOR EVERY BUYER, THERE MUST BE A SELLER

You would think that in a market such as the FOREX that moves around such a large amount of money, liquidity would never be a problem. However, the truth is that there has to be a seller for every buyer and a buyer for every seller for transactions to be executed.

When orders are too large at a certain price, exceeding the opposite orders for that level, the price has to move to a point where there is enough counterpart interest to match them. Prices that are listed on the Interbank through the EBS show how much and at which price banks agree to buy or sell a currency. They choose the price and are in no way forced to transact if they believe that it is not in their best interest to do so.

The volumes of bids and offers are shown for each price level, and of course, there are prices at which there are none. All these constitute limit orders placed in the market.

Thus, at the moment a market order for a certain volume is placed at a given price, it will have an effect on spreads and will move the price accordingly. Depending on the volume and level of the opposite orders available, the price will settle at a higher or lower level, immediately, causing a widening of the spreads and sharp changes in prices, because there are no intermediary orders to absorb the current quote. Later on, another order can enter the market at an intermediate price between the widened bid-ask spread, and thus a new change in spreads and prices will occur.

Slippage means that there is no one to take the other side of the transaction at the exact moment the order is placed in the market. You are being given the nearest best price according to the volume of matching orders. Changes occur very fast, especially at news time, because higher volumes enter and exit continuously. Thus you can be quoted a price that is not available any more less than a second later. This is why you get requotes or invalid prices because there is no more interest left at that particular level. The *spread* is defined by the price levels where there are effectively existing bids and offers. If all the intermediary limit orders were canceled at the same time, the spread could widen because a higher offer and lower bid could exist at that moment. This only means that nobody is agreeing to effect a transaction at any price between those levels. Spreads and slippage are a natural part of the trading scene and are the result of agreements or refusal to transact between market participants and thus are impossible to avoid.

PAPER TRADING

A FOREX demo account is basically a practice account that allows traders to use virtual credits instead of real money, but with actual real-time price feeds and conditions, on the FOREX market. It is important for every individual who wishes to invest in the currency markets to acquire a solid grounding in basic financial concepts and to learn as much as possible about technical and fundamental analysis. Then practice as needed to apply this knowledge in a live situation to make sure that it is understood.

Paper trading (or demo trading) is often overlooked because most traders are impatient to jump into the market and gain their first real-money profits. However, nobody should be trading with real money until they have at least obtained good results consistently in their demo account with real-time conditions (not only backtesting).

Of course, being able to get excellent results on paper trading will not guarantee that you will have the same outcome when you are trading with real money because the emotional part of trading doesn't show up (or at least not at the same level) until you are using real money. However, you will be able to determine if your strategy or system works and gauge its probabilities while you learn all the mechanical details of the platform. This is very important because not every trading software system offers the exact same features, and styles of trading allowed will differ a little from one broker to another.

All retail brokers allow their potential customers to test their platforms, some for a limited time and others with no limited. Precise knowledge of the software is needed to be able to act as fast as possible and avoid making mistakes. I have integrated a demo account into my AI software platforms to help achieve a more realistic trading environment.

You also can experiment with various trading styles and different brokers in different time zones, test various systems simultaneously, and define more precisely the trading style that suits you best. There also are different styles of platforms. Some you can access directly online; others need to be downloaded to your computer. Most of them integrate news and charting packages in addition to the price feed, as well as a history

and reports of your trading activities. It is a good idea to try several of
them so that you can master all the different mechanics. For example,
some allow you to place contrary orders on the same currency pair,
whereas others use those contrary orders to close an existing position.
Some require a single margin or even no margin on two contrary positions, whereas others require a margin guarantee on both the long and
short trades. With certain platforms, you will be able to do a stop and
reverse with just one click by opening a contrary position of double the
value of your existing position or plan a detailed sequence of interdepen-
dent orders to be executed if the first condition is met, whereas others
won't have this feature.

With my AI software, I have had the luxury of thousands of traders over
the years providing feedback as to what features they like and don't like,
what enhancements increase the efficiency of the platform, etc. This has
allowed me to build what I believe to be the single best, most robust and
flexible trading station on the market. If you want to learn more about it,
you can visit *www.JamesDicks.com*.

The following are the basic questions you should ask before you
attempt to trade live with your own real money on any platform:

1. How do I to place a market order?
2. How do I place a pending order (buy/sell limit or buy/sell stop)?
3. How do I set a stop loss?
4. Are automated trailing stops available, and if so, are they on my side
   or the server's side?
5. Can the target profit and stop loss be set at the moment of the entry,
   or do they have to be set afterwards?
6. Are the spreads on the platform fixed or variable, and if so, what is
   the usual range?
7. What are the swaps (overnight interest) earned or paid on open
   positions that last more than 24 hours?
8. What is the lot size that can be traded (standard, mini, micro,
   or nanolots)?
9. Can partial lot sizes be used (e.g., 0.45 microlots, 1.2 lots, etc.)?
10. Does the broker offer the possibility of calling the dealing room
    directly by phone if my Internet connection goes down?
11. Is live support available?

12. Are the trading history and reports clear enough to be used afterwards for tax purposes? Although this is a responsibility of the trader, you should be able to get manageable reports under the point of view of accounting.

DISADVANTAGES OF DEMO TRADING

Most of the real circumstances of trading can be easily overlooked when you are paper trading. Unless you commit yourself to treat your demo account in the same way as you would a real-money account with the same set of rules and discipline and a starting capital that is proportional to the one you will be using when you switch to a real account, the following are the most common pitfalls that you might face:

1. *Careless handling of real risks.* Losses that you may incur are not real losses, so you won't be able to learn to deal with your real emotions when facing a loss.

2. *No fear is involved.* Whenever you start losing, and even if you get a margin call on a demo account, you simply can start a new one all over. So you won't be able to learn how to handle the fear of losing, which is a very powerful emotion in real trading.

3. *No real commitment to develop a concise money management.* Since you can chose to trade with any huge amount, you could be tempted to take excessive risks because, in the end, it is not real money, and you could develop a bad habit that will continue when you start on a live account.

4. *You can develop greed.* Given the great amounts that can be involved in a demo account and the larger position sizes that you can trade because of this, if you start making lots of money, you could become greedy and be under its control.

To avoid those pitfalls, you must trade on a demo as if it were real money. For example, if you are planning to start trading live with equity of $2,000, open a demo account with that same amount of funds. Trading a higher amount would be fun and boost your ego for a while, but it wouldn't be applicable thereafter to real life. Add to this the fact that you might lose your sense of proportion and make huge mistakes afterwards.

Paper trading should be just for learning purposes. It's also a good way to test a system or strategy to see if it really works before going live with it and losing your money. Keep in mind that if you are unable to produce acceptable gains on a demo account, chances are that you won't on a real-money account either. The good part of a demo account is that you can make all the mistakes you need to acquire experience and confidence, which you then will be able to apply under real conditions.

FOREX demo accounts are also very useful for experienced traders, who employ them to bring their trading strategies to perfection, test new changes without risking funds, or practice a new system while evaluating its results in total safety.

C H A P T E R

HOW TO KEEP YOUR PROFITS

MONEY MANAGEMENT

A good understanding and handling of money management is the key to a successful career as a FOREX trader. Although you don't need to have a master's in economics and finance to be able to trade and earn a profitable income from your trading activities, a certain degree of financial education assuredly is an asset. This is why I am writing this book and what my organization really does. We provide education, training, and support. There are simply not enough places to go to learn such things as trading the FOREX. Actually, if primary education were even a little geared toward some sort of basic financial education, maybe we would all be a little better off.

Understanding what lies beneath price movements, how the market is structured, what the exchanges of foreign currencies are designed to satisfy in the current economy of the world, why and how currency values change, and how those changes affect overall political and economical stability is basic knowledge that has to be acquired. In particular, a thorough understanding of the spread and bid and ask prices and how they interact and the implications of trading on margin is needed to establish and implement a sound set of rules for money management of your own trading account.

As you have seen before, the bid-ask spread is the difference between the price at which a currency pair is offered to be sold and the price at which it is actually purchased. If the ask or offer price is $10 and the bid is

$12, you get a $2 difference, which is the spread. When you are trading on margin, you are buying and selling currency pairs for a much higher value than the money you have in your account. The margin can be so small because the exchange rates don't usually move beyond 2 percent of their value. This capability, or leverage, allows traders to obtain great profits in a small time span, but this also represents a high risk. With proper money management, you can effectively manage this risk.

If you want to invest in speculative activities, the most important thing to consider is that you should only use risk capital, that is, money that you don't need for your daily expenses or other projects, money that you can afford to lose should problems arise.

Never invest what you can't afford to lose. If you don't have the necessary starting capital all at once, set aside a small portion that you will dedicate solely to FOREX trading. In fact, even if you have a fair amount of money available to assign to your trading, break it into equal portions, and use only one portion at a time. In this way, if things go wrong, you still have another portion to start over, and your risks are minimized. Trading is not gambling. Despite the high leverages available, where you can risk all your account and reap a handsome profit, this would be based on luck, and luck is for gamblers. Trading is a business, and as such, it has to be undertaken with clear goals and asset administration.

As soon as you decide to get into real-money trading, and assuming that you have already spent a few months paper trading on a demo account, you should carefully examine what your goals are, how much money you can expect to earn based on your capital, and above all, whether your goals are realistic. Make sure that your expectations are realistic and based on the real experiences of people you can trust.

The first step in real-money trading should be to open a small test account with little money thus little risk. Try a mini account or, better, a micro account, where you can open positions and trade for 1 cent a pip. This seem like a ridiculously small amount, but remember that you are still learning, and you need to make sure that your profits are stable and consistent before increasing your capital and position sizes.

A final word about capitalization: Many people are attracted to FOREX trading because it offers them the dream of starting a home-based business and a chance to be their own bosses and quit a probably boring day job. How many businesses can you start without initial working capital? If you are thinking of getting a steady monthly income from your FOREX activities, you have to prepare the ground very well from the start. Plan all the steps to get to your goal because this will not happen overnight. Remember, we're not in this to be lucky but to be successful!

How much startup capital do I have? How much do I need for my living expenses? How much time do I need to practice, learn, apply, and obtain profits from my trading system in a consistent and steady manner? All this has to be taken into account. Write down your plans and goals, with precise schedules and numbers. Remember to be realistic in your expectations. A high percentage of return is possible in some months but will not last over time. A small and steady increase will last longer. Anything on the order of 2 to 5 percent a month is fairly possible to obtain with discipline and good money management. This would represent about 0.1 to 0.25 percent daily profits, which is achievable. Use the power of compounding: 5 percent a month represents 60 percent a year, noncompounded, and 80 percent if you compound the profits made monthly. Remember the rule of 72: 20 percent doubles your investment in 3.6 years, and 40 percent doubles your investment in 1.8 years. Pick a realistic return-on-investment goal for you, and stick to it.

A SIMPLE CALCULATOR

This is a simple calculator that you can build in any spreadsheet application that will help you to determine the appropriate stops, targets, and risk-reward management based on your specific plan and risk appetite. It is composed of five variable cells, with their respective descriptions, where you will introduce values based on different situations, and seven fixed formula result cells, with descriptions, that will give you the lot size for the trade, the value per pip, the amount of maximum loss, and the price at which to set the stops and targets for both short and long positions depending on the actual price that you will have entered above.

	A		B
A1	Account	B1	1,000.00
A2	Risk %	B2	2%
A3	Actual Price	B3	1.4500
A4	SL (pips)	B4	50
A5	R/R	B5	1:5
A6	Trade Size (lots)	B6	0.04
A7	PIP Value	B7	$0.10
A8	Max Loss	B8	$20.00
A9	SL Buy	B9	1.4450
A10	SL Sell	B10	1.4550
A11	TP Buy	B11	1.4575
A12	TP Sell	B12	1.4425

Let's assume that you are working with columns A and B and cells A1 to B12. Column A is for the descriptions, as follows:

Account = account *equity* (not to confuse with account balance because positions should be calculated with respect to the net equity remaining in the account).

Risk % = risk percentage (which should be in a 1 to 3 percent range as a maximum for ideal money management).

Actual price = the actual price of the currency pair.

SL = stop loss (the number of pips or points needed depending on your strategy and time frame).

R/R = risk/reward (the ratio between risk and reward you would like to apply to your trade. For example, 1:5 would be a reward that is 50 percent higher than the risk; that is, in the case of a 50-pip stop loss, you would need a 75-pip target profit).

The remaining descriptions will have fixed formulas: Cells B6 to B12 won't be changeable after the calculator is built.

Trade size = size (in lots, mini lots, or microlots; you can configure the formula to show as integers or decimals at will). In the figure shown, size is in microlots, namely, 0.04 lot, and the result is obtained by multiplying the pip value by 10. The formula is the next B cell ("Pip value") divided by 10.

Pip value = value per pip on that particular currency pair for the trade size (in the figure it is calculated with a fixed $10 per standard lot, $0.10 per microlot). The formula is account equity times risk percent divided by stop loss, or B1 times B2 divided by B4.

Max loss = maximum amount of loss expressed in U.S. dollars or your deposit currency of choice. The formula is pip value times stop loss, or B7 times B4. It also could just be account equity times risk percent, or B1 times B2, which will give the same result.

SL buy/sell and TP buy/sell = prices at which to set the stops and target profits for both long and short positions. It is divided by 10,000 to get the last two digits of the decimal price in the case of four-decimal currency pairs or by 100 in the case of JPY two-decimal currency pairs. Formulas include

$$\text{SL buy} = B3 - (B4/10{,}000) = \text{actual price} - (SL/10{,}000)$$
$$\text{SL sell} = B3 + (B4/10{,}000) = \text{actual price} + (SL/10{,}000)$$
$$\text{TP buy} = B3 + [(B4/10{,}000) \times B5] = \text{actual price} + [(SL/10{,}000) \times R/R)]$$
$$\text{TP sell} = B3 - [(B4/10{,}000) \times B5] = \text{actual price} - [(SL/10{,}000) \times R/R)]$$

In this way, you will only have to change the details of the first five B cells and will immediately obtain the position size needed to open the next trade. I also have money-management capabilities built into my AI software, and you can access this calculator at *www.JamesDicks.com*.

PERCENTAGES TO RECOVER IN CASE OF LOSS

Maximum drawdown is the largest percentage drop in your account equity. The following table shows the percentages of profit needed to recover your trading account to breakeven based on different percentages of equity loss.

Percent of Loss on Capital	Percent Profit Needed to Recover Up to Breakeven
10%	11.11%
20%	25%
30%	42.85%
40%	66.66%
50%	100%
60%	150%
70%	233%
80%	400%
90%	900%

As losses increase, the percentage required to recover to breakeven increases much faster because it grows geometrically.

This emphasizes the importance of a sound money management to avoid huge drawdowns because it is very difficult to recover from big losses. Respect for risk is one of the characteristics of professional traders. And risks are controlled through proper money management.

MANAGING RISK

Every business or investment has some risks involved, including the risk of loss. It is always possible that a trade will go wrong and turn against your chosen direction. Being aware of risks can help to minimize them, although there isn't any guarantee that they can be eliminated.

EXCHANGE-RATE RISK OR EXTREME VOLATILITY

The FOREX is highly volatile, and changes in rates can be sudden and totally unpredictable. You have to be prepared to cut your losses—and fast. Correct timing is the key. Don't let your positions run too far away. The price can run up or down very quickly. It is better to close with a small loss and try again later than to hope endlessly that the market will come back.

CREDIT RISK AND FOREX SCAMS

Be very cautious to check your broker's background before signing up for an account and especially before sending your money. Run away from any investment program that guarantees that you will make a big profit with little risk.

In the United States, brokers should be properly registered with the Commodities Futures Trading Commission (CFTC) and be a member of the National Futures Association (NFA). In other countries, offshore brokers should be registered with an equivalent institution.

In addition, your broker should handle pricing with honesty. Since there is no central marketplace and the broker is the one who establishes execution prices, you can only rely on the broker's reputation and reliability.

COUNTRY RISK OR POLITICAL/ECONOMIC INSTABILITY

Countries that participate in the FOREX market can represent a risk when they limit their currency flow. Choose to trade currency pairs that are among the most liquid and free markets to be sure that you don't get caught in a bad trade. Lack of liquidity can be an obstacle to closing a position because there is no counterpart at the moment to perform the exchange. This is why exotic or seldom-traded currencies represent a high risk.

ELECTRONIC OR SYSTEM FAILURES

Besides risking that your own equipment could crash or a power outage could block you from managing your open positions, sometimes the platform's server can fail. When this happens, you are unable to cancel or modify open orders or enter new positions until the technical problem is solved. Be sure to check whether your broker has alternatives, such as a phone dealing desk or a mobile platform, to palliate this risk. Another issue is problems with a broker's data feed from the liquidity provider. Although such problems usually are solved quickly, your orders could be slipped or closed at a price other than you anticipate. While placing trades, always set a stop, even if it is a safety stop far outside the market. In this way, if anything does happen to your trade, you still have a level of protection.

LEVERAGE AND TRUE LEVERAGE

Usual leverage can be anything between 1:1 and 1:500. This refers to the margin needed to secure a position. Thus 1:1 leverage would mean that for opening a trade with 1 lot, you would need to have at least $1,000 for the margin (more if the main currency is not the U.S. dollar), plus the spread × $10, plus your stop loss × $10, plus maybe a little more room just in case. At 1:500, you would need only 0.20 percent of the value of the lot (or $200 to $300) plus the mentioned additions to open that same position.

True leverage is the full amount of your position divided by the amount of money deposited in your trading account. However, true leverage is the proportion of the overall position size. Indeed, if you open 1 lot with only $300 in your account, you are using the full 1:500 true leverage. Now, if you open a position that, including the spread and risk, totals $300, you would be using 1:1 true leverage. This would be, for example, 300 units (3 nanolots; pip value $0.01 per nanolot).

If you are using microlots (pip value $0.1), you would be using 1:10 true leverage. Should you open more positions, the total added value of your trades would vary the leverage accordingly (3 positions at 1:10 = 1:30 true leverage), and the leverage will keep growing (which, in fact, is also growing your risk) as you keep adding.

Let's say that you don't want to risk more than 2 percent of your account, so you want to use 20 pips maximum risk per trade. On this same $300 account, you can open a position of 3 microlots (3000 units) at 2 percent risk with a 20-pip stop. This will give you the above-mentioned 1:30 true leverage, which is a conservative ratio, and with any amounts, the risk percentage doesn't change (only the required stops and corresponding position sizing should you need more or less than 20 pips). If you are risking 2 percent of your total equity, you will never lose more than 2 percent of your total equity, independent of any leverage used.

If you want to raise your stops—let's say that you need 60 pips, still at 2 percent risk—you would only open one microlot. Your position then will be at 1:10 true leverage. However, you still would lose only 2 percent of your account if stops are hit. Raise your stops to 100 pips, and decrease the position to 600 units or 6 nanolots. Your position now would be at 1:2 true leverage, but you still would lose only 2 percent of your account if stops are hit. And so on.

Also remember that the calculations have to be made on your account's equity, not the balance. You could have several positions open and going down, and thus your equity would be decreasing. The remaining equity is the only available capital at that moment.

Position size has to be adjusted while growing (*and* while decreasing). In fact, if you maintain the same 2 percent risk and 20-pip calculation, you'll be automatically adding lots (or mini-, micro-, or nanolots) to your position as soon as the proportion allows it. You also can decide to increase the stops instead and keep the original number of lots should you want to trade on higher time frames.

There are numerous ways of looking at leverage and risk. I like to keep things simple, so I think about them separately. Risk is the percentage of your account that you're willing to lose on a trade. Let's say that you have a $10,000 account (for a $500 account, see my comments below). If you trade 0.5 lot of GBP/USD, every 1-pip movement will affect your account by $5. Thus, if you set your stop loss 40 pips away from entry, then the risk is $40 \times \$5 = \$200$, which is 2 percent of your $10,000 account. Viewed this way, none of this has anything to do with leverage. Risk is the product of position size (0.5 lot in this example) and stop-loss point (40 pips from entry).

Leverage determines the amount of money you need in your account (margin) to be able to take the trade. Let's say that GBP/USD is currently priced at $1.45, and your broker is offering you 100:1 leverage. Then the margin you need is 0.5 lot $\times$ $100,000 per lot/100 leverage $\times$ 1.45 = $725, which is 7.25 percent of your $10,000. If the leverage were only 50:1, then the amount required would be 0.5 $\times$ 100,000/50 $\times$ 1.45 = $1450, or 14.50 percent; that is, at 50:1, you need twice the margin than at 100:1, and so on. Thus, at 50:1, you are locking up 14.50 percent of your account balance, leaving the remaining 85.50 percent free (unused or available margin) to place on other trades. None of this alters the fact that the risk is still 2 percent, meaning that if your stop loss gets hit, you lose $200.

A standard account allows a minimum position size of 1 lot, a mini account allows 0.1 lot, and a micro account 0.01 lot. This, assuming a minimum-size trade on GBP/USD in a standard account, each pip move alters your account balance by $10; in a mini account, $1; and in a micro account, 10 cents.

As a general rule, you shouldn't place more than 1 to 2 percent at risk on any one trade. This will allow your account to survive many losses. Preserving capital will keep you in the game. Of course, if you're new to the FOREX, you should start trading in a demo account to practice your understanding of the preceding and to get a feel for the mechanics of trading.

Take, for example, a $500 mini account: 2 percent (risk per trade) of $500 is $10. Thus, given that each pip is worth $1, the maximum distance your stop loss can be away from entry is 10 pips. Obviously, this gives very little room to move. Hence, with only $500, it would be better to trade in microlots. It is said that to trade a standard account (at 2 percent risk per trade), the ideal amount required would be a minimum deposit of $25,000; proportionally, then, a mini account would require $2,500 and a micro account $250. At 2 percent risk, each of these allows you to place a stop loss 50 pips from entry.

OVERTRADING AND OVERCONFIDENCE

Overtrading can be interpreted in two ways: opening too many positions with regard to your account equity or trading beyond a certain quantity of positions in a single day because you feel that you need to be "always in the market." It is so easy to jump compulsively into a trade without regard for your strategy or for the consequences, which often can be costly. *Overconfidence* can lead to overtrading because you feel all powerful and think that you will keep winning more and more. As a result, you incur excesses and overlook the warning signs. Revenge trading is the inverse behavior and another type of overtrading, where you keep desperately opening positions after you have lost many previous ones in the hope of recovering the losses. Such behavior is enhanced by emotions such as anger and frustration.

How can you determine if you are overtrading? The following are some symptoms that can help you to identify and correct this erroneous trading style:

- You don't have a trading signal, or at least the signal is not very clear.
- You check all the possible time frames, currency pairs, and indicators available, switching from one to another looking for a "confirmation" justifying your need to be in the market.
- You open a trade as soon as you enter your trading platform without much previous analysis.
- You see opportunities and trends everywhere, and if you don't trade, you feel that you are missing out on potential profits.
- You feel frustrated when you think of an entry point but fail to enter, and then it goes the way you predicted.
- You want to stay awake from Sunday to Friday so that you don't miss any trade; you sleep very little and scour the charts every 5 minutes looking for another trade.

- You can't bear to be away from your trading platform. In fact, this is one of the reasons I created the James Dicks FOREX alerts—so that you don't have to sit at your computer Sunday through Friday. My traders do that for you, and when they enter a trade, they will send out an alert so that you can quickly see what they are looking at and make a decision to enter the trade or not.

- Maybe you have a working trading plan and system, but you often bend the rules and justify this with a series of weak excuses: "I'm risking so little that it won't matter"; "This time only"; "This is the perfect setup, and I don't want to miss the profits"; "The market is moving a lot; I've got to jump in"; and so on.

- You think that the more you trade, the more profits you will make. You open a lot of random positions because behind any of them lies assuredly the "big home run" that will make up for all your previous losses. You trade carelessly and furiously, with despair and excitement and contradictory emotions throughout the entire process. You enjoy the rush and stress and think that they are a normal part of trading. Anything else would be boring.

Overtrading reduces your win-loss ratio and increases your costs because every time you open a trade, you are paying the spread and commissions if your broker is an electronic communications network (ECN).

Trading should not be seen as an adventure or a hobby. It is a business and a money-making opportunity, where you can succeed if you treat it as such. If you constantly lose or have huge losses followed by extraordinary wins without a system and a planned strategy, you are trading carelessly and just gambling. Trying to get revenge after a string of losses is very common. This attitude is lead by a mixture of fear and anger and only brings about more losses and frustration. Keep your money management under strict control. Many traders increase their position size after a series of bad trades in the hope that a single winning trade will allow them to recover all. Trade what you see in the market, use your system, and follow your plan. Losses are part of the picture, and money management will take care of them. Money-management rules are very easy: Your winning positions should be bigger than your losing trades.

If you are new to FOREX trading, do not get involved in scalping. This is a very risky and difficult strategy that requires a strong personality, total control, focus, and a clear mind that is free of negative or positive emotions. A strict discipline is needed to enter and exit many dozens of trades in a short time span.

Overconfidence is perhaps the trickier state of mind for a trader. The ego boost that a series of winning trades can give you is even worse than the effects of a losing streak. Wait for the market to come to you. Chasing the market is a common mistake. After every small move, there is almost always a retracement, where you can enter at a better price.

OVERLEVERAGING

The extreme leverage allowed by some FOREX brokers—a relative proportion that can go up to 500:1, which means controlling on the markets an amount of money 500 times greater than what you are required as margin—can induce a trader very easily to overleverage his or her positions and risk a total margin call. The most important and first thing to do is to protect your working capital.

Working with only a small percentage of your total equity is not easy when trading on very small accounts. For this reason, you should find a broker that allows microlots or even nanolots, in which every pip has a value of 1 or 10 cents. A microlot is equivalent to controlling $1000; a nanolot would be $100. In this way, you can trade with a greater confidence and manage your risk more efficiently by setting your stop losses at the exact level where they have to be and avoid being stopped out on tight settings because you can't afford to risk more.

Depending on your trading style, you will need to open much smaller lot sizes, especially if you are scaling or averaging down into a losing position, which is not a recommended trading style but can be done with a careful plan. Scaling involves splitting a single position into several parts to enter at a better price on a trade after a signal given by your system has proven that the entry and direction can have good probabilities. Always protect your trading account; the best way to make it grow is to use compounding and make continuous small, consistent profits instead of hoping that you will hit the jackpot. Remember, FOREX trading is not gambling. When you use smaller positions, you are limiting your risk and also avoiding huge drawdowns that would limit your available margin and thus your trading ability.

It is of fundamental importance to determine how much you can afford to lose because this is what will allow you to choose the most suitable type of leverage. Using leverage judiciously allows you to maximize your profits and minimize your losses and, above all, to keep trading for a longer time.

TRADE EXPECTATIONS

Many traders worry about how many pips they are "leaving on the table." Currency rates are constantly moving, giving and taking, even in a small range. Thus there will always be "pips on the table" for traders to take or lose.

The price moves (on average and based on the slowest markets such as Asia) about 10 pips every 5 minutes, then reverses, then again, etc., even in a tight channel, as you might have seen (barely 15- to 20-pip ranges). On a 1-minute chart, you can't expect much more per trade unless the pair starts trending (which seldom occurs in Asia) or unless you stay in the trade by managing your stops and watching the higher time frame (5 minutes). This is especially true if your entry is conservative.

However, in more volatile market conditions, trades can yield a better return. Thus maybe you would have to find better trading conditions, such as the Europe–New York market, where a conservative entry will not hamper evolution of the trade.

There are thousands of pips of the table (and many more if you consider all the pairs that are moving at the same time). Cherish the ones the market is willing to give you; there are always plenty of opportunities throughout the day.

I often make light of how badly traders want to be in the market, myself included. I like to trade. I enjoy the process. I am not a gambler and really do not like to lose. I focus on good money management, but even that and my plan sometimes suffer at the hands of boredom. I can be at home sitting around late at night after everyone has gone to bed, nothing on television, and the only thing left to do is pull out my laptop, open up my AI software, and start looking for a trade. I will analyze everything with nothing really to trade. In such a situation, the next thing that happens is that you start seeing things that aren't there. You place a trade, and the trade goes against you. Then you get mad, and you cost-average down or revenge trade. And then you take a loss. I always say that I can make any chart look good. It is true. Stare at any currency pair or stock, for that matter, and if you want to get into the market, you will convince yourself that the trade looks good. Just remember the rule of 72, and don't force trades. If things aren't going well for you, simply stop trading and take a break. Come back with a clear head and a positive mental attitude, and then you will be ready to trade some more.

TRADING PSYCHOLOGY

7

MASTERING
EMOTIONS

TRADING PSYCHOLOGY

Most traders can spend years trying to find and develop the "right" system with the expectation that it will yield excellent results and make a lot of money for them. However, very few would dedicate as much time to delve deeply in their own psychology as human beings and as traders, thus neglecting the most important part of the FOREX trading scene: the individual trader.

Having a good system, coupled with a sound money management and a disciplined trading plan, is fundamental indeed. But it will not work completely unless the trader is able to understand all the psychological barriers than could affect the decision-making processes and the ulterior reactions that stem from any positive or negative outcome of the decisions made. Trading must include all these elements in a balanced way for the trader to succeed in this business.

What is the first thought that comes to your mind when your trade has a negative outcome? The first thing you probably blame is "your system." You "knew" you shouldn't have taken the trade; you look for what could be wrong in your strategy, even if the system effectively gave the trading signal. Seldom, however, do you look inside your own self to see what really happened at that moment.

What is a mistake? In your day-to-day life, being wrong or making a mistake is something bad and signals incompetence. You are conditioned to strive and fight to always be right, so it is very difficult at the beginning to be able to accept that losses are only a normal part of the trading environment.

It is said that only a small group of traders is able to achieve the goal of obtaining consistent and continuous profits. Do they have a special gift that differentiates them from others? The reason behind their success is persistence. They are not set back because of mistakes. On the contrary, any mistake they make is a lesson to learn and another chance to try again, to do it better, and in the end, this persistence is what makes all the difference.

You accept the concept that failing to obtain money from any given trade is a mistake. However, this is not true. You make mistakes when you don't follow the guidelines of your trading plan. You make mistakes when you violate the rules of your system. Here are a few examples of what would be a trading mistake and what wouldn't.

First trade: Your system gives the signal to take a trade. You do so, and the outcome is profitable. You make money with that trade. You followed the rules. This confirms that the system works and reinforces your confidence in it, as well as your self-confidence as a trader. No mistakes were made.

Second trade: You take the signal, but it ends up being a losing trade. You lose money. You followed the rules. You understand that it is not possible to win every trade that you make and that it is part of the whole outcome of your system, a given percentage of winners and losers. You keep your confidence because you respected the guidelines of your system. No mistakes were made.

Third trade: You do not take the signal, and the trade would have been profitable. You do not lose, but neither do you gain any money. You feel frustrated because you didn't follow the rules of your system. You lose self-confidence as a trader. You made a mistake, which was not taking a trade when the system gave you the entry signal.

Fourth trade: You do not take the signal, and the trade would have been a losing one. You are glad that you didn't lose any money. This is a risky outcome because you might start thinking that you are better than your system. Thus, thereafter, you will continue to have second thoughts on every trade that is signaled by your system because subconsciously you are certain that your "feeling" is more accurate than the system. You start developing overconfidence, which is fatal to your confidence into the system and most probably to the final outcome of your trading activities. You made the same mistake as in the third trade: not taking a trade when the system gave you the entry signal.

Fifth trade: You don't have a signal from the system. You don't take any trade. You are disciplined and enter trades only as signaled by the system and the rules. You feel confident as a trader and trust your system. No mistake was made.

Sixth trade: No signal, but you take a trade, which turns out to be profitable. You make money. As in the fourth trade, this is very dangerous and leads to overconfidence because you will start thinking that you do not need the system at all, that you know better. You will start trading based on your own thoughts. You have lost confidence in the system. You made a mistake, which was taking a trade when the system did not give any entry signal.

Seventh trade: No signal, but you take a trade, and it is a losing one. You lose money. You start thinking that your strategy is not good. You will think twice next time before entering a trade if it is not signaled by the system. You regain confidence in the system. You made a mistake by taking a trade without a signal from the system.

Mistakes are independent of the results (money gained or money lost). A huge win can be a huge mistake, and a small loss can be a positive outcome. Mistakes are only related to your ability to respect the rules and follow the discipline of your trading system and plan. The same concept applies to entry and exit strategies and includes money-management rules, such as entering a trade with a bigger position size than what your system has calculated previously based on your plan.

HOW CAN YOU HANDLE MISTAKES?
The basic approach to avoiding mistakes is to have a trading plan, which will include the system itself, how and when to enter and exit the market, money management, how much will you risk on every trade, and any additional detail relative to the trade itself. Then a very important element is to be able to exert a strict discipline and follow the outlined trading plan.

Another important issue is that your trading plan should be in line with your personality and beliefs. If any of the elements of the plan contradict your belief system or your action pattern and habits, it will be much harder to develop enough discipline to follow its guidelines.

At the moment you created the plan, you were not trading, so there were no psychological obstacles to developing the plan after a thorough analysis of all possible situations. In this way, you can be assured that if you follow your plan to the letter, you will be making the best decision, and this will help you to get the best results. The system eliminates most worries and concerns because you only have to follow the plan point by point with confidence and steadiness.

There are four steps that I find useful in successfully handling the concept of "making mistakes" when trading:

1. Change your beliefs.
2. Find out what the mistake was.
3. Study the consequences of the mistake.
4. Implement an action so that the mistake doesn't happen again.

Change Your Beliefs

Your beliefs will determine, to a certain extent, your mental fitness. Your beliefs represent your attitude in life toward anything that surrounds you. They also shape your emotions. You agree or disagree with a certain point of view independent of the right or wrong of it. You trust your view. But how many of those beliefs are really helping you to see the real picture? To change your beliefs, you would have to examine what lies at the root of your belief system, look for evidence that sustains a different point of view, and investigate further.

Begin to see every mistake as a learning experience and every losing trade as a lesson that you will have to accept and understand fully instead of feeling frustration and disappointment. Find out what happened and why. In this way, you will be able to change the beliefs that are presently limiting your success.

Find Out What the Mistake Was

Reexamine the situation that led to a loss, and identify the mistake itself. Find out its nature, why it happened, what the conditions were, and what you did or didn't do. Were you following the system? Did you break any rules of your plan? What were you feeling at that time? You need to search as deep as you can to find the real motives that caused the mistake.

You also will need to find out about mistakes that had a positive outcome; this can be a little more difficult because you will tend to overlook the details of a successful trade. Examine every trade you make under the same parameters. Keep a thorough record of all the circumstances involved so that you can easily discover if taking that particular trade was a mistake or not.

Study the Consequences of the Mistake

Make a list of all the consequences of a specific mistake, good and bad. Also make a list of all the possible lessons that you can learn from what happened. For example, one of the lessens could be that not following the system will cause you to lose confidence in it and be out of winning trades when you should be in or in losing trades when you should be out.

Implement an Action So That the Mistake Doesn't Happen Again

You need to change your behavior so that the mistake doesn't happen again. Every mistake can be changed into a trading success if it is thoroughly assimilated in your mind and action. In this way, you can commit other mistakes, but not this particular one again. If the mistake comes from your system, redefine and refine the strategy so that you don't encounter further problems in following its rules and signals in the future.

As soon as you understand that the result of your trades has nothing to do with a mistake, you will be opening your mind to hundreds of possibilities, and you will be able to finally comprehend the very nature that lies behind every apparent mistake. Taking action properly will lead you to a successful trading career, where you never stop learning. The process will be slow and probably repetitive, but your attitude when dealing with mistakes and your constant work at finding out and correcting the situation gradually will shape your future as a trader and, most important, as a human being.

EMOTIONS OF TRADING

Emotions are intense mental states that come from the subjective mind instead of an effort or consciousness. They usually manifest as strong feelings, such as love, hate, fear, pleasure, happiness, pride, etc. Emotions can be positive or negative.

Any kind of emotions can interfere with your trading because a trader is a human being at any time independent of the degree of experience possessed. Having emotions is a normal human condition; determining how to deal with them so that they do not disturb or represent an obstacle to your trading success is what counts.

NEGATIVE EMOTIONS

Negative emotions are one of the main factors that cause trading failures. The focus of the trader is mostly on fear, failure, greed, self-sabotage, ego, self-destruction, etc. As a result, enormous amounts of energy are diverted from the normal learning process. Of themselves, emotions are not a bad thing; they are normal reactions that normal human beings experience when confronted with different situations. However, how to handle those emotions is the key. Being able to overcome a failure, control oneself, and move the focus to a new trading opportunity are necessary to let go of the past and keep on track, with persistence, on the path to success. If you are unable to let go of the bad trades, disappointment will take over and obstruct little by little any further attempt at entering winning trades.

POSITIVE EMOTIONS

Positive emotions are the result of a desire for happiness and success, such as when you have closed a successful trade, accomplished a certain goal, or finally solved a problem. When you experience positive emotions, they can enhance your life and uplift you.

However, overconfidence, excessive exhilaration over a series of winning trades, and the rush that comes from the challenge and expectation of making huge profits also can hinder the outcome of your trades.

STRESS AND CONFUSION

An excess of information—too many books, too many systems, too many gurus, too many indicators—can get in the way of acquiring essential knowledge. Traders still fail despite all the fancy tools, multiscreen monitors, superfast computers, and vast amounts of data that become too much to absorb. Too many news services; too many signal services that often give contradictory opinions; all the chat rooms, traders' forums, and webinars; and the latest guru with his or her "from 1K to 1 million in 2 months" 100 percent successful and foolproof system all push us into complete and exhausting confusion because of information overload. This raises your stress level, which will have a negative effect on your trading decisions.

There is nothing wrong with studying and absorbing as much realistic information about your career as you can. But more important is how you apply all that information. Successful traders will look only for the most relevant and essential data that can help them to refine their trading systems and that they can apply to their own psychological traits, personal situations, and trading styles.

HOW CAN YOU USE EMOTIONS TO YOUR ADVANTAGE?

Emotions definitely can be used in a positive way. They are a valuable source of information that can help us in making the right decisions. The goal is not to get rid of them, but rather to learn to control and use them for the best outcome. You shouldn't avoid them; on the contrary, you must get in touch with your deeper feelings and thus know yourself more thoroughly. Disappointment or frustration appears when losing; happiness and excitement arrive when you are winning. It would be extremely difficult not to feel anything and become like a robot.

The first step is to learn to focus your emotions on your positive trading and life goals, dreams, and projects. When you experience a loss, you should review the trade and then use the fear of making that mistake again to help you get out of future trades earlier or plan your exit strategies more carefully. This would be a positive outcome that will help you to succeed in the future. A negative outcome would be using hope to stay in a losing trade in the expectation that the market will reverse. This should be avoided.

Negative emotions have a tremendous impact on your mind and body. They will affect all your thinking processes and become an obstacle to your trading. You can't feel happy, confident, and peaceful when you are having a negative emotion. You can't be in control either. The emotion takes hold of your mind and leads to wrong assessments or decisions.

Accept your losses as part of the business. Learn from them, and try not to repeat the mistake in the future. Take some time off periodically in your daily schedule to relax your mind and your body. In this way, you can take the attention off the negative feelings and turn toward more positive thoughts. You could try to use some sort of meditation routine as a means to achieve peace of mind. Among other activities, physical exercise is an excellent way to get rid of all the accumulated stress, and it also keeps you healthy and thus more fit and energized when you come back to the trading charts. Listen to good music, music that elevates your mind and spirit and calms your senses. Let go of the past. Don't cling to past failures. Move on to the next challenge because there will be many to come, and they all will be interesting and yield additional knowledge and certitude. You cannot change the past, and you don't know what the future will bring about, but you can assuredly change the *now,* which is the place where you should try to live the most. Changing the *now* will automatically change any future outcome. Prepare yourself, and be confident about your skills and experience.

HOW TO GAIN CONFIDENCE IN TRADING
You should prepare yourself by acquiring an adequate skill level through the study of technical and fundamental analysis, plus a sufficient amount of screen time. Go back to the basics. Review your trading plan periodically, as well as your system and strategies. Be sure to understand all the steps, and make sure that you follow them as per your trading plan. Check the reasons why you sometimes do not follow the rules.

To avoid stress buildup, work with small position sizes until your successful trades become consistent and steady. When you start winning, even if small, you should reward yourself in some way for the success. Learn from your mistakes whenever they occur. Accept losses as part of the business experience. Some traders even have more losers than winners as a percentage, but they cut the losses as soon as possible and let the winners run, so their risk-reward ratio is high even if they win less than 50 percent of the time. Use positive affirmations, and visualize your goals. Feel like a winner, act like a winner, be a winner! Do not waste any time or energy on negative emotions or doubts.

Choose a strategy that fits you and that you understand and like. There are hundreds of systems, but it is better to master a single one or, at best, two or three depending on market conditions. This will allow you to be completely focused on the price action instead of wandering around the details that you do not fully grasped.

Observe your thought processes. Be aware of what you think, especially when taking a trade. Thoughts tend to materialize, independent of whether they are positive or negative. Do not judge yourself; observe and detect any negativity arising. Replace negative thoughts with a positive counterpart. Use visualization as a means to make the negativity disappear, replacing it with a powerful and positive energy that fills your mind and body with renovated impulses. Feel strong, feel calm, and feel that you are in control.

Avoid the company of negative people, don't view negative movies, and avoid negative surroundings. Read positive books and quotes, think positive, and speak positive. Thoughts should inspire you to improve and get better in all areas of your life that you want to improve. Try to be specific about your goals and the steps you will undertake to reach them. Reinforce the positive with your ability to focus by remembering great moments where you had a successful outcome, happy moments, and beautiful places. Surround yourself with harmony, order, and beauty.

NEGATIVE FORCES
Negative forces are overwhelming behavioral patterns that you direct against yourself and that invariably will lead you to a loss.

Self-destruction. Individuals who are self-destructive tend to minimize themselves and thus their future evolution. They don't have a clear sense of self-identity and fluctuate between other people's ideas and ways of being. Contradiction and confusion are common.

Doing too much. This is another form of self-destruction through exhaustion. People undertake too many projects and activities for short spans of time, touching superficially on everything and mastering nothing. They are too busy to pay attention to results; they always feel that they aren't doing enough. This leads to permanent dissatisfaction and unfinished issues and projects.

Distraction. Not living in the *now* can be a very powerful negative force. Your energies are diverted from the actual present activity, and your mind wanders about, for example, regretting the past, worrying about others' opinions, fearing the future, and being absolutely overwhelmed by the present. Such people are not living, nor are they focused on what has to be done *now.* Thus they have no real control over what happens in their lives.

Inefficiency. A lot of people continually complain about not having enough resources to get the job done. Meanwhile, they are wasting the few resources they have. They waste time, money, and energy and at the same time think that they are productive because they are always moving things, going here and there repetitively, taking more steps than needed to realize an activity, not planning carefully in advance what has to be done, checking once and again the same point obsessively, and not scheduling and organizing their activities in a logical fashion.

Poor discipline. Discipline is erroneously seen by some people as something enforced on you by someone else. This is wrong. You are the one who decides to follow up a series of rules; you choose to be your own master. A lack of discipline leads to poor focusing ability, inconsistency, and impatience. It can only be resolved by building up one's own self-esteem.

Insufficient training. Skills have to be built. Natural talent can be a wonderful asset, but if you lack the needed foundation that comes from a thorough apprenticeship in any career or technical field, sooner or later you will be whipsawed by the forces of good and bad fortune. Building your attitude through discipline and adequate learning is a must. Most people want to reap the rewards right now and procrastinate at developing all the needed skills that will yield those rewards. Practice makes perfect, day after day. Most people just react in the moment and are swung around any way the wind blows while feeling overly powerful and neglecting any kind of preparation. Know your own limitations, and strive to push them further away from yourself through education and a thorough practice of what you have learned.

A TRADER'S CAPITAL SINS

There are seven capital sins: *pride, avarice, envy, wrath, lust, gluttony,* and *sloth*. A trader's capital sins would number eight because you have to add *fear* to the deadly list.

Pride. Overconfidence is one of the biggest causes of bankruptcy in FOREX trading. You think that you know it all, you risk a little too much, you win, excess of confidence is reinforced, and suddenly you lose grip on an unexpected market reaction because of the cloudy vapors of glory stemming from your ego. You will need to continuously criticize your strategy with perspicacity, keep studying the market as it changes continuously, and always find out the cause for the outcome of your trading.

Avarice. Greed or excessive and unrealistic ambition is, in fact, caused by a subconscious fear. It is impossible to become rich in a week without making an effort to learn and investing your own time, hard-earned money, and dedication. There is no free lunch, and you will have to be persistent at acquiring the necessary skills if you want to succeed.

Envy. Some traders are always comparing themselves with other apparently more successful traders, trying to copy their strategies, clinging around to get their trading calls or signals, and asking for directions. Always doubt that anyone has really found that elusive Holy Grail. Analyze by yourself, use your own common sense, and develop and build your own system. It will save you a lot of money in the end.

Wrath. Anger and revenge will cloud your judgment. You feel that the market is against you, price always moves in the opposite direction of your trade, and your broker is after you and wants you to lose, hunts your stop losses, and separates you from your money and potential profits. Watch closer: If price is always going against your trade, most probably you simply made a mistake. Assume your losses, wait for another opportunity, reinforce your discipline, and above all, do not try to get even or revenge-trade. This is the best way to lose even more and faster. Refine your money-management rules, reduce your risks, and

correct the flaws that your system could have. This is the only
way to recover and win in the end.

Lust. The ultimate technological gadgets will not help you to advance
a millimeter in your trading career. Worse, excess in any field can
be counterproductive. Too many screens and too much time
watching the charts lead to stress and anxiety, eye strain, and a
state similar to hypnosis and delusion. You will begin seeing
nonexistent signals, or you will be paralyzed and fascinated by
screen movement when it is the moment to act. Never spend more
than eight hours a day watching your computer monitor; if you
trade and analyze full time, it is even better to make several small
pauses during the day because a focused activity has a relatively
short time span, something around two or three continuous hours,
maybe even less. Stay healthy. If your health declines, you will
not be able to apply your methodology as well, and the odds will
start piling against your success. Your ability to manage your
screen time and overall daily life schedule efficiently will
determine your success or failure.

Gluttony. Respect your stops. Take profits with prudence and
intelligence. You can never catch a complete rally. Not all trades
will be winners. One pip more can become 50 pips less.

Sloth. Nothing happens by chance. Gambling is not trading. You need
to design a plan and trade following its rules. Barely using vague
hunches or intuition or other people's random calls is the same as
tossing a coin—heads or tails, bulls or bears. The only path to
success is through a methodical and systematic approach.

Fear. Fear is paralyzing. But you can use it to your advantage! Employ
the fear emotions to help you get out of trades much sooner. You
risk not being able to trade another day! Control the fear, and
make it work for your benefit.

HOW TO GET OUT OF A BAD TRADE

There's no "perfection to the pip" with so many different prices at different
brokers and times—only ranges (which on longer time frames I would say
have $+20/-20$ accuracy). This seems like a lot, but remember that you
should not be seeking to catch the very bottom or top and then bring the
position to its very utmost perfect exit target. As in a sandwich, the meat is
in the middle.

Scalping is a different thing, of course. In longer time frames, though, it is better (and easier) to plan on that middle range.

Every system (paired with the trader himself or herself) has an average win-loss ratio that is the result of previous thorough testing. For example, a certain system can have a win-loss ratio of around 75:35. This means that for every 100 trades, you have to be prepared to accept a third of them to be stopped out.

Now, what is a "good trade"? How can a losing or stopped-out trade be good? A good trade is a position that has been taken *based on the rules,* the rules of the system itself *and* your own money-management rules. In this way, you can have good losing trades and *bad winning* trades. Let's say your money-management rule is "not to risk more than 2% on a single trade," plus your system's rules. You suddenly decide to have a go at gambling and open a position with half the money in your account and enter the trade without waiting for the entry rules to be met. Suddenly, you're lucky! The trade goes in your direction, and after a few minutes, you close the trade with positive pips. Wow, what a winner!

In fact, *no!* That super-duper "winning" trade is a *bad* trade in your books because you broke every rule of your trading plan, and in so doing, you put at risk much more than what your money-management rule says. And finally, you didn't execute the trade with discipline. Next time you happen to do this, who can guarantee you'll be as lucky?

Every trade taken by the rules is a *good* trade. Every trade in which you break the rules and do not follow your trading plan and your personal discipline is a *bad* trade.

Now, how do you get out of a bad trade? Fast! Exit strategies should always be planned carefully in advance because you will never know if a trade is good or bad unless you are in it! Planning how to exit a position is one of the most important parts of a trading plan. Entries are less important than exits unless your style is to be scalping.

To get out of a trade, you have a choice among several techniques. For example, you can use trailing stops, which help in securing the profits while letting the trade run further. With trailing stops, you go on tracking the positive movement of the trade, and as soon as it moves in the opposite direction, you exit the trade. Stops never should be changed back because you would not be securing your profits anymore! Initial or fixed stops are intended to take you out of a trade when it has moved against you.

Another good exit strategy is to place a profit target. You can exit the trade as a whole or scale out your position in several installments.

For example, if your money-management rule allows you to take 3 lots (standard, minilots, or microlots), you break the position in three parts. You open a trade, for example, in EUR/USD at 1.2600 with a 30-pip stop. When the trade is 30 pips into profits, you close one of the lots and move the stops on the other two positions to breakeven. Breakeven stops are usually set to the entry price or at one or two additional positive pips. In this way, you have locked some profits, and if you are stopped out, you won't lose any money, and you have two "free trades" to move on further if the price keeps rising. If it does and moves to 60 pips of profit, you close the second lot, and let the last third lot run as long as possible, using trailing stops or just leaving the stop to breakeven. This strategy takes the fear out of the picture and decreases the risk of drawdowns of your system while also allowing you to profit more from a single position.

If you have open orders at news time, it would be preferable to close a trade before the trailing stops get hit because big whipsaws could stop you out anyway with much less profit. This especially happens when the result of economic releases is very different from what was expected. Another fundamental time to watch is when institutional representatives are making public announcements.

Finally, a good stop-loss strategy is to use the nearest support or resistance by examining the charts and noticing where the price has bounced many times and reversed. Previous lows or highs, pivots, and Fibonacci levels are usually quite safe. You should place the stop at around 1 or 2 percent away from the support or resistance. Prices usually will test those levels or even break them a little and come back. You should leave a prudent distance so that the trade can breathe and go beyond until it returns.

HOW TO DEVELOP AN EXIT STRATEGY

To implement a successful exit strategy, you should consider the following factors: the total time that you plan to stay in the trade, the amount of risk that you will allow yourself to take (this pertains to money management more properly), and finally, where and when will you want to get out of your position. This will all depend on your trading style and your trading personality. A long-term trader will set profit targets over many years, making many fewer trades. He or she will study specific trailing stop levels to lock some profits in order to limit the potential drawdown. The primary goal of a long-term trader is to preserve capital. Profits can be taken incrementally, especially on huge positions, to avoid volatility at the moment of closing. Strategies will be oriented mostly toward including fundamental factors that can influence the markets over a larger time span.

A short-term trader will set targets at nearer-term levels, such as pivot points, Fibonacci retracements, trendlines, or other technical zones. Stop losses will be calculated to get out immediately if the position is not performing. Exit strategies will be devised by taking account of short-term technical studies or fundamental events.

Accurately gauging risk is very important when you are investing. You need to determine how much you can afford to lose, which, in turn, will have an effect on the duration of your trades and what kinds of stop losses or exit strategies you should use. If you want less risk, use a tighter stop. If you want the greatest possibility of profit from a longer-term trade and can afford it, set wider stops, and decrease the size of your position accordingly. Stops always should be set at levels where the normal market volatility is less likely to reach them.

A TRADER'S TEN COMMANDMENTS

1. *You can't predict the future.* Long-term technical analysis is useless in the short term. It is not designed to predict, but rather to explain past behaviors of the market. It can be used to have a probable idea about the possible future behavior and chances that the past will repeat itself.

2. *Don't be prejudiced.* You always must examine both sides of the picture. Having a bullish or bearish bias can cloud the obvious signals that your system will present. Plan accordingly so that you can be prepared for both sides in any eventuality. Don't try to find signals where they are not to justify your particular and subjective point of view. The market has no feelings.

3. *Be flexible.* Follow a logical and structured thought pattern instead of pure intuition and instinct. This will help you in limiting losses over time based on a plan. Do not cling to your positions; assume the losses, and move on.

4. *Trade with the main trend.* Although you can trade against the trend if you are aware of the probabilities and ratios of pullbacks and corrections, it is better to trade with the major trend unless you are just looking for a few pips. You will have more chance of success and will be able to get more pips in a much safer manner and faster. Do not chase the market. Let it come to you.

5. *Trust your analysis.* If you have carefully planned your trading session, that is all you need to build confidence and operate according to your

own rules. Design your system, test your strategies, and calculate your money management with respect to your available balance. If everything is ready and you feel right with what you have designed, work with confidence and discipline.

6. *Have a plan.* Never face the market without having a plan. It has to be based on a working methodology that you will be developing day by day, which includes what your working conditions are for that specific trading day. If you don't have a plan, you put probabilities against you.

7. *Know "How much" and "When."* Always keep track of and readjust your money-management rules as needed. You should not change the percentage or amount of capital that you can afford to risk too much ("How much") in each trade. You also have to study carefully "When" to increment that risk to obtain more benefits, using leverage in your favor.

8. *Keep it simple.* Thinking that the more complicated a system is, the better results you will get is a wrong belief. Simple is always better. At first, it can seem to you that something is missing if you use only one or two indicators; you will have the impulse to add another, and yet another, and can end up with a chart in which the price is no longer visible under so many lines and signs. Besides, following too many indicators can lead to trading paralysis because many will contradict each other, and it will be more difficult to get them to a consensus, so no trade and no profits.

9. *You will not get rich quick.* Don't even try FOREX trading if you are wishing to become rich in one night: Greed can blind you. The FOREX is a profession, and as such, it needs to be studied as thoroughly as any other career. You have to invest time and money to become a real professional.

10. *Keep control.* Keep your emotions under control. Keep your trading under control with a proper plan. Emotions are one of the most important aspects of FOREX trading; at least they represent 60 to 70 percent of a trader's activity. Those who succeed understand that they have to handle their fear and greed and eliminate anxiety and stress before starting the workday, checking the trading space and keeping it clear of any negatives, and understanding the daily impulses and emotions that influence them at the moment. Leave your ego out of the picture, reeducate your natural impulses, and add a great deal of healthy discipline.

BECOME A PRO

FOREX trading has to be treated as a job—with a proper (and limited) schedule that accommodates in your life the best market hours for your strategy, as well as the rest of your obligations—family, maybe still a standard job, recreation, friendship, study, and (most important) proper rest and sleep.

As for a standard job, you should have the proper tools, and these include not only a good Internet connection but also a good computer and alternative elements when one of the others falters. You should "build your office" like you would for any other type of working situation. It should be free of distractions, have a good and anatomic chair if your strategy asks for long hours of screen time, and you should plan for frequent short interruptions to relax your eyes if you have been looking at the screen for an hour, etc.

Never trade if you feel sleepy (imagine that your job involves operating a very dangerous machine). Indeed, the FOREX won't cut your hand, nor will you slip and fall on the factory floor, but you could risk your account because the risk of committing a mistake is very much higher when you aren't able to focus properly (from lack of sleep, too many hours doing the same thing, physical pain because of improper furniture, a lower attention capacity because of a drink or two, etc.).

Choose your trading session by carefully taking all these elements into account. Set yourself a daily goal in pips *and* in time spent at the screen. If you do not meet your goal, tomorrow is another day, and the markets never stop.

TAXES AND LEGAL ISSUES

Individuals and businesses related to securities are classified into three different categories for tax purposes. Those categories are dealers, investors, and traders. *Dealers* are defined as market makers. As an individual trader, your business could fall into any of the two remaining categories.

This is an important thing to plan in advance. Most FOREX traders consider themselves to be *investors* because their activity involves obtaining a return on their money. However, the tax benefits are not the same. As a trader, you can get a series of tax deductions from your income, such as the costs of your trading education, financial software, books and study materials, seminars, business-related trips, and meal expenses; accounting, legal, and tax advice; and brokerage fees and commissions; office equipment such as computers, phones, and Internet connection fees; overnight interest paid on your trading account; home and automobile expenses; and others.

You can use your trader status to create a small sole proprietorship. Your ordinary business expenses would be placed on Schedule C, and your income or loss would be reported on Schedule D because it is still considered capital.

No self-employment income is calculated on the total income, and your trading losses are still limited to $3,000 per year but can be carried over indefinitely.

The benefits of this choice are good, but there is also another way, which might be better under several points of view, to operate your trading business. This would be to create your own trade corporation by incorporating your business.

Establishing a trade corporation allows you to possess a new legal entity from which to conduct your trading. This has short-term advantages, a better and much wider protection for your assets, and other advantages for family financial planning. Assuredly, you will be incurring in extra costs for setting the business up and overall operational costs, but the benefits are clearly more valuable.

What kind of corporation is the best for you? You can find three types of corporations: One of them is a regular corporation, named the *C corporation;* then you have the *sub-S corporation,* which is named after the tax code section that lists and defines its benefits; and finally, you have the *limited-liability corporation* (LLC), a corporate structure that is relatively new and was designed to overcome some of the structural difficulties of the sub-S corporation.

The preceding applies to residents of the United States. Different laws and tax systems apply for other countries. I would recommend that you to approach a specialized law and taxes service in your location to help you to define what type of business is more convenient based on your particular situation

For me, personally, I use a limited-liability corporation (LLC) whenever possible.

MIND OVER MATTER FOR HUGE PROFITS

AFFIRMATIONS

Affirmations can be defined as positive declarations in which the content is stated as being true. The word *positive* is the clue because this is the way affirmations should be phrased, instead of using negative words. For example, instead of affirming, "I am free of debt," you should say, "I have enough money to satisfy all my obligations."

Affirmations are used in a repetitive way to gradually reinforce their power. They are phrased in the present tense even if the goal to be reached hasn't yet manifested (e.g., "I am successful" instead of "I will be successful").

When I was in the Marine Corps and still today, although not as much today, I wake up every morning and say, "Another glorious day." Ooh-Ra! This is an affirmation. I start every day off like this, and I am able to build on that positive mind-set throughout the day.

What is less understood is that even if you think that you don't use affirmations (consciously, that is), in fact, you use them continuously, day after day, but you are not aware of it! Your beliefs and thoughts are constantly running through your mind. They are built over your entire life, and their content is a heterogeneous mix of other people's beliefs, old childhood rules, wrong or right decisions you have made based on life experience, and external influences from the media, which can be contradictory at some point.

Those unconscious affirmations are running free, out of your control. However, it is possible to bring them to your awareness and control the flow and content so as to be more precise about what you really want to manifest in your life.

Your present is the result of your past affirmations! You will become what you always tell yourself, whether it is good or bad!

If you are not satisfied with the results you have gotten so far, which are the by-product of your thoughts and beliefs, you need first of all to change the content or expression of your thoughts and beliefs. Transforming your thoughts will transform your results, and this is done through conscious affirmations.

Negative thought patterns are repeated unknowingly again and again, and the cycle has to be broken and brought to the light so that you can examine the contents of your thoughts and discard all that are negative and replace them with positive affirmations. Examine for a moment, for example, your deepest thoughts and beliefs about money. Are there any "imposed" beliefs (e.g., phrases or statements that you were told in childhood) that could be blocking your attainment of success?

Affirmations can help you to "clean the slate" so that there are no more hidden obstacles in your path to successful trading. You have control over your conscious mind, but the unconscious mind operates under the radar, feeding you automatically all those thoughts and phrases you have been collecting throughout the years. Your unconscious mind is also connected to emotions, which make you react based on past programming. The subconscious mind even has power over the conscious mind in cases of conflict. For example, you decide that you want to be a successful trader and make lots of money, but there's a hidden belief that tells you that "being rich is evil." Even if you understand on a conscious level that this is not so, the power of your earlier programming will win, and you will find yourself doing counteractions against your primary goal, which is "making lots of money."

I always tell people in my presentations that to be successful, you have to have a plan, and before you can build your plan, you have to set goals, both long and short term. Before you can take this step, you have to recognize that we all have a different set of values and that at different times in our lives we have to maintain balance. This balance often will shift as our needs shift in different ways. You simply cannot have a goal that is outside your values, such as saying that you want to make a million dollars trading and subconsciously thinking that being rich is evil. Build your plan around your goals and values, and then you will start to see a difference. You must write this down. If you write your plan down with your long- and short-term goals, your mind will build a mental picture around it, and you will work subconsciously to accomplish it.

When you repeat positive statements about the changes that you want to see in your life, you are reprogramming your subconscious mind. It takes some time to replace the old statements and develop new ones. However, if you keep repeating the new beliefs, your effort will bring about the desired results, and they will become a part of your automatic behavior.

HOW DO YOU CREATE A POWERFUL AFFIRMATION?
First of all, the most important part is the wording; it has to be effective and believable. If you are unable to believe what you are affirming, it will not have enough power to create the change.

The second part is your mood when repeating the affirmation. If you don't believe it, feel doubts, or even have a cynical reaction to it, your feelings about the affirmation will be negative, thus increasing the negative patterns about the whole subject in your mind. For example, you could affirm, "I am a successful trader." However, it might not yet be completely true, so you can't relate to the statement, and it even could trigger a contrary reaction. In this case, you could add, "I am becoming a successful trader, and I am in the process of making lots of money with my trading." This would bring the reality much closer and still be positive and dynamic. The more you add positive emotions to your affirmations, the sooner they will come to fruition in your life.

COUNT YOUR BLESSINGS!
Another important part is to act as if you have already reached the goal, expressing gratitude for your blessings. You also can add other affirmations of positive things that you already have in your life, looking around for all the great blessings you have and transforming them into positive gratitude affirmations:

"I am grateful for my health."

"Thank you for my learning ability."

This will boost your self-esteem and help in the process of building a positive environment for the affirmations to take root and grow up to your desired results.

When you open your heart and are grateful for what you already have, you are telling the universe that you are ready and willing to receive more! No matter what the circumstances of your actual life, there is always something to be grateful for. By being grateful, you create a positive state of mind that will attract all that is positive to your life. Similar attracts similar, either way, so better to do it in the right way to obtain the right results!

Thoughts that you have frame how you experience things and people around you. If you are negative, distrustful, and cynical and you are always looking for the worst, then your feelings and actions will follow the same path. You need to change the way you think in order to make self-improvements. Thoughts that are gloomy and negative do not come out of thin air. You have unknowingly been repeating negative thought patterns, and your actions follow these patterns. Repeated use of positive affirmations will break your negative thinking.

"I am worthy. I am positive. I am confident."

"I am intuitive. I am a winner. I am intelligent."

"I am patient. I am grateful."

HOW DO YOU AVOID THE COMMON MISTAKES?

First of all, define exactly what you really want. The more precise your goal is, the more chances it has to develop and be attained faster. It is your job to find out what you really want in life and in your trading career. How far do you want to go? Are you prepared for greater success, or will you settle for a moderate but consistent income?

Then, know that it is perfectly right to want abundance, happiness, and prosperity in your life. Sometimes it can be difficult to define a precise goal because all the traditional and religious education and beliefs tend to diminish your self-worth and your sense of deserving. You deserve to be happy and prosperous and collect the fruits of your hard and dedicated work.

How, then, can you define what is that you really want? You could start by making a list of all the things you don't want. What would you change? What do you want to get rid of? Try making your list as complete as possible. You then can start creating the positive affirmations item by item that will help you to change progressively all the things or situations you definitely don't want to be a part of your life or your trading.

Choose to experience trading in a positive way every minute. You will think more clearly, see the market more clearly, and trade better.

To trade like the pros, you have to learn to think like the pros. Condition your subconscious to be in line with your desires. Encrypt those affirmations into your brain to achieve lasting success.

POWER OF NETWORKING

Networking includes connecting with different cultures, ages, special-interests groups, and networks themselves. Strong connections are constantly being made—following up, keeping in touch, identifying and making contact with spheres of influence, and forming strategic alliances where everybody wins, as well as brainstorming groups. Networking is a way of living, a life skill, more than something that you do with a purpose in mind. This is one of the big reasons that I created the James Dicks FOREX Network, so that as a FOREX trader, you can connect with other individual traders who are trying to accomplish the same or similar success trading in the FOREX. I encourage you to check it out at *www.James-Dicks.com*. There are three basic and universal rules on which its principles are grounded: abundance, reciprocity, and generosity.

> *Abundance.* Opportunities are open and plenty for everyone. There are many alternatives from which to chose, many careers, jobs, customers, ideas, and so on.
>
> *Reciprocity.* What you give out comes back to you multiplied. If you give out help, you get back help; give out love, you get back love; give out information, you get back information. It might not come instantly or from the same person to whom it was given, but the balance is always restored.
>
> *Generosity.* The fundamental philosophy of all successful networkers is to treat everyone the way they would like to be treated themselves. This is the determination to give your time and share your knowledge with other people, with the sole aim of helping them to get answers to their questions or reach their goals, without any expectation of receiving something back from them.

STRATEGIC ALLIANCES

A *strategic alliance* is the union of two or more people who subscribe to an agreement to undertake or develop certain activities and share common goals with the purpose of obtaining benefits for every one of the participants. Such networks can grow with each member's additional external activities, which then can be shared and added to the global diversity of age groups, cultures, and interests, forming a stronger and much larger network of networks and bringing to each of them under an enormous sphere of influence that can be positive or negative.

People who know a lot in one or two areas in which they are usually specialists are prone to becoming a sphere of influence in the networks in which they participate. The interaction with other people who are also spheres of influence in other subjects allows them to acquire a good general knowledge of many areas.

The important qualities a network should possess are integrity, honesty, ethics, and sincerity among all its participants because mutual trust is vital for a network to exert a positive influence on all its members and obtain the desired results.

BRAINSTORMING GROUPS

Those are formal or informal gatherings where people unite with a common and definite agenda of sharing mutual knowledge or creative ideas and solutions or studying a particular subject in detail. Networking is basically about information sharing. Thus every networker should be very well informed and eager to update regularly the information he or she possesses through every learning means available—reading books and the press, using Internet resources, and paying attention to the information that is shared through their own networks.

Communication in our times is becoming faster every day, thanks to technology, and we have much less time to share adequate and useful information with our peers. There is too much information to process and absorb, and there are too many electronic solicitations throughout the day. Thus, creating or participating in a network is more important than ever.

The following are two of the most important places to engage in networking in the trading scene:

Forums. Trading forums are a source of invaluable information. There are various levels and focus in each of them, some specialize in trading systems, others in general information for newest participants, and still others in all the different personal experiences of seasoned traders as well as newcomers. This sharing enriches each individual's perception, and it also allows you to find other people who are working in the same field, going through similar steps in the evolution of their trading career, and get some advice from the ones who have already been through the pitfalls of the industry. Although trading is mostly a solitary activity, because of the focus needed, creating relationships with other traders is very important to have an adequate perspective.

Mentored trading communities. Some of the most experienced traders can decide to create trading groups, in which they give back to others in terms of knowledge, techniques, and intuition, all that they have learned and applied throughout their trading life. Also, groups of traders who share the same system can gather to trade together and compare their own results, thus the James Dicks FOREX Network.

FUNDAMENTAL ANALYSIS

C H A P T E R 9

ECONOMICS

WHAT DOES ECONOMIC RELEASE MEAN?

An *economic news release* is a press report issued by central banks, the Federal Reserve, governments, large financial institutions, and research and analytical organisms stating economic decisions and data that are the result of their periodic calculations to gauge performance of an economy. Such releases are usually done rendered public through the main financial press.

FOREX traders, especially those who directly trade the news, are very attentive to the results and data offered and apply fundamental analysis to interpret those figures. Then they act on the market's reaction to the data.

The main areas of economic releases are divided into balance of payments; gross domestic product (GDP) and output reports; confidence and sentiment reports; leading indicators; prices, salaries, and wages; spending figures; monetary policy; and employment and housing.

FUNDAMENTAL ANALYSIS

Fundamental analysis is usually centered on financial and economic data, but it also can be influenced by political decisions. In this way, a trader can get an idea of how strong the offer and demand of the currency in question can be.

Fundamental analysis includes examination of the revision of macroeconomic indicators, the stock markets, and political decisions (such decisions influence confidence in the governments and the climate of stability of the country in question). The greater trust there is in a government, along with rising macroeconomic indicators, the higher will be the level of confidence of a trader in making the necessary decisions.

In determining fundamentals, traders consider rates of growth, the GDP, types of interest, the existing inflation rate in a country, the monetary mass, the foreign currency reserves, and productivity. Sometimes governments, through their central banks, try to exert an influence on the markets with the purpose of preventing their currencies from getting too far away from a certain level and, in this way, avoid imbalances. These interventions usually have a remarkable impact, but they are usually of short duration.

To avoid imbalances, a central bank could enter the currency market as an investor, buying or selling its currency against another. Sometimes several central banks might intervene in the market together.

Traders consider the expectations on the possible evolution of a currency or several currencies based on macroeconomic factors, the news about a particular currency, or the potential events that can occur in a country that would have an influence on the quotation of its currency. Therefore, traders look for macroeconomic variables to be able to predict the future behavior of a currency.

To this end, governments publish the frequency and evolution of these macroeconomic variables so that traders can see the previous result, the forecast, and the government's release, along with any revisions of prior data that was released in the previous month. When the variable figures do not agree with the forecast, this usually produces abrupt movements in the market that will provide benefits for the trader.

Among the variables released, several are important in primary analysis:

Economy growth. This is usually gauged through the quarterly published GDP figure. This variable is important because it will tell us how the economy of a country is evolving. When you see that the GDP of a country is growing, you are aware that there is movement of capital, which shows higher consumption and savings. Companies then are encouraged by that consumption and investments that can be made. Excessive growth, however, would lead to inflationary tensions, and therefore, there could be an increase in rates from central banks. At first, a higher than forecast GDP would push the currency quotation from a country to the rising side, whereas a lower GDP would harm the currency quotation and cause it to drop.

Price developments—inflation. The appreciation or depreciation of a currency against another is usually neutralized by the change in differential of the interest rates. Currencies with higher interest rates are often seen as more attractive owing to the possible containment of inflation and an implicit higher profitability. This variable is released monthly. A higher than expected consumer price index (CPI) will push the exchange rate upward, whereas a lower CPI will push the exchange rate downward.

Unemployment. This indicator usually is difficult to predict, but its weight is important and has immediate impact on both the income and consumption of families. If the nonfarm unemployment figures are greater than estimated, then the currency of the country goes to the floor. If the rate of unemployment is lower than estimated, that helps the appreciation of the currency. The same applies to the hourly earnings indicator.

Trade balance. The equilibrium point of a currency quote occurs when a country has a stable balance of payments. When the country has a trade deficit, it then experiences a reduction in its currency reserves, causing a depreciation in the value of its currency. It is necessary to consider that a cheap currency favors exports of the country but increases import prices. In midterm, this causes a drop in imports and an increase in exports, thus, as a result, stabilizing the trade balance and producing an appreciation of the currency.

Stock market. Variables such as growth, inflation, unemployment, and trade balance are not the only indicators that can favor the appreciation or depreciation of a currency. Every day, currency evolution has a greater correlation with asset markets, especially with stocks. When investors consider a country as a good place to invest, that market of stocks or assets will be boosted by the arrival of other currencies, and therefore, the value of the country's currency will remain robust.

Thus, when you see that the variables are positive, this will encourage an increase in the quotation of the currency, but if the variables are negative, this will indicate a decrease in the currency.

DOW THEORY

The basic principles of the Dow theory are

1. *The averages emphasize everything—the news, data, and inclusively misfortunes or wars.* This leaves us with a clear view of the tendency of the market.

2. *The markets move in tendencies.* Every market has a tendency, with these three types—primary, secondary, and tertiary.

    - *Primary trend.* This trend usually lasts more than a year, and movements are extensive and constant.

    - *Secondary trend.* This trend can last months, but fluctuations of this trend are included in the primary trend. Any corrections that may have been made are one-third or two-thirds of the previous section and are usually 50 percent.

    - *Tertiary or minor trend.* These are variations within the secondary trend.

3. *Principle of confirmation.* The averages would have to confirm a possible change of tendency, as much to the upside as to the downside. The movement in only one of the averages does not confirm, in itself, a change of effective tendency. However, you can see in advance how by using two moving averages, you can confirm a possible change.

4. *The volume moves with the tendency.* The movements in favor of a trend will always be accompanied by a volume greater than the potential correction. If you are in a bull-market phase, the volume will be increased in the up moves and will be less in the descents. If you are in a bear-market phase, the volume goes up in a fall and declines in rises.

5. *The tendency will be effective while there is no change confirmation.* This is intended to avoid premature exits of a trend. A trend will continue its effectiveness if there is no change in the averages. This allows us to follow the advice: "Let profits run; cut losses short." A lateral trend or a possible correction does not indicate a change in the main trend.

6. *The trends have three phases.* Phases of a bullish trend:

    - *Phase of accumulation.* In this phase, investors who think that an economic recovery is possible enter the market aggressively, considering that this has a rising potential. These investors, who usually are better informed, enter very aggressively when the currency does not have the attention of the mass media. Even so, the feeling is of discouragement and therefore is pessimistic. The buying positions are accumulated by investors who are better informed until the demand starts pushing, causing the quotes to rise. These movements can be considered by the public in general as a bounce from the bearish tendency.

- *Phase of tendency or fundamental.* This phase is characterized by an improvement in the economic conditions, where the buys by traders are growing. In this phase, many traders realize that a change has happened in the main tendency, and they enter progressively. The movements of this phase usually are ample.
- *Phase of distribution or speculation.* At this stage, the economic conditions are usually very good. In this phase, a large number of traders will enter the market. Strong rises in the currency start appearing in the media. Traders who entered in the first phase begin to sell their positions because they believe that the currency has already gone too far and anticipate a fall.

Phases of a bearish trend:

- *Phase of distribution.* Traders who have been participating in the increase from the start of the first phase start unloading their positions. At this time, the news is still good, and the market correction that occurs is considered by the public to be minor or intermediary inside the rising tendency. In this phase, traders still wait for a strong bullish movement.
- *Phase of panic.* In this phase, the selling strength is highly superior to the buying strength, and the depreciations pile up. Panic sells often occur. Traders usually will sell strong positions to the market, provoking very sharp falls in which many traders lose their money. After this phase, either a sideways correction or a recovery of the bearish tendency usually occurs, which is often minimal. In this phase, there is usually a high volume in the descent that is often smaller than the volumes that occurred in the rising phase.
- *Phase of discouragement.* In this phase, the news about the currency starts getting worse, but it may not have any influence on prices. Traders who are in this phase are usually those who held up their positions during the phase of panic or those who bought late, believing that the prices were still low. The media stops paying attention to the currency, and falls start smoothing out.

FUNDAMENTAL INDICATORS

ECONOMIC INDICATORS FOR THE UNITED STATES

- Balance of payments
  - Current account balance

- o   Trade balance
- o   Net foreign security purchases
- o   Goods and services imports
- o   Export price index
- GDP and output report
  - o   GDP
  - o   Institute of Supply Management (ISM) manufacturing
  - o   Philadelphia Fed survey
  - o   Empire State manufacturing survey
  - o   Durable goods orders
  - o   Business inventories
  - o   Wholesale inventories
  - o   Factory orders
  - o   Industry productivity and costs
  - o   Capacity utilization
  - o   Industrial production
  - o   Richmond Fed manufacturing survey
  - o   Chicago Purchasing Managers Index (PMI)
  - o   ISM nonmanufacturing
  - o   Energy Information Administration (EIA) crude oil stocks
  - o   Monthly budget statement
- Confidence and sentiments report
  - o   Consumer confidence
  - o   University of Michigan sentiment
  - o   ABC consumer comfort index
  - o   Fed beige book
- Leading indicators
  - o   Empire State manufacturing survey
  - o   Chicago PMI
  - o   ISM nonmanufacturing
  - o   Richmond Fed manufacturing survey
  - o   Philadelphia Fed survey
- Prices, Salary, and Wages and Spending Figures
  - o   Personal consumption expenditures (PCE) deflator
  - o   CPI and core CPI

- ○ Producer price index (PPI) and PPI core
- ○ Employment
- ○ Nonfarm payrolls
- ○ Unemployment
- ○ Manufacturing payrolls and average hourly earnings
- ○ Personal consumption expenditures
- ○ Industry productivity and costs
- ○ GDP price index
- ○ ISM manufacturing and prices paid
- ○ Personal income
- ○ Import price index
- ○ Export price index
- ○ Advance retail sales
- Monetary policy
  - ○ Fed Open Market Committee (FOMC) rate decision
  - ○ Minutes of the FOMC meeting
  - ○ Fed governor speaks
  - ○ Fed chairman speaks
  - ○ Beige book
- Employment
  - ○ Employment situation
  - ○ Nonfarm payrolls
  - ○ Unemployment
  - ○ Manufacturing payrolls and average hourly earnings
  - ○ Unemployment rate
  - ○ Personal income
- Housing
  - ○ Building permits
  - ○ Construction spending
  - ○ Housing starts
  - ○ Mortgage Bankers Association (MBA) mortgage applications
  - ○ Pending home sales
  - ○ New home sales
  - ○ Existing home sales
  - ○ National Association of Home Builders (NAHB) housing market index

DESCRIPTION AND EFFECT OF EVENTS

Gross National Product (GNP)

The GNP measures the economic performance of the global economy. This indicator, on a macro scale, is the sum of consumption, investment and governmental spending, and net volume of transactions. The GNP refers to the sum of all the goods and services produced by U.S. residents, either in the country or abroad. The higher this number is, the better it is for the currency.

Gross Domestic Product (GDP)

The GDP refers to the sum of all the goods and services produced in the United States by domestic or foreign companies. The differences between GNP and GDP are nominal in the case of U.S. economy. GDP figures are more popular outside the United States. As a means to make things easier to compare the performances of different economies, the United States also issue figures for GDP. The higher this number is, the better it is for the currency.

Consumption Spending

Consumption is possible thanks to the personal and eventual income. The decision of consumers to spend or save is psychological in nature. Consumer confidence is also measured as an important indicator of the tendency for consumers who receive eventual income (additional income to that needed for basic survival) to exchange their saving behavior for a spending behavior. The higher the consumption spending index, or consumer confidence, is, the better it is for the currency.

Investment Spending

Investment spending or private domestic gross spending is made up of fixed investments and inventories. The higher the number is, the better it is for the currency.

Government Spending

Government spending has a strong influence because of its size and its impact on other economic indicators owing to special expenditures. For example, the military expenses of the United States had a significant role in totality of employment in the United States until 1990. The expense cuts in defense matters that occurred at that time increased short-term unemployment figures. The higher the number is, the better it is for the currency.

Net Trade

The net trade volume is another major component of GNP. Internationalization and the economic and political developments that have occurred since 1980 have had a strong impact on the ability of the United States to compete abroad. The trade deficit of past decades has diminished the evolution of the global GNP. This GNP can be examined from two points of view: product flow and cost flow. The higher the net trade figure is, the better it is for the currency.

Industrial Production

The industrial production indicator is given by the total production of factories, utilities, and mines of a nation. From a fundamental point of view, it is an important indicator that reflects the strength of the economy and, as an extrapolation, the strength of a specific currency. For this reason, FOREX traders use this economic indicator as a potential trading signal. The higher the number is, the better it is for the currency.

Capacity Utilization

Industrial capacity utilization consists of the total industrial production divided by total production capacity. The term refers to the maximum level of production that a factory can output under normal operational conditions.

In general, utilization of capacity is not a major indicator in the FOREX market. However, there are situations where its economic implications are useful for fundamental analysis. A "normal" figure for a stable economy is 81.5 percent. If the number is 85 percent or more, the data suggest that industrial production is overheating and that the economy is reaching its maximum capacity.

High figures of capacity use tend to predate inflation, and the expectation in the FOREX market is that the central bank will increase interest rates as means to avoid or fight inflation.

Generally speaking, the higher the capacity utilization figure is, the better it is for the currency.

Factory Orders

This indicator refers to the total factory orders of durable and nondurable goods. Nondurable goods are food, clothing, light industrial products, and products that are designed for the maintenance of the durable goods. Durable goods orders are analyzed separately. This indicator has little significance for FOREX traders, but in general, the higher this figure is, the better it will be for the currency.

Durable Goods Orders

This consists of products whose useful life is greater than three years. Examples of durable goods are vehicles, electrical appliances, furniture, jewelry, and toys. Orders are divided in four main categories: primary metals, machinery, electrical machinery, and transportation.

To mitigate the volatility that pertains to big military orders, the indicator includes discrimination between defense and nondefense orders. This indicator is quite important for the FOREX market because it gives a good indication of consumer confidence.

Given that durable goods have a higher cost than nondurable goods, a higher figure in this indicator shows the spending propensity of consumers. For this reason, a high number generally is bullish for the domestic currency.

Business Inventories

Business inventories consist of items produced and stored for future sale. The compilation of this information brings little surprise to the market. Furthermore, financial handling helps to maintain control on business inventories in unsurpassed ways. Because of this, the importance of this indicator for FOREX traders is limited.

Construction Data

Construction data represent a significant group of indicators that are included in calculation of the U.S. GDP. Additionally, housing traditionally has been the engine that brought the U.S. economy out of the recessions that occurred after World War II. These indicators are classified into three main categories:

1. Housing starts and permits
2. Single-family home sales, new and existing
3. Construction expenses

The construction indicators are cyclic and very sensitive to interest-rate levels (thus to mortgage rates as well) and to the available-income level. However, low interest rates by themselves probably can't generate a high demand for housing. As was demonstrated by the situation in the early 1990s, despite a historical low level of mortgage rates in the United States, housing barely increased in a marginal way as a result of the lack of employment security in a weak economy. In addition, despite the recession in 2000–2001, the cost of homes, for example, in California practically didn't go lower.

Home starts of between 1.5 and 2 million units reflect a strong economy, whereas a figure of a million units suggests that the economy is going through a recession. Thus the higher the home figures are, the better result they will have on the currency.

Inflation Indicators

Traders watch inflationary data very closely because the preferred way to fight inflation is to raise interest rates. Higher interest rates tend to give support to the local currency. To measure inflation, traders use the economic tools that will be analyzed below. By itself, a higher inflation rate is bearish for a currency.

Producer Price Index (PPI)

The PPI is compiled from most sectors of the economy, such as manufacturing, mining, and agriculture. The sample used to calculate the index groups nearly 3400 articles (commodities). Some of the proportions of the most important groups that are used for calculation of the index are food: 24 percent; fuel: 7 percent; vehicles: 7 percent; and clothing: 6 percent. Unlike CPI, the PPI does not include imported goods, services, or taxes. The higher this number is, the better it is for the currency.

Consumer Price Index (CPI)

The CPI reflects the average change in retail prices for a basic basket of products and services. CPI data are compiled from a price sample for food, clothing, fuel, transport, and medical services that people acquire daily. The proportions of the most important groups for calculation of the index are housing: 38 percent; food: 19 percent; fuel; 8 percent, and vehicles: 7 percent. The higher the CPI is, the better it is for the currency.

Even though the Federal Reserve takes the position that the indexes tend to exaggerate the strength of inflation, both the PPI and the CPI are tools that help traders to gauge inflationary activity.

GNP Implicit Deflator

This index is calculated by dividing the actual GNP dollar figure by the constant GNP dollar figure. The higher the number is, the better it is for the currency.

GDP Implicit Deflator

This index is calculated by dividing the actual GDP dollar figure by the constant GDP dollar figure. Both GNP and GDP implicit deflation indexes are released quarterly, along with the respective GNP and GDP figures. These deflation indexes generally are considered to be the most significant measurement of inflation. As long as this number is high, it is better for the currency.

Merchandise Trade Balance

This is one of the most important economic indicators. Its value can trigger long-duration changes in monetary and international policies. The trade balance consists of the net difference between exports and imports of a particular economy. The number includes six categories:

1. Food
2. Basic materials and industrial supplies
3. Consumer goods
4. Vehicles
5. Capital goods
6. Other merchandises

A separated indicator that pertains to this group is the merchandise trade balance of the United States with Japan. The higher the merchandise trade balance is, the better it is for the currency.

Employment Indicators

The unemployment rate is a significant economic indicator in many areas. This measures, naturally, the solidity of a country's economy. Unemployment rate is a delayed economic indicator. It is important to remember this, especially in times of economic recession. While people are focused on health and recovery of the working sector, employment is the last indicator to react.

When an economic contraction causes a job shortage, it takes time to regenerate a psychological confidence about an economic recovery at management levels before new jobs are added. At an individual level, the betterment of the employment situation can be clouded when new jobs are added in small companies and thus don't reflect completely in the data.

Employment reports are significant for the financial markets in general and for the FOREX in particular. These data are considered very seriously in the FOREX during transitional periods of recovery and contraction. The reason behind this importance in extreme economic situations lies in the panorama it paints about economic health and the degree of maturity of a business cycle. A decreasing unemployment figure signals a mature cycle, whereas the opposite occurs when the unemployment indicator increases. The greater the unemployment data are, the worse it is for the currency.

Nonfarm Payroll (NFP)
In general, the most used employment figure is not the monthly unemployment rate, which is given as a percentage, but instead the nonfarm payroll. This figure is calculated as the proportion of the difference between the total labor force and the employed labor force divided by the total labor force [(TLF − ELF)/FLT].

These data are complex, but they generate a lot of information. In the FOREX, the standard indicators watched by traders are the unemployment rate, the manufacturer payrolls, the nonfarm payroll, average income, and average working week. Generally speaking, the most significant employment data are the manufacturer and nonfarm payrolls, followed by the unemployment rate. A higher NFP is better for the currency

Employment Cost Index (ECI)
The ECI measures salaries and inflation and provides a comprehensive analysis of the compensation given to workers, including salaries, commissions, and wages, as well as additional benefits. The higher the number is, the better it is for the currency.

Consumer Spending Indicators
These consumption indicators are based on data that are relative to the volume of retail sales and are important for FOREX traders because they show the demand level from consumers and their sentiment, which represents initial data necessary for calculation of other indicators such as GNP and GDP. The higher the consumer spending indicators are, the better it is for the currency.

Retail Sales
Retail sales are a significant indicator of consumer spending for FOREX traders because the figure shows the strength of consumer demand and at the same time consumer confidence. As an economic indicator, retail sales are particularly important in the United States. Unlike other countries, such as Japan, the core of the U.S. economy is the consumer. If consumers have enough additional income or enough credit because of it, more merchandise will be produced or imported. The figures for retail sales create an economic process of impulse to the manufacturing sector. The seasonal aspect

also is important for this economic indicator. The months that are watched more closely by FOREX traders as to retail sales are December because of the Christmas holidays and September, the month of return to school. Also, November is becoming a more and more important month owing to the changes in previous post-Christmas sales to pre-December sale days.

Another interesting phenomenon occurred in the United States. Despite the economic recession of the early 1990s, the volume of retail sales was unusually high. The profit margin, however, was much smaller. This occurred because consumers turned their preferences to discount stores.

Traders watch retail sales closely to evaluate the global strength of the economy and thus the strength of the currency. This indicator is issued monthly. The higher the number is, the better it is for the currency.

Consumer Sentiment

Consumer sentiment is the result of a household survey designed to measure directly the individual tendency to spend money to increase or maintain at the same level the expenses related to the satisfaction of actual household needs and thus implies a gauge of the actual labor market. The higher this number is, the better it is for the currency.

Auto Sales

Despite the importance of the automotive industry in terms of production and sales, the level of vehicle sales is not an economic indicator that is widely taken into account by FOREX traders. American vehicle manufacturers have experienced a long and constant loss of market share that only started reversing in early 1990s. However, the internationalization of vehicle manufacturing has grown more and more, given that American vehicles are being assembled outside the United States and German vehicles are being built inside the United States.

Owing to this confusion, vehicle sales figures can't be used easily in FOREX fundamental analysis.

Leading Indicators

The following economic indicators are leading indicators:

- Weekly average production of manufacturing workers
- Weekly average of state employment claims
- New orders for consumer goods and materials (inflation-adjusted)
- Sales performance (companies that receive slower deliveries from suppliers)

- Contracts and factory orders for products and equipment (inflation-adjusted)
- New building permits
- Changes in the nondelivered factory orders and in durable goods
- Changes in prices of important materials

The higher these figures are, the better it is for the currency, except for the weekly state employment claims (unemployment claims). The higher those unemployment levels are, the worse it is for the currency.

Personal Income

Personal income is the income received by individuals, nonprofit institutions, and private investment funds. The elements of this indicator include commissions and wages, income from rent, profits, dividends, interest earnings, and payment transfers (Social Security, state unemployment insurance, and veteran's benefits). Commissions and wages reflect the underlying economic conditions.

This indicator is vital for the sales sector. Without an adequate personal income and a tendency to buy, durable and nondurable goods purchases by consumers will be limited. For FOREX traders, personal income is not significant. However, when it is high, this is positive for the currency.

JAPAN'S MONETARY POLICY

During the long economic depression in Japan from the beginning of the 1980's through the fourth quarter of 1991, monetary policy essentially consisted of the application of a very low interest rate since 1995, a zero interest rate since 1999, and a quantitative easing since 2001. The purpose of such a policy was to lower expectations about future interest rates.

However, there is a problem because a more effective way to reduce interest rates and at the same time stimulate the economy would be to increase expectations of the private sector about future price levels. Quantitative easing can induce expectations of a higher price level, which, in turn, can lead to a depreciation of the current value of the currency, especially if the quantitative easing is expected to be permanent. The commitment to a zero interest rate until inflation was controlled was not effective in inducing inflationary expectations or escaping from a liquidity trap.

Especially between 1998 and 2003, the policies of the Bank of Japan were not helpful in fighting deflation, which can be a very costly mistake.

A zero interest rate implies that there is no other way to use the overnight interest rate as an instrument of monetary policy.

The monetary policy meetings of the Bank of Japan produce a guideline for money-market operations in the periods between meetings, and this is written as a target for the overnight interest rate, which is to be achieved with open-market operations. After the March 19, 2001, meeting, the operating target was changed to a target on overnight bank reserves, which had experienced a significant increase, thus generating a zero interest rate.

The Bank of Japan executes open-market transactions two or three times a day. As it intervenes in the money market, it represents an interest-rate target operating procedure, which helps it to fix the noncollateralized overnight interest rate in the Interbank market. Additionally, the Bank of Japan has a steady program of buying Japanese government bonds.

Since 1998, the monetary policy meetings of the Bank of Japan have been held on a preannounced but somewhat irregular schedule, usually around the tenth and twenty-fifth of each month. Interest-rate decisions are announced immediately after the meeting. No press conference or further information or discussion is given. The minutes of the meetings are released after six weeks or more. The Bank of Japan issues a monthly report of recent economic and financial developments that summarizes all the economic information that has been used in the discussions during the monetary policy meeting.

JAPAN ECONOMIC INDICATORS

The Economic Structure of Japan

The economy of Japan can be compared with the economy of developed European countries. Japanese companies see financing from banks as more reliable than the use of market of equities and bonds. Employment, at least in the big companies, is usually a lifetime career. The economy can be divided in two large groups: multinational corporations and small family enterprises.

The main indicators of Japan's economy are the balance of payments, the CPI, the GDP, the industrial production index, leading and coincident indices of business conditions, machinery orders, money supply, retail sales, unemployment, the wholesale price index (WPI), and the Tankan index.

Tankan Index

This index is based on the surveys that Japanese companies hold four times a year. It shows business confidence. The Tankan index is one of the key indicators of the Japanese economy.

A positive economic trend usually is shown by Tankan values higher than 0, which is considered as normal; however, higher values provide good support for the yen and are good for the entire economy of Japan.

Money Supply

The money supply strongly affects the rate of the Japanese currency, the yen. If the supply is growing slowly, the Bank of Japan needs to decrease the interest rate, which has a negative influence on the yen. In the same way, deflation (represented by a fall in prices) has a negative effect on the Japanese currency.

FOREX CURRENCY CARRY TRADE

The *carry trade* is a well-known FOREX strategy that takes profit from the different interest rates between two currencies; if one currency has a relatively low interest rate, it can be sold against another currency that has a higher interest rate, and the trader will profit from the positive difference that results. Every day, speculators have a steady deposit of positive interest, or swap, in their trading accounts, and this can be an important incentive for traders. For example, if you open a position in a FOREX currency pair where the higher-interest currency is 7 percent and the lower-interest currency is 2 percent, the swap can yield 5 percent as long as the market doesn't change.

The term *carry trade* without further modification refers directly to currency carry trades: Investors borrow low-yielding and lend high-yielding currencies. It is principally correlated with global financial and exchange-rate stability, and its use decreases when there are global liquidity shortages.

However, even when the differences between interest rates can be profited on, important risks still remain. The market obviously still can change and go against the trader's position, although the continuous daily rise in the interest amount in the account may help to attenuate the potential losses. With the exceptionally high leverages that are used to profit from those differences, even a small variation at a given moment can lead to huge losses.

THE YEN CARRY TRADE

In earlier years, many trillions of dollars were accumulated on the yen carry trade. Interest rates set by the Bank of Japan allowed profitability on borrowing the Japanese yen to acquire other currencies.

For several years in the recent past, Japan had a 0 percent interest rate. The rate was increased to 0.5 percent but remained much lower than the rates of other countries. On the other hand, Japan has a very high level of savings, around US$15 billion (much higher than the total U.S. GDP). Because of the low interest rate, Japanese investors save in other currencies, accumulating around US$6 trillion in foreign assets. This, in turn, increases the value of those foreign currencies. Other investors have borrowed the yen to invest in the global markets. However, in the recent months, the lowering of interest rates in all major currencies has caused the yen carry trade to begin unwinding.

UNWINDING OF THE YEN CARRY TRADE

The yen carry trade can only be profitable if there is stability in most currencies or if they are rising against the yen, especially the U.S. dollar. If the dollar falls, the trade would bring up a loss independent of the positive interest-rate difference.

Now that the United States, Europe, and other countries have lowered their interest rates, this signifies the end of the carry trade. The global economy has entered a recession. There is a slowdown in the overall economies of the world. Thus the interest-rate differential has narrowed, and there is no longer an incentive to borrow the Japanese currency. Local investors have started to sell their investments in dollars and euros and take their money back to Japan. The yen has started to increase in value.

This increases the risk of losing a huge amount of money on those trades as the yen is rises against the dollar and the euro, and as a consequence, people have started selling their foreign investments, which, in turn, reevaluates the yen even more as the demand is increased.

The other currencies depreciate, and this harms Japanese exports because they become more expensive, thus reducing the general demand and leading to a lower growth in the economy and possible deflation.

INTERVENTIONS

Interventions are the result of decisions by central banks to intervene in the economy by using their reserves and buying or selling their foreign-currency assets in order to stabilize the value of their own currency. Interventions represent quite an interesting opportunity for traders because they can be an indicator that the currency involved has a lower value with respect to fundamentals, especially if what triggers the intervention is highly negative, such as the national debt or a natural catastrophe.

The sharp fall of one currency leads the counterpart asset to rise fast, and thus traders can speculate to what extent there could be an intervention, which would have as a result a series of price movements in the near term. They can then take a position previous to the potential intervention and make profits on those moves, exiting after the effects of the intervention have ended. This can be very risky, however, because such traders are operating against the current trend, and large capitals losses could result in a very short period of time because of the fast-moving market.

Some indicators will signal if there is a possibility of intervention. Interventions usually will occur at the same price level as previous interventions. This is not always true, though, because sometimes the intervention is canceled by the central bank if it costs too much. Another clue can be found in speeches by finance officials, such as announcements or threats of possible future interventions. Those words sometimes can be enough to give impulse to the markets. However, if there is no reaction, with time, such announcements will have lesser and lesser impact because their credibility decrease. Finally, FOREX analysts can determine fair estimations of levels where an intervention may occur, especially those who work for the main banks or investment companies.

How can you trade when an intervention is occurring? First of all, you should identify the previous intervention levels and evaluate the actual expected price level to make your decision. Then, of course, always trade with a stop loss and a target level so as to limit losses and lock in some profits. Leave enough room on the stops though, to mitigate against sharp movements that may occur after the intervention. The targets for profits should be set at the same levels that were attained in the previous intervention. Finally, open your trade with a reduced position size. Remember that you will be trading against the main long-term trend, so there are high risks of a margin call if the intervention doesn't happen during the time span that you have considered.

Although interventions can be extremely profitable, trading them is mostly for pure speculators. There are several ways to identify the moment when an intervention is most likely to happen, but it is always a good idea to be prepared by using a very low leverage and a well-planned smart money management through the use of stop losses and the setting of targets to lock profits.

GROSS DOMESTIC PRODUCT (GDP)

The gross domestic product (GDP), also called *gross domestic income* (GDI), is one of the instruments that allows measuring the income and output of the national economy of a particular country. It represents the total value in dollars of all the goods and services produced in a given year inside that country.

The most common approach to measuring and quantifying GDP is the expenditure method:

$$GDP = consumption + gross\ investment + government\ spending + (exports - imports)$$

Consumption and investment in this equation represent the expenditures on final goods and services. The net exports (exports minus imports) adjust this by subtracting the part of this expenditure that is not produced domestically (the imports) and adding back the income coming from what has been produced locally (the exports).

GDP per capita is often used as an indicator of standard of living in a given country; the explanation is that theoretically all citizens benefit from an increase in their country's economic production. The advantage of using this figure is that GDP is measured frequently, and information is given four times a year. The standard of living in different countries can be compared because GDP is measured in practically every country of the world. Finally, the calculations are consistent between countries, so the same things are measured and the comparisons can be done at the same level.

However, per capita GDP is not really a strict measure of the standard of living because it measures particular types of economic activity within a country, such as exports and imports. For example, if a country exports 100 percent of its production but does not import anything, the GDP still would be high, but the standard of living would be poorer.

GDP rather is used as such an indicator because the standard of living tends to increase when GDP per capita increases. It is not a direct measure but a relative measure. Also, it can be used to gauge working productivity. An alternative to GDP as a country's economic health measurement is the human development index (HDI).

TRADING THE NEWS

If you are considering trading the news, subscribing to a timely news feed is paramount. There are several free services around and many public media that announce the economic results almost as soon as they are released. However, obtaining the data exactly at the moment they are issued is of great importance in determining the success or failure of a news trading strategy.

Usually, the main financial media will offer both free and paid news services, with some differences as to the timing of the release. It is also crucial to select a trustable news source because sometimes the media tend to be slanted toward one side or the other, thus influencing the public through rumors or distorted expectations previous to the releases, especially in what concerns forecast figures.

The continuous operability of the FOREX market and the fact that economic data are always being released throughout the day from any of its participant countries constitute a great advantage. Besides, the currency markets not only will react to economic data coming from a single source but also to any financial or political news coming from every corner of the world. Usually there are always at least six or seven important releases daily that will affect any of the eight major currencies from the countries that traders follow more closely. This adds up to many opportunities to trade the news.

The following are the eight major currencies: U.S. dollar (USD), euro (EUR), British pound (GBP), Japanese yen (JPY), Swiss franc (CHF), Canadian dollar (CAD), Australian dollar (AUD), and New Zealand dollar (NZD). Some of the derivatives with the greatest liquidity, based on those currencies, are the following currency pairs: EUR/USD, USD/JPY, AUD/USD, GBP/JPY, EUR/CHF, and CHF/JPY.

When trading the news, you can easily choose which currency and economic releases you will be paying attention to. However, since the U.S. dollar is mostly present as counterpart of all currency trades, U.S. economic releases usually have the heaviest impact on the behavior of the markets.

Trading news is not as easy as it may seem. There are the actual figures reported, but the previous forecasts and rumors have to be taken into account, and revisions to previous releases may change the picture completely. Extreme volatility at news time makes the trades harder to achieve. One has to be very careful not to be stopped out before the move has been given a chance to progress.

There is a saying, "Buy the rumor; sell the fact." You have to keep up with what is getting the focus of the market at any moment. The effects of economic releases can last for hours and even days after they have been issued.

The most common way to trade the news is to examine the charts previous to a particular big number to be released and look for periods of consolidation in preparation for that release. You then trade the breakout that ensues after the figures have been made public. Since the effects usually last for more than one day, you can either trade news intraday or based on the daily charts in a more conservative way.

WHEN ARE THE NEWS RELEASES ISSUED?

If you are planning to trade news releases, you should pay extra attention to the following times based on each market involved. The following list shows the approximate times (Eastern Time) when the most important economic releases are usually published.

Market Hours

Country	Currency	Time (EST)
United States	USD	8:30–10:00
Japan	JPY	18:50–23:30
Canada	CAD	7:00–8:30
United Kingdom	GBP	2:00–4:30
Italy	EUR	3:45–5:00
Germany	EUR	2:00–6:00
France	EUR	2:45–4:00
Switzerland	CHF	1:45–5:30
New Zealand	NZD	16:45–21:00
Australia	AUD	17:30–19:30

APPROXIMATE VARIATION IN PIPS BASED ON THE NEWS

In the following 20 minutes after the news is released:

Unemployment (non-farm payrolls)	124 pips
Interest rates (rate decisions from the Fed)	74 pips
Trade balance	64 pips

Inflation (CPI)	44 pips
Retail sales	43 pips
GDP	43 pips
Current account balance	43 pips
Durable goods	39 pips
TIC report or foreign acquisitions of U.S. assets	33 pips

In the continuation of the day when the news is released:

Unemployment (nonfarm payrolls)	193 pips
Interest rates (rate decisions from the Fed)	140 pips
TIC report or foreign acquisitions of U.S. assets	132 pips
Trade balance	129 pips
Current account balance	27 pips
Durable goods	126 pips
Retail sales	125 pips
Inflation (CPI)	123 pips
GDP	110 pips

WHAT ARE CONTRARIAN INDICATORS?

You may have heard the saying, "Buy the rumor; sell the fact." *Contrarian indicators* are news, data, and opinions that imply a certain path and direction for any given currency pair, whereas, in reality, the result is totally opposite. They are very important when you are timing market moves because they can provide warning signs of possible market reversals.

It has been noted in some research in experimental psychology that people usually tend to overreact to news events, especially when the events are unexpected and/or of a dramatic nature. The most recent information has more weight than previous data.

When this reflects on the markets, you will see that extreme movements in prices will be followed almost immediately by strong movements in the exact opposite direction; the stronger the first move, the greater will be the reversal. This is caused by the panic that overcomes investors in the face of new information, and this expands to the rest of the market. As a conclusion, you could deduct that when the market is most bearish and everybody is selling, there is a good opportunity for buying, and inversely, when other investors are buying and the market shows a strong bullish impulse, there is a good opportunity for selling. If your estimation about the overreaction of the market is correct, you will profit because the markets always make a correction over time.

A contrarian indicator is one that indicates that a currency or stock actually will do the *opposite* of what the indicator says. When a particular currency pair or stock starts to get a huge amount of press coverage or advertising, it is time to pay attention for the imminent reversal. In the case of a currency pair, the more it is advertised that the pair will be rising (or falling), the more it is the time to go in the opposite direction. When everybody is long or short, it's time to get out and go the other way.

TECHNICAL ANALYSIS

10

TECHNICAL INDICATORS

TECHNICAL ANALYSIS

In a technical analysis, you look at the price and volume data to be able to predict future movements. The basis for a technical analysis was given by Charles H. Dow, whose methods were based on the behavior of investors, on psychology, and on the movements of prices. When an analysis is made based on the movement of prices, you will be doing a technical analysis.

As you can see in charts that are not more than a compilation of movements in the market price of a particular currency, the beginning of a technical analysis is that any market moves in trends and in the statements of encouragement of traders. Therefore, all the information necessary to conduct a technical analysis is in the chart of a particular currency.

The analysis of trends is necessary for trading in the FOREX because in the FOREX you can gain in a bull market and a bear market as you buy one currency and sell the other. The trend lines are a simple reference that will be useful in confirming the direction of the trend in a currency.

The advantage of technical analysis is that all the factors that affect the prices of currency, both rational or irrational (e.g., economic data, hopes, and feelings), are expressed in a single element that represents the agreement between buyers and sellers at a given time. This element is the quotation, which synthesizes the future expectations and estimates that investors have about each currency and that determine the price.

With a technical analysis, you can detect when a trend is about to change or continue, and you can determine areas that can serve as starting points for an operation. However, as stated previously, it is necessary to operate with coldness and discipline, not being influenced by feelings, euphoria, or discouragement and not being carried away by the atmosphere in the market.

In order to make a technical analysis, your approach will be based first on the tendency in the market, which can be primary, secondary, or tertiary. A primary tendency can last for years, and a secondary tendency can last for months. Tertiary tendencies are variations within a secondary tendency.

Technical analysis uses indicators and patterns. Indicators are mathematical operations on the range of prices that exist in a chart, whereas patterns are forms that are often repeated over time.

The second important point of a technical analysis is the resistance and support levels because some levels remain constant over time and are difficult to break upward (resistance) and can break downward (support). Certain resistance or support levels are difficult to break because traders determine whether it is good to break them or not. But when a rupture of a support or a resistance level takes place, the prices tend to go toward the following level of support or resistance. However, there can be false breaks in a given level, and this occurs because traders are not attracted to break this particular level.

What you find in the charts that your broker gives you will be explained in the next section, and that information can be displayed in different ways.

TYPES OF CHARTS SHOWING PRICE ACTION

PRICE ACTION

What Is Price Action?

Price action is the direct result of order flow: buyers and sellers in the market at a given moment and at a certain price level. Price action will show you the particular bias (more buyers than sellers, or vice versa), the speed at which operations are being performed, and where the buying and selling are occurring (the levels of support and resistance). You can gauge when a breakout is real and where a reversal is probably going to happen. Indicators are born from the continuous flow of this price action and thus depend on it. The indicators only can show what is happening or has happened a few moments ago. For this reason, your understanding of and ability to interpret price action become an essential component of your trading. They are a way to get to the core that lies behind the origin of indicators and of most of the technical signals in the market.

Basic elements are the condition of the bars or candles themselves. You will have up bars, down bars, inside and outside bars, and pin bars or Pinocchio bars. How they relate to one another and form patterns is also taken into account, as in double highs or double lows.

Here are some of the basic definitions of price-action patterns:

A *Pinocchio* or *pin bar* (PB) has a very long nose pointing in one direction, but it is lying about the direction it will take thereafter (thus the name). Its close has to be lower than the open and its direction down, nose pointing up, for a bearish pin bar The inverse, nose pointing down, direction up, close higher than the open, is the case for a bullish pin bar.

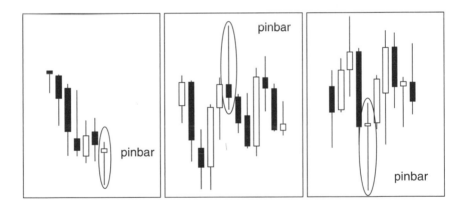

A *double-high lower close* (DBHLC) shows two sequential bars with the same high, the second bar closes lower than the first bar's low, and the direction is down, or bearish. Inversely, a bullish *double-low higher close* (DBLHC) will show two sequential bars with the same low, the close of the second bar is higher than the close of the first bar, and the direction is up.

Outside bars can be bearish or bullish, a *bearish outside bar* (BEOB) will engulf the first bar, its close being lower than its open and the close of the first bar, with the direction down. The *bullish outside bar* (BUOB) has an upward direction, also engulfs the previous bar, and its close is higher than its open and than the open of the previous bar.

inside bar

The *inside bar* setup needs three candles or bars for confirmation. The previous bar is bigger, the inside bar is contained within the length of the previous bar, and the third bar must break both of the first two bars for validity, as you can see in the figure above. The direction will be up or down depending on which side breaks first.

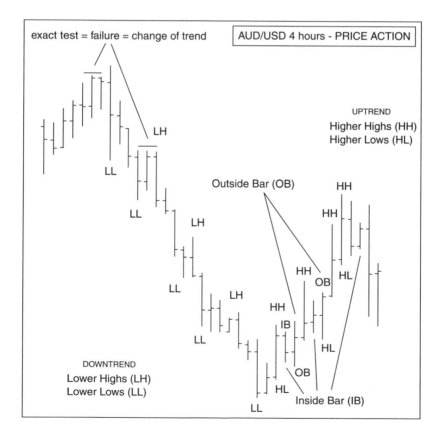

The price on any given time frame is in an uptrend if it continuously makes *higher highs* (HHs) and *higher lows* (HLs) and in a downtrend if it continuously makes *lower highs* (LHs) and *lower lows* (LLs). Any other behavior will give consolidation patterns such as ranges, triangles, pennants, rectangles, etc. The trend continues until the behavior remains in place and is broken as soon as there are no higher highs and higher lows occurring for an uptrend or lower highs and lower lows occurring for a downtrend. After a trend is broken, there is usually a period of consolidation until the trend resumes or reverses.

Different time frames can have different trends, so it is important to be able to differentiate uptrends and downtrends as well as consolidation patterns. Price can be rising on a daily chart but meanwhile can be performing a correction or retracement over shorter periods. You have to train your eye to spot the movements, and a good exercise to do is to take a chart and mark the lows and highs as in the figure above (with LL or HL for lows and HH and LH for highs). First take a higher time frame, such as 4 hours, and mark the trendlines that result from the union of higher or lower highs and higher or lower lows. Then switch and do the same on a shorter time frame, such as 30 minutes. Identify the new highs and lows, and draw the corresponding trend-lines. Now you are able to see the trend in both time frames. You can decide to trade based on the shorter time-frame trend or wait until both align and the price starts moving in the same direction as the higher time-frame trend.

ADVANCE AND RETREAT

The two essential moves that can be seen on a chart are impulsive moves and corrective moves. An *impulsive move* is a strong advance in the direction of the trend, usually fast and long, followed by several candles in the same direction. *Corrective moves* are the inverse and usually follow an impulsive move. The price action retreats, but the strength is very low. Small bars or candles show with no particular alignment. They usually prepare the next impulsive move.

An impulsive move is the result of a large amount of capital entering the market, where buyers or sellers come in at a particular level and with a specific direction in mind. It also can be triggered by a price cascade, such as by reaching a huge amount of pending stop-loss orders (exiting contrarian positions or entering new positions in the same direction as the move). These are the moves with the most consistency because the order flow is heavily biased in one direction. Being able to identify impulsive moves provides us with great trading opportunities.

Corrective moves, on the other hand, are usually the result of two possible situations: profit taking after an impulsive move or a mixed number of buyers and sellers sitting at a certain level, which could become a reversal point. Very often the next move after a correction is a continuation of the previous impulsive move. This type of move has a much lower and unstable order flow and offers a much smaller number of opportunities for good trades.

Gauging the time elapsed between moves is useful in order to have an idea of how much time you will have to wait for the next continuation move. Although not exactly accurate, the price wave usually has a particular frequency (different in every time frame) that can be measured and help you to identify impulses and corrections and give you a rough idea about the possibilities of success for a particular entry. Counting the bars when a pattern is formed is also important in verifying the consistency and potential of the given pattern. For example, wedges and triangles usually complete or exit their patterns at between two-thirds and three-quarters of the move. It is quite rare that they go all the way to completion. Finally, observing the time variable in a consolidation pattern will give you an idea of the potential breakout that has to come later. The longer this time is, the greater is the possibility that the following breakout is a legitimate one. Also, it will break with more strength after a long period of ranging.

LINE CHARTS

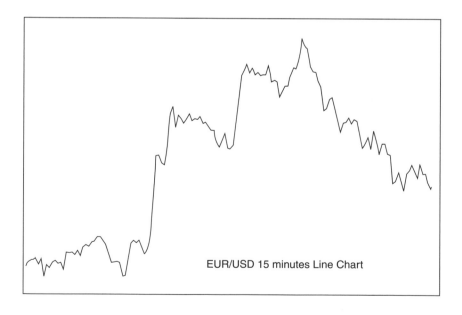

EUR/USD 15 minutes Line Chart

In *line charts,* the closing price is displayed as a point, which is then connected to all the other points through a line, called the *price line.* This line offers very little information but can show the general trend in the price of a particular currency. Every different time scale will show the closing price point for that specific time frame. In some trading platforms, you are able to plot the chart based on a different price (e.g., open, high, or close), but the standard is usually the close because the fluctuation in price during that time frame is not as important as the point in time where the pair closes for most traders.

Other possible settings are an average price between the open (O), close (C), high (H), and low (L), or (O + H + L + C)/4, or other less common settings such as the average of high, low, and close, or (H + L + C)/3, or (H + L + 2 × C)/4, or (H + L)/2, etc. The average of the four prices is best because it is easier to work with and takes out most of the noise.

The line chart is much harder to interpret, especially for beginners, and some chart patterns are not as easier to spot. It can be of general use to have an overview of the price movement, but I would not recommend it for hands-on trading because other types of charts can give much stronger signals and indications.

BAR CHARTS

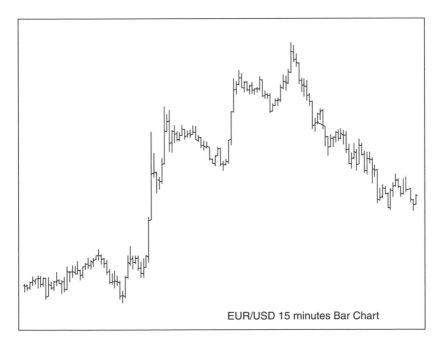

EUR/USD 15 minutes Bar Chart

A *bar chart* can show three or four types of prices, the opening and closing price and the high and low on *OHLC bars* or simply the high, low, and close prices on *HLC bars*. The top indicates the highest price for the period, the bottom shows the lowest price, and the vertical bar indicates the trading range for the given period. The horizontal dash on the left side is the open price, and the dash on the right side is the close price. On HLC bars, only the right dash is seen.

The bar chart is one of the most popular charts, and it offers a fair amount of information about the price movement of the currency pair. High and low prices are united by the vertical bar showing the trading range, and visualization of market movements is much better than on line charts because you can see where the price has closed with respect to the opening price and thus see if the market is going up or down.

CANDLESTICK CHARTS

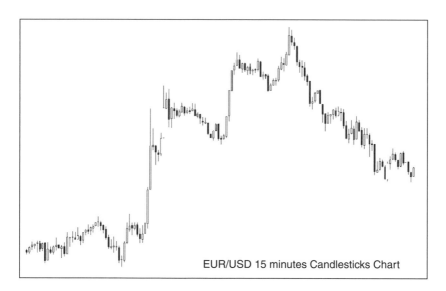

EUR/USD 15 minutes Candlesticks Chart

Candlestick charts are very similar to bar charts in the type of information they offer, also containing price direction information. However, the graphic display is easier to interpret.

Opening and closing prices make the body of the candlestick. When the opening price is lower than the closing price (up candle), the body is left blank or white. When the opening price is higher than the closing price (down candle), the body is filled with color or black (this can be interpreted as "void" and "filled" because a void candlestick will be lightly weighted and will "float up" and a filled candlestick will be heavy and "fall down").

Upper shadows or wicks show the high of the price and lower shadows show the low of the price for the time period selected. There is a series of patterns that are considered to have prediction qualities. The names of the patterns make it easier to remember what a particular pattern means; in addition, some of the patterns are good for identifying market reversal points.

These are the most commonly used charts. However, there are also other ways to represent price action graphically.

HEIKEN-ASHI CHARTS

Heiken-Ashi charts were invented by the Japanese and look like candlestick charts, but they use a different method to calculate and plot the candles.

EUR/USD - Heiken-Ashi - 1 hour Chart

Unlike candlestick charts, in which each candlestick shows four different values of the open, close, high, and low prices (independent of each other), Heiken-Ashi candles use the preceding candle and are calculated based on their relationship:

Close: This is the average of the open, close, high, and low prices (OHLC/4).

Open: This is the average of the open and close of the preceding candle.

High: This is the highest value among the high, open, and close prices.

Low: This is the lowest value among the high, open, and close prices.

In this way, they are related to each other. When calculating the open and close prices of every candle, you need to know the preceding open and close prices, and the high and the low are affected in the same way by the preceding candle. For this reason, the candles appear on the chart with a certain delay. This can be a good feature when you are trading very volatile currency pairs and also when you engage in scalping very short time frames such as the 1-minute chart because it prevents you from entering too early and making mistakes by trading against the market. However, trading with Heiken-Ashi candles by themselves is not the best option, especially in higher time frames, because the action is delayed, and you could be entering too late. You should have another chart open to see the normal candlesticks or bars along with this indicator.

When the market is bullish, Heikin-Ashi candles have big bodies and long upper shadows but no lower shadow. When the market is bearish, Heikin-Ashi candles have big bodies and long lower shadows but no upper shadow. Reversal candles are similar to doji candlesticks, with a very small body and long upper and lower shadows.

There are five primary signals that identify trends and buying opportunities:

- Hollow candles with no lower shadows indicate a strong uptrend; they signal to keep on the long side and gather more profits.

- Hollow candles signify an uptrend; you might want to add to your long position and exit short positions.

- One candle with a small body surrounded by upper and lower shadows indicates a trend change; risk-loving traders might buy or sell here, whereas others will wait for confirmation before going short or long.

- Filled candles indicate a downtrend; you might want to add to your short position and exit long positions.

- Filled candles with no higher shadows identify a strong downtrend; stay short until there's a change in trend.

RENKO CHARTS

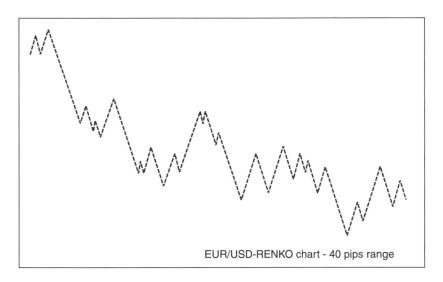

EUR/USD-RENKO chart - 40 pips range

Renko charts also were invented by the Japanese. In this type of chart, the time and volumes are not taken into account. The chart is concerned only with price movement.

Renko candles look like small boxes or bricks (*renga* in Japanese) with no upper or lower shadows. The size of the box can be changed based on a chosen set price value. The smaller the size, the higher will be the number of boxes needed, so more details of the price changes will be shown on the charts.

The chart is built by placing a box in the next column as soon as the price surpasses the top or bottom price of the preceding box by a given amount. In the chart above, the range established is 40 pips. White or hollow boxes are used when the direction of the trend is up, whereas black or filled boxes are used when the trend is down.

This type of chart helps traders to identify very efficiently the main support and resistance levels. The signals to buy or sell appear when the direction of the trend changes, and the boxes alternate colors.

For example, a trader will sell when a black box is placed at the end of a series of rising white boxes. Some caution should be exercised, though. Since this type of chart was designed as a means to follow the general price trend of a particular asset, you often can get false signals when the color of the boxes changes too early, thus producing a whipsaw effect.

POINT AND FIGURE CHARTS

This is a chart that records period-to-period price movements but doesn't take time into consideration. Point and figure charts are composed of a series of columns with Xs or Os. An X is used to state a rising price, and an O represents a falling price. This helps in filtering out price movements that are not significant and also in determining what the main support and resistance levels are. When the price moves beyond those levels, traders will place their orders.

30											X								
29											X	O	X		X				X
28											X	O	X	O	X	O			X
27											X	O	X	O	X	O			X
26											X	O		O	X	O			X
25									X		X			O	X	O	X		X
24							X	O	X					O	X	O	X	O	X
23							X	O	X						X		X	O	X
22				X		X	O	X								O	X	O	X
21				X	O	X	O	X								O		O	
20			X		X	O	X	O	X										
19	X		X	O	X	O	X	O	X										
18	X	O	X	O	X	O	X	O	X										
17	X	O	X	O		O		O	X										
16	X	O	X				O												
15	X	O																	
14	X																		
13	X																		
12	X																		
11	X																		
10	X																		

The first thing defined here is the *box size,* or the number of points that the currency pair will have to move to justify the drawing of a new box. Every time the price changes more than that amount, another X or O is added. For example, in the chart above, the box size is 1, and every time the price goes up an additional point, another X is drawn. Xs and Os are not mixed in the same column. If the price goes down after a previous rise, a new column will be drawn to the right.

PIP RANGE BAR OR CANDLESTICK CHARTS

Pip range bar charts were designed by Vicente Nicolellis, a Brazilian broker and trader, in 1995. He wanted to solve the problem of handling the extreme volatility of local markets and finally decided that the best way to achieve this was to take time out of the equation, focusing solely on price. This is similar to a point and figure charts approach, where only price changes are recorded.

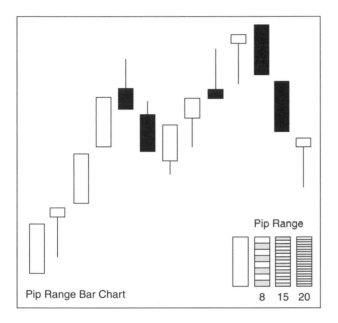

Constant ranges are used to define the bars or candles. Usually, you can find ranges of 8, 10, 15, 20, and 30 pips. A new bar is opened as soon as that range has been covered and the price opens higher or lower, starting a new range with the same pip value. You can apply to these charts the same indicators you would on normal bar or candlestick charts.

These charts are particularly interesting when you are facing a stalling market, where there is a long congestion of prices, which in a normal chart would be reflected in several short-bodied bars or candles. In this way, attention can be focused on the essential changes in price itself, taking out the usual noise of sideways markets. When a range is complete, a new bar opens independent of the time. You could have a single bar for a whole day of trading if you are using a 30-pip range and the price hasn't gone over or under that range for the duration of the day. As soon as the market goes over the 30-pip range, a new bar will open, starting at the closing level of the preceding bar, and the 30-pip range will have to be completed again to allow a new bar to open later on. Conversely, if the range is covered in a few minutes and the price keeps going in a fast move, you will have several 30-pip range bars or candles showing those changes.

TREND INDICATORS

MOVING AVERAGES

The *moving average* (MA) is an indicator that shows the average value of the price of a currency pair over a set period. It is generally used to measure momentum and define areas of possible support and resistance, as well as for checking the direction of a trend. The most commonly used detection of upward or downward momentum is through the cross of two moving averages, one short term and the other longer term. When the fast MA crosses above or below the slow MA, it indicates a possible change in trend.

There are several variations in the calculation for this indicator. An MA can be simple, exponential, smoothed, or linearly weighted.

AUD/USD - 1 Hour Chart

Moving Averages (50 periods) applied to Close Price

Simple	———
Exponential	■■■
Smoothed	·············
Linear Weighted	– – – – –

Simple Moving Average (SMA)

This is a simple, or arithmetic, MA calculated by adding the closing price of the given instrument for a number of time periods and then dividing this total by the number of time periods.

Exponential Moving Average (EMA)

An EMA is similar to an SMA, with the difference that more weight is given to the latest data. An EMA is also known as an *exponentially weighted moving average.* This type of MA shows a faster reaction to most recent price changes in comparison with an SMA. EMAs are used, for example, in the moving average convergence-divergence (MACD) indicator and in other oscillators. The most commonly used values to gauge long-term trends are the 50- and 200-day EMAs.

Linearly Weighted Moving Average (LWMA)
This type of moving average, like the EMA, also assigns a higher weighting to the most recent price data in a proportional regression. Each price of a given set of periods is multiplied by its relative position in the data series, and then they are all added and divided by the total number of time periods. For example, in a 25-period LWMA, the price of the last period is multiplied by 25, the preceding one by 24, and so on and then divided by the sum of all the multipliers.

AVERAGE DIRECTIONAL MOVEMENT INDEX (ADX)
This indicator was developed by J. Welles Wilder to identify the presence of a trend in a given financial instrument. The ADX is composed of three lines: the index itself and two lines known as the *directional movement indicators* (DMIs) in the index's positive and negative directions (+DI and −DI).

This indicator provides an objective value for the strength of a trend. It is nondirectional and related to the respective directional indicator, so it

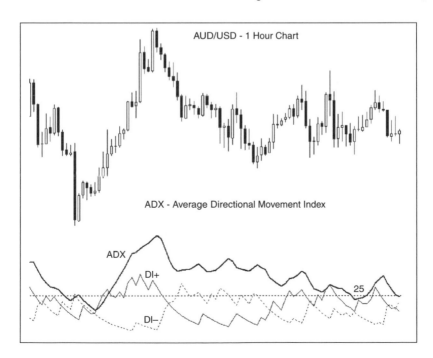

AUD/USD - 1 Hour Chart

ADX - Average Directional Movement Index

ADX

DI+

DI−

25

will provide a measure of the strength of the particular direction. When it rises, the trend signaled by the directional indicator that has crossed above the other one will be stronger; when it falls, the trend will be weaker.

Directional Movement Index (DMI)
The DMI indicates the potential trending of a currency pair. The scale for the DMI goes from 0 to 100. It is composed of two lines, the +DI and the −DI (positive and negative directions). The ADX is a moving average of the DMI. Its value should be above 25 for a trend to have the needed strength for its definition.

Positive Directional Indicator (+DI)
The +DI is a component of the ADX that is used to measure an uptrend. When the +DI slopes upward, it indicates that the uptrend is getting stronger. The beginning of the uptrend will be signaled by this line crossing above the negative directional indicator (−DI).

Negative Directional Indicator (−DI)
The −DI is another component of the ADX that is used to signal a down-trend. When the slope of the −DI starts rising, it indicates that the down-trend is getting stronger. When it crosses above the +DI, this signals the beginning of a new downtrend.

BOLLINGER BANDS
Bollinger bands are an indicator developed by John Bollinger that allow users to compare the volatility and relative price levels over a time period. This indicator consists of three bands that follow the price action of a given currency pair.

The middle line is an SMA of the set periods (the chart above is set to the standard of 20 periods). The upper band is commonly set to 2 standard deviations plus the given SMA value, and the lower band is set to the SMA minus 2 standard deviations. The standard deviation is a statistical unit of measure that offers an assessment of the volatility of a certain price. In this way, the bands can react quickly to price movements and reflect periods of high and low volatility. Bands will widen when there is a greater volatility and will stretch when the volatility is very low.

The number of periods of the moving average, as well as the number of deviations, would have to be adjusted to the usual behavior of the specific currency pair as well as the time frame that is being used. The default setting is 20 periods and 2 standard deviations. Properly set Bollinger

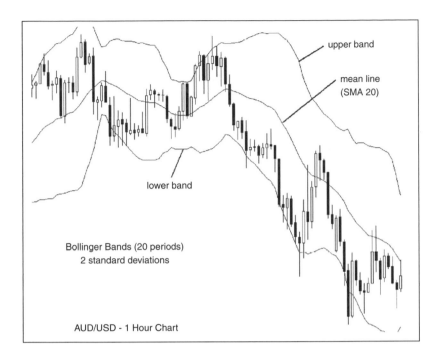

upper band

mean line
(SMA 20)

lower band

Bollinger Bands (20 periods)
2 standard deviations

AUD/USD - 1 Hour Chart

bands should hold both support and resistance of the price reversal swings, that is, the higher low in a downward move turning to the upside and the lower high in an upward move turning to the downside. The price of this second low or high should not penetrate the bands. Those higher lows or lower highs are formed as a reaction after a strong fall or rise. The price has corrected, and it rallies again in the former direction, failing to reach the previous bottom or top.

Bollinger bands allow traders to identify periods of high volatility and extremely low volatility. In particular, they help in gauging when prices are reaching unsustainable extremes and are near a reversal to the mean. Periods of lower volatility, when the bands are very narrow, lead to a breakout. However, the bands will not give any indication of the future direction of prices. This should be determined with the help of other indicators and general technical analysis.

A signal that can be taken from the configuration of the bands is the double bottom or double top. When prices penetrate below the lower band and remain there, resting above the band, this is a signal for a long position, which will be confirmed when the price rises above the middle band. When prices penetrate above the upper band and a second attempt fails to break through, and the price remains below the band, this is a signal for a short position, which will be confirmed when the price falls down and reaches the middle band.

It is important to note that the second low or the second high has to remain above the bands, although the remaining lows can be higher or lower than the others.

This indicator can be used for trend following because the price will tend to remain near one of the bands, for straddling breakouts when there is a very tight zone, and also for counter-trending by profiting from trend exhaustion, as in the preceding example of double bottoms and double tops.

Note that just touching the bands is not a signal in itself; this will only indicate that prices are reaching an extreme with respect to their mean, becoming overbought or oversold. However, when trending, prices can continue the path of one of the bands and fluctuate between the band and the middle line without crossing to the other side.

COMMODITY CHANNEL INDEX (CCI)

This oscillator was developed by Donald Lambert, and it is used to help determine overbought and oversold conditions of a particular currency pair. It is also often used to identify cycles in trends because it allows a trader to see the potential peaks or troughs in the price line and to estimate possible changes in the direction of the trend. Usually crosses of the zero

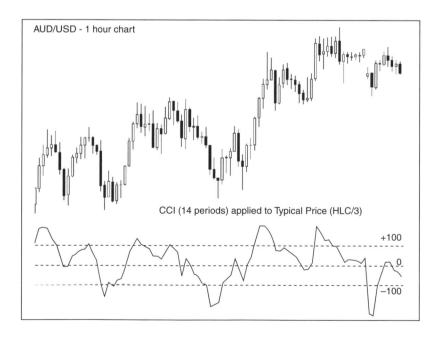

line indicate a buy or sell opportunity, and values above 100 show a possible overbought condition. Meanwhile, values below 100 will alert of a possible oversold situation.

The formula for its calculation is as follows:

$$CCI = price - MA/0.015 \times D$$

where MA is a moving average of the price and D the normal deviations from that average.

PARABOLIC STOP AND REVERSE (SAR)

This indicator is part of a strategy that uses a trailing stop point level in which the position has to be reversed when the level is broken and the trailing stop has been hit. It is used to evaluate the best entry and exit points. This method was developed by J. Welles Wilder. If the currency pair is trading below the parabolic SAR (PSAR), the market is bearish, and you should sell or stay in your short positions. If it trades above the PSAR, you should buy or stay long.

This indicator determines not only the direction of a particular currency pair but also its momentum and the location of the points at which

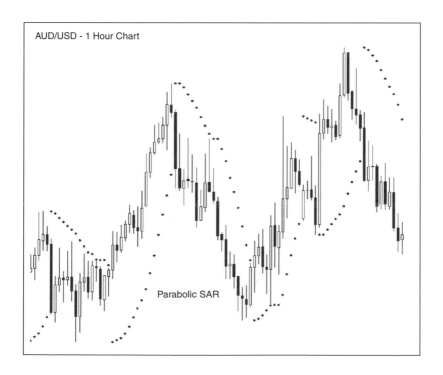

AUD/USD - 1 Hour Chart

Parabolic SAR

it is higher and thus has a greater probability of changing direction. It is shown on the charts with a series of dots placed at a relative distance from the prices depending on the settings. Common standard settings are step 0.02 – maximum 0.2, but I have been having much better results with a step 0.03 – maximum 0.6 setting for scalping and in smaller time frames.

When the most recent high price has been broken, the PSAR changes its side, and thus the direction is usually reversed, placing itself at the most recent low price. The SAR then starts rising or falling faster as the trend develops, and at a certain point, the dots catch up with the price action. This is when a turning point is near. It is better to use the PSAR in trending conditions because it will not work as well in a choppy or sideways market.

MARKET AND VOLATILITY INDICATORS

AVERAGE TRUE RANGE (ATR)

This indicator measures the volatility. It was introduced by Welles Wilder in his book, *New Concepts in Technical Trading Systems.*

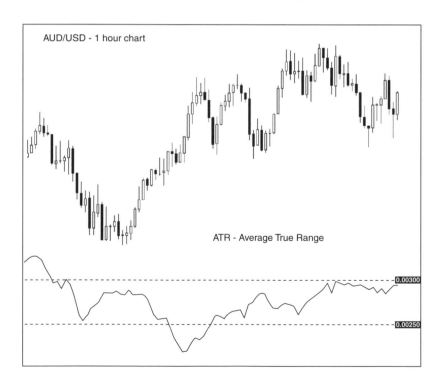

The true range indicator is the greatest result of the following calculations:

- The current high less the current low, or
- The absolute value of the current high less the previous close, or
- The absolute value of the current low less the previous close

The average true range is a moving average (20 days is the most commonly used time period) of the true ranges of every individual period considered. Higher volatility will show a higher value of ATR; lower volatility will show a lower value of ATR.

BULLS AND BEARS POWER

This indicator was designed by Dr. Alexander Elder. It consists of two different oscillators, and it is used to evaluate the relative strength of bullish and bearish sentiment. Extreme conditions of optimism or pessimism are detected in the markets, which show the states of mind of most of its participants, and the trader thus can profit by trading against them. When the market is rising, the trader will go short; when the market is reaching its lowest point, the trader enters and buys.

Calculation of this indicator includes an exponential moving average that is subtracted from the high prices in the case of bull power and from

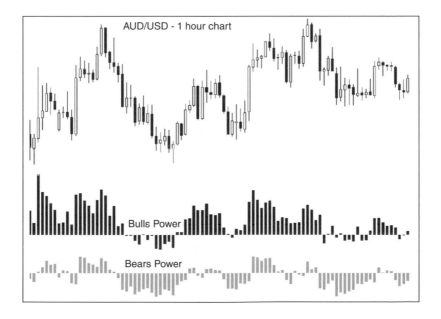

the low prices for bear power. Both are usually shown as histograms, as you can see in the figure below.

Interpretation of the moving average is relative to its slope: When the average rises, there is a bigger bullish sentiment in the market. When it falls, the sentiment is more bearish. The turning point is when prices can't be pushed any higher, which shows as the high value in the indicator; the low shows the turning point for a reversal up, when sellers can't drive the price any lower. Both turning points show the maximum power of each group.

When bulls power is positive and rising, bulls are stronger; the values become negative when they are particularly weaker. Bears power is usually negative and shows a positive value when the market is under complete control of the bullish sentiment.

How to Use This Indicator

For entering a long position, the trend should be up, bears power rising and bulls power making a higher peak. The strongest signal comes when bears power is rising from a bullish divergence.

When prices reach a new high but the bulls power reaches a lower peak, it is time to place a short position. The trend must be down, bulls power falling, and bears power can be showing its lowest values or be decreasing from a bearish divergence. The best trading opportunities can be found when there are divergences between the bulls or bears power indicator and prices.

MOMENTUM

The momentum indicator measures the rate at which the price or volume of transactions of a certain currency pair accelerates. As soon as this acceleration is seen in price, most traders will enter the market because it is very probable that the momentum will continue in the same direction. This is used mostly in short-term strategies and not recommended for beginners.

Calculation of momentum is based on the change in price multiplied by the trading volume for a given period. The volume is an important element of this indicator because it determines the strength and potential durability over time of a certain change in prices. If the volume is low, the move will have little momentum.

VOLUME

The volume indicator shows the number of contracts that are being traded for a particular currency pair during a specific period, depending on each time frame. Each bar indicates the number of transactions realized, and as

long as the current period is active, the value will go up with every additional trade that is made.

Volume is commonly used to gauge the strength or importance of a market move. The higher the volume during a particular price move, the more significant the move will be.

However, what does your broker's platform volume indicator really measure? Unless you are trading directly with a major liquidity provider, it will show the volume of transactions performed at any given point on a time scale (thus depending on it), not only the open effective orders (buy or sell) but also the positions that are closed in both directions. But only for that brokerage!

It is not a reflection of the whole FOREX market, but the proportional part of transactions that occurred on the specific platform on which you are trading. This explains why in certain situations (e.g., during the Christmas holidays or on other special dates) there might be a huge discrepancy between prices and volumes among several different platforms because the "population" of traders on each of them can have its own behavior that is different from that of others at key moments, while they behave under a general average in normal situations (e.g., although every broker has customers from every corner of the world, I am convinced that many of them concentrate a higher number of traders from one or another nationality depending on the broker's origin, and this has a special incidence on certain holidays).

For example, the volume of a 5-minute candle that shows 18 transactions at 13:55 can contain

- One buy and six sell trades (including the eventual counterpart that brokers usually place on the market)
- Eleven trades closed, of which
    - Two because of a sell: target reached or manual close
    - Three because of a buy: target reached or manual close
    - Six stopped out with stop losses or trailing stops (three sells and three buys)

In my opinion, this illustrates the number of different reasons why volume on the indicator fluctuates and makes it difficult to get a true appreciation of what is really happening because the indicator lacks the necessary details, especially when it includes counterpart transactions as well as stopped-out trades.

It is not the same to see a decrease in prices because of a bearish sentiment as it is because a retracement (very well measured, in the case of stop hunting) has closed all the long positions in play. This can lead to confusion and would be what is usually called a *bear trap* or a *bull trap.*

Therefore, because what is measured by this indicator is not absolute in terms of the totality of the market but instead reflects every broker's own particularities, it will not provide a trustable view of actual price behavior and cannot be an accurate gauge of the actual market climate.

UNDERSTANDING OSCILLATORS

OSCILLATOR

An *oscillator* is a technical analysis tool that fluctuates inside a band of two extreme values based on the results of a trend indicator that allows discovery of short-term overbought or oversold conditions. When the value approaches the upper extreme, the currency pair is considered to be in an overbought condition, and conversely, when it approaches the lower extreme, the pair is considered to be in an oversold condition. Such points would be probable points of swing reversal or correction. They are very useful when the market is ranging in a sideways motion in periods of consolidation. The most common oscillators are the *moving average convergence-divergence* (MACD), the *stochastic oscillator,* and the *relative strength index* (RSI).

MOVING AVERAGE CONVERGENCE-DIVERGENCE (MACD)

The MACD is another trend indicator based on momentum and market sentiment that shows the relationship between two moving averages of price. It is calculated by subtracting the EMA of the higher number of periods from the EMA of the shorter periods. Another EMA of an even shorter period is used as the signal line and serves as a trigger for buying or selling. The standard values are 26, 12, and 9, respectively.

In the figure below, the value resulting of the subtraction of both moving averages is represented as a histogram.

The MACD can be used in several ways, and the most common interpretations are crossovers and divergences. Crossovers are twofold: When the

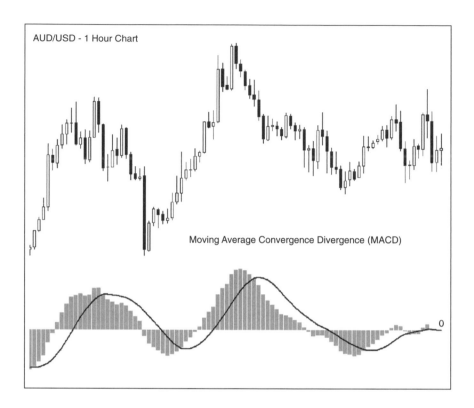

MACD histogram changes to positive when crossing the zero line, this is an early signal of a possible signal cross upward. When the signal also crosses above the MACD histogram, this is confirmation of the former cross of the zero line and a signal to buy. When the MACD falls below the signal line, this is an indication that it might be time to sell the currency pair.

Divergences, which will be discussed at the end of this chapter, are used when the direction of the price of the currency pair diverges from the direction of the MACD and signals a possible end of the current trend.

STOCHASTIC OSCILLATOR

The stochastic oscillator is a technical indicator based on momentum that compares the closing price of a currency pair with its price range over a given time period. The formula for this indicator is as follows:

$$\%K = 100[(C - Lx)/(Hx - Lx)]$$

where x = number of previous trading sessions
C = the most recent close price

Lx = the low of the x preceding trading sessions
Hx = the highest price traded during the same x sessions period
$\%D$ = three-period moving average of $\%K$

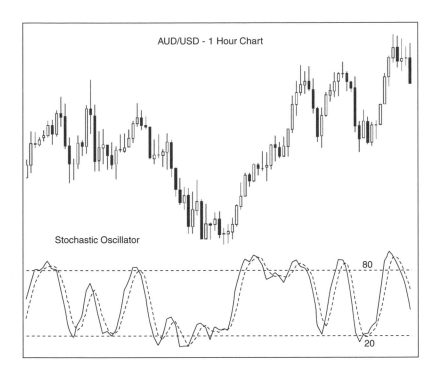

The theory on which this indicator is based is that prices tend to close near their high when the market is in an uptrend and that they tend to close near their low when the market is trending down. The signal is given when the %K line crosses through the three-period moving average called the %D.

RELATIVE STRENGTH INDEX (RSI)

The RSI indicator is based on momentum and compares the size of recent gains with recent losses so as to determine the overbought and oversold conditions of a currency pair. It is calculated using the following formula:

$$RSI = 100 - 100/1 + RS$$

where RS is the average of x days' up closes divided by the average of x days' down closes.

The RSI ranges from 0 to 100. A currency pair is said to be overbought as soon as the RSI approaches the 70 level. This means that it might be getting overvalued, and there are fair chances for a possible pullback of prices. Conversely, if the RSI approaches the 30 level, this means that the currency pair is possibly getting oversold and thus undervalued, with a possibility for a reversal in prices.

The RSI is an excellent tool to be used as a complement to other market indicators. However, it is not a stand-alone indicator because large and fast rises or falls in prices can create false signals that could induce a trader into error.

AN UNIQUE INDICATOR: ICHIMOKU KINKO HYO

Ichimoku kinko hyo is a trend-trading charting system in itself. Its primary strength is that it uses multiple data points to give the trader a deeper and more comprehensive view of price action. Ichimoku is a very

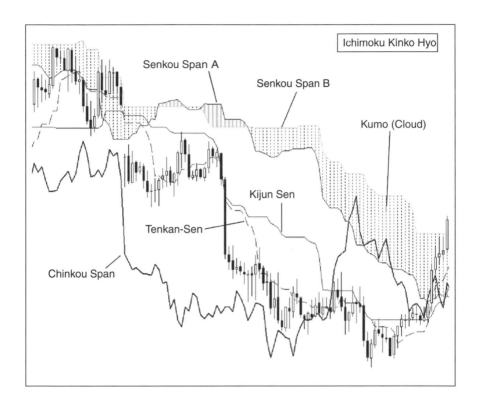

visual system, and it enables traders to quickly discern and filter the low-probability trading setups from those with higher probability.

The kumo (or "cloud") is the very core of this system. It enables you to immediately distinguish the prevailing trend and the relationship of the actual price with regard to that trend and provides a deep, multidimensional view of support and resistance as opposed to just a single, unidimensional level that is provided by other charting systems. This more complete view represents a much better the way to see how the market truly functions, where support and resistance are not merely single points on a chart but rather are areas that expand and contract depending on market dynamics.

DIVERGENCES

Divergences are divided into classic or regular (bullish and bearish) and reverse or hidden (bullish and bearish).

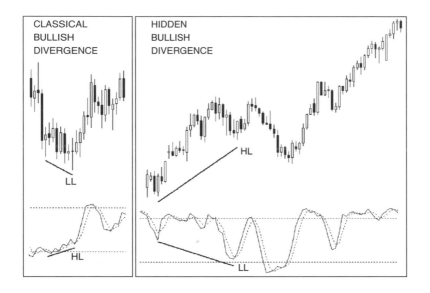

Bullish (Buy)

Classic or regular = price LL + oscillator HL
Reverse or hidden = price HL + oscillator LL

Bearish (Sell)

Classic or regular = price HH + oscillator LH
Reverse or hidden = price LH + oscillator HH

It can be useful for you to remember this phrase: "Tops down, bottoms up," to evaluate divergences. Whenever the tops are involved (lower and higher highs on the price or on the indicator), the movement that usually ensues is bearish or downward; whenever the bottoms are involved (lower and higher lows in any of both), the movement that most probably follows will be bullish or upward.

Divergences act as an early warning system, alerting you when the market could reverse. However, they do not have to be used as a trading signal. Relying only on divergences would give too many false signals. But if you use them along with a particular setup and strategy and confirm the entries with other indicators, your trades will have a high probability of being successful with relatively low risk.

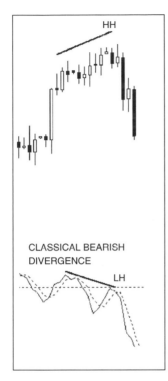

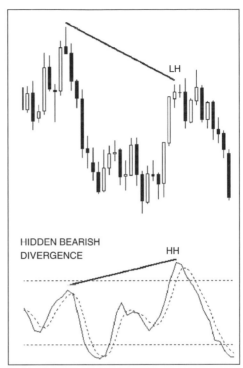

On the other hand, it is not recommended to trade against the direction given by this indicator. Classic or regular divergences usually appear when the trend is about to change. Reverse or hidden divergences can indicate continuation of the actual direction and thus allow keeping you in the trade for a longer time and bigger profits.

CHAPTER

11

TECHNICAL PATTERNS

CANDLESTICKS

Candlesticks were developed as a means to perform technical analysis, thanks to the Japanese, who first used them to trade rice in the seventeenth century. A rice trader named Homma from the town of Sakata has been credited with their development and charting style. Afterwards, Charles Dow started his own version around 1900, using very similar principles. Through years of trading and refining, they have been evolving up to the presentation that you can see today.

The basic principles behind candlesticks are as follows:

- Price action is more important than the reason behind the moves.
- All the fundamental data are already reflected in the price.
- Markets move because of expectations and emotions of fear and greed in buyers and sellers.
- Markets fluctuate.
- The actual price doesn't always reflect the real value of a currency.

BASIC PARTS OF A CANDLESTICK

The data that are reflected on a candlestick chart are the open, high, low, and close prices. The chart consists of a body, which is the hollow or filled portion, which represents the range between the open and the close prices, and wicks or shadows on both sides, representing the high and low price ranges from open or close. The high is signaled by the top of the upper shadow, and the low is marked by the bottom of the lower shadow. If the close price is higher than the open price, the candlestick is bullish, and its body will be drawn as hollow; if the open price is higher than the close price, the candlestick will be bearish and will be drawn with a filled body.

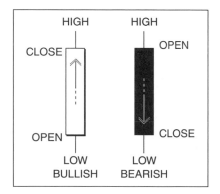

Candlesticks provide a fast overview of price action and are easy to interpret. Relationships between open and close and high and low are easy to compare at a glance. The essence of candlesticks is the information about the relationship between the open price and the close price. Bullish or hollow candlesticks indicate buying pressure; filled or bearish candlesticks indicate selling pressure, and the longer the body is, the more strength the direction has. Short candlesticks, inversely, are a signal of consolidation and little market movement.

GENERAL OVERVIEW

Long versus Short Bodies
Long-bodied candlesticks show a strong buying or selling pressure. The longer they are, the greater distance there is between the open and close prices, indicating a significant advance in prices and more aggressive moves. Usually longer candlesticks will show in the direction of the general trend (hollow are bullish and filled are bearish), but this also depends on their position in the overall pattern of the chart. This type of candlestick can signal a potential support level or a reversal after an extended rise or fall.

Marubozu candlesticks are even more powerful because they don't have any shadows or wicks, thus signaling that control of the price action of the market is in the hands of buyers or sellers for the complete period they represent.

Short-bodied candlesticks indicate a stalling market where there has been very little change in prices during the period.

Long versus Short Shadows

Upper and lower shadows or wicks provide information about the trading action. The longer the body is, the more intense is the buying or selling pressure. Short shadows indicate little action, mostly circumscribed to the open and close prices.

When one of the shadows is long and the other is short, this indicates that one of the sides dominated during that trading period; an longer upper shadow with a short lower shadow shows that buyers were more active in the first part of the session, leading prices to a higher level, and that sellers forced the price to go down, closing at a weaker point. A longer lower shadow indicates that sellers were dominating and driving the prices down but were overcome by buyers later on, ending with a stronger close.

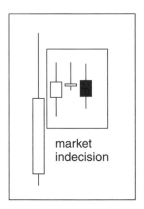

There are candlesticks with long shadows and a very small body, called *spinning tops*. Such candles represent indecision in the market and that both buyers and sellers were highly active during the period represented, driving prices much higher and much lower than the open and close prices but closing near the opening price in the end. A spinning top signals a possible change in the actual trend, especially if it shows after a long hollow or filled candlestick.

Doji

This type of candlestick alone is a neutral pattern. The candlestick forms when the open and close prices are practically at the same level, with various types of shadows, long or short depending on the price action during that period. The candlestick looks like a cross, an inverted cross, or a plus sign; sometimes even one of the shadows is not present, as in the case of a dragonfly doji.

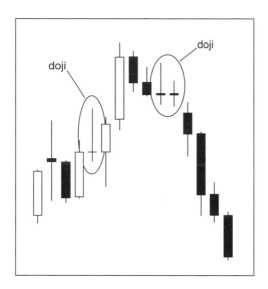

Similar to the case of the spinning tops, a doji is a signal of indecision in the market and thus a potential turning point because both buyers and sellers didn't get control. It shows equilibrium between offers and bids; buying and selling forces are getting even, which could represent a weakening of the previous trend and a close potential change. However, by itself, a doji is not enough to be a powerful signal of a trend reversal, and you would need more confirmation before taking a trade.

BULLISH PATTERNS
See the Appendix.

BEARISH PATTERNS
See the Appendix.

REVERSAL PATTERNS
See the Appendix.

CONTINUATION PATTERNS
See the Appendix.

CHARTISM PATTERNS

Chartism is a system of analysis and prediction for financial instruments and is a part of technical analysis. It is based exclusively on the study of patterns that are drawn by the curve of prices on a chart. Its use started at the beginning of the twentieth century and was consolidated around the 1930s because the amplitude and depth of the crisis of 1929 generated the need to evolve new analysis techniques in the stock market to get better information than what was being offered by fundamental analysis.

Chartism is a graphic analysis that focuses solely on the prices and volumes of transactions. Its purpose is to determine the price trend, that is, to gauge if it is in a bullish or a bearish phase, and help to identify the movements that the price wave realizes at the moment of a trend reversal. It is based exclusively on the study of the patterns that are drawn by those price waves. The entire set of patterns is studied and codified in detail, and each one of them indicates the possible future evolution of prices with a given risk factor.

Chartism has three basic principles:

1. All the elements that affect a particular asset are reflected and included in the price.
2. Price rates move in trends.
3. Movements and patterns of price rates always repeat themselves.

With these principles, the chartist analysis affirms that if you know the price, you do not need to analyze why it is moving because it is enough to be able to identify clearly the trend of the particular rate and check how it is moving so as to control and anticipate any changes in trend. Chartists believe that by studying past actions, the future probable behavior of the market can be predicted. For this, several chart patterns are used and studied in detail.

REVERSAL PATTERNS

DOUBLE AND TRIPLE TOPS OR BOTTOMS

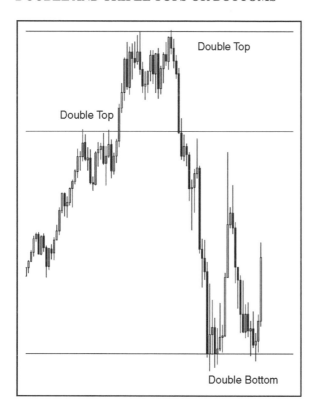

Double tops and double bottoms are major reversal patterns that form after long-term trends. They are made up of two consecutive peaks or down moves mostly to an equal price with a recession between extreme points. They usually indicate a change in trend from bullish to bearish, or vice versa, but a reversal will not be confirmed as long as the key supports or resistances are not broken.

The recession between the two extreme points must be at least 10 percent because a shorter distance could represent a normal bump into a resistance or a support. In addition, there must be a certain indication that there has been an increase in the selling or buying pressure before the price attempts a second time to break the resistance or support level.

The need for confirmation of a definite break of the support or resistance helps to prevent making a decision too early. The trend remains in place as long as those levels hold.

Triple tops or bottoms are a similar pattern that also indicates a possible reversal, but having three consecutive highs or lows followed by a break of the support or resistance. Triple tops usually are formed on shorter time frames, unlike triple bottoms.

Before forming completely, the pattern will look like a double top or a double bottom. You also can find a pattern made up of three equal highs or lows in a rectangle or in an ascending or descending triangle. The triple top or bottom, like the double top or bottom, should be observed, and you should wait for a breakout to occur. If there is a failure to break above or below the peaks, the reversal is near, but only after support or resistance has been broken will you really have confirmation of the move.

HEAD AND SHOULDERS (H&S) AND INVERTED H&S

Head-and-shoulder patterns usually form after an uptrend, indicating reversal of the actual trend after it has been completed. It is a bearish indicator.
It consists of three consecutive highs, with the middle high being the highest of all three, similar to a head with two shoulders; the two lateral highs
are mostly equal in height and width and lower than the head. The lows
formed at support of the shoulders and the head constitute the neckline.
When this neckline is finally broken after completion of the pattern, the
projected price fall is calculated with respect to the distance from the top of
the middle high, or head, to the neckline. This distance in points is to be
subtracted from the price level at the neckline, and the result is the probable price target. Of course, other indicators should be taken into account,
such as, for example, Fibonacci levels and pivot lines, to have a more accurate perspective on setting the target profit.

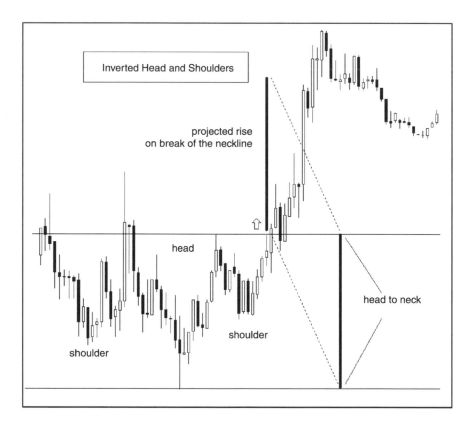

An inverted head-and-shoulders pattern is the reverse and indicates a
possible bullish reversal under the same conditions as its bearish counterpart. In this case, though, the volume patterns would be more important to

define a confirmation of the reversal. The middle low, or head, is deeper than the lateral lows that form the shoulders, which should be equal in height and width. The neckline in this case will constitute a resistance, and when it is broken, the projected price target will measure roughly the distance from the bottom of the head, or lowest low of the pattern, to the neckline; the point range will be added to the price level at the neckline to define the target price. As a general rule, volume increases are absolutely required to confirm the bottom version of this pattern.

FALLING AND RISING WEDGES

Wedges are patterns that begin wide in which prices contract as they move higher or lower. The resulting shape is a cone with a lower line that slopes up as highs converge for a rising wedge and an upper line that slopes down as lows converge on a falling wedge. Conversely to symmetric triangles, where there is no definite slope or trend, rising wedges are bearish and falling wedges are bullish. This is confirmed by a support or resistance breakout, which is represented by the horizontal line formed by the price convergence.

A wedge is usually a reversal pattern, but it also could be considered a continuation pattern if the slope of the wedge goes against the actual trend. As a reversal pattern, the slope will be in the same direction as the prevailing trend.

Rising wedges will form after a continued uptrend, where you can see that prices stall at the horizontal level, indicating that the power of the bullish sentiment is fading away. This horizontal level will act as a resistance that holds, and the slope acting as support has to be broken to confirm a change in trend. Falling wedges, on the contrary, will form after a continued downtrend, and prices will tend to agglomerate at the same level, forming the horizontal boundary of the wedge, which will be the holding support. The falling slope resistance has to be broken to confirm the change in trend. In both cases, one should wait for the break to be retested through a correction move to confirm that either the support has become a new resistance or the resistance has become a new support. Volume is more important in confirming the breakout of a falling wedge.

Both falling and rising wedges are consolidation patterns where either side of the market, depending on the case, is losing strength and momentum. They are particularly difficult to recognize because the trend apparently is continuing and there are still higher lows on rising wedges and lower highs on falling wedges. However, the failure to cross the boundary formed by the horizontal line is a signal that upside or downside momentum is losing its potential, and finally, when the resistance or support is broken, you can see that the contrarian side of the market has won, and prices will cross up or move down against the prevailing trend.

ROUNDING BOTTOM OR TOP
The rounding bottom is a longer-term pattern that can be witnessed on daily or weekly charts. Rounding tops are less usual. The round bottom is also called a *saucer* and is a long period of consolidation turning from a bearish trend into a bullish trend.

Usually the low of this pattern will be marking a new low in a bearish trend. However, there can be a series of lower lows while it is forming. The first part is a long price fall; then comes a slightly decreasing consolidation period where lower lows are slowly creating a horizontal support zone. When seen as a whole, the shape of the round bottom is like a V pattern.

The second part of the pattern will develop after about the same number of periods as the first declining part, creating a shape that is mostly symmetric. The confirmation of a change in trend from a bearish decline to a bullish rise will be the breakout of the starting reaction high from where the decline started in the first part. An increase in volume is usually expected in this second part.

Round Bottoms

BUMP-AND-RUN REVERSAL

The bump-and-run reversal (BARR) was developed by Thomas Bulkowski. It was originally named *bump and run formation* (BARF), but such an acronym wouldn't have gotten much approval on Wall Street, so he changed it to BARR, although the original name would have been quite representative of what happens in the markets when this kind of formation occurs.

The pattern develops in three phases: lead-in, bump, and the final run. The first phase can be quite long and is the base off which the trendline is formed. There is a steady and slow advance in prices and no particular surprises or excessive surges. The angle that Bulkowski determined to be optimal is 30 to 45 degrees of steepness.

The second phase is a sharp and sudden advance, where prices move further away from the trendline, creating a steeper angle, usually nearly doubling the previous one (around 45 to 60 degrees). The bump represents the unsustainability of such an advance for a long time, and prices hit a high and decline a little bit. Prices make a small peak or a series of descending peaks toward the initial trendline. Volume in this phase is usually low, whereas it increases in the previous advance and in the subsequent second attempt to rise higher.

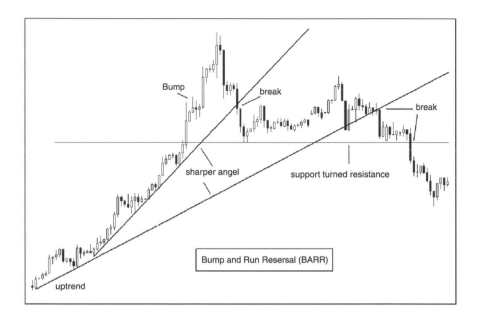

The final phase is the run, and prices start declining heavily with an increase in volume and reach the trendline, which then is broken. A retest of the broken trend line will confirm the run, and support will transform in resistance. This is usually followed by a period of consolidation, as you can see in the figure above. The decrease in prices most commonly will be equivalent to the previous long advance.

CONTINUATION PATTERNS

FLAGS AND PENNANTS

Flags and pennants are usually short-term continuation patterns that indicate a small consolidation of the markets before a resumption of the previous move. This consolidation has to be preceded by a steep advance or decline with heavy volume and strength and commonly marks a midpoint of the overall move.

The first part of the move is called the *flagpole,* and it represents the distance from the first break of a resistance or a support to the highest high or lowest low of the flag or pennant. The previous breakout is one of the conditions necessary for this pattern to be considered valid.

The subsequent flag will be a small rectangle pattern whose direction slopes against the trend of the preceding move or flagpole. The price usually will be located between two parallel lines.

In the case of a pennant, you will have a small symmetric triangle instead of a rectangle that will converge proportionally as the pattern reaches its maturity. There is no significant slope, and the prices will be located between the converging trendlines.

These patterns are usually of a short-term duration. A break above the resistance formed by the high of a flagpole will signal that the previous rise is resuming. In the case of a bearish flag or pennant, a break below the support formed by the low of the flagpole will signal a resumption of the previous move down.

The subsequent estimation of the distance that can be targeted in the second advance or decline is made by applying the length of the flagpole as a projection starting from the break after the consolidation period. The credibility and probability of success with this pattern are strongly determined by the presence of a strong advance or decline, with confirmation being made by a high volume on that initial move or flagpole; then the consolidation and further break will add to the strength of the completed pattern.

TRIANGLES

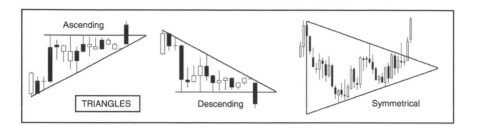

Symmetric

A symmetric triangle commonly is formed as a continuation pattern along the evolution of a trend. It must have at least two lower highs and two higher lows. When you connect those points, the lines will converge to form a symmetric triangle. Price range is wider at the beginning and goes on contracting near the end point. There are also some conditions in which symmetric triangles indicate an important trend reversal. The direction of the next move will be determined only after there has been a breakout of the converging range. The volume will be decreasing progressively as the triangle extends in a tight consolidation. This is a medium- to long-term pattern.

The breakout of the tightening range usually happens midway or near the 75 percent point of triangle development. The time duration will be evaluated from the point where both upper and lower lines converge back to the start of the lower trendline base. If the break occurs much earlier than the 50 percent point, the signal may be a weak or nonvalid one. Volume should be increasing as well, particularly in the case of breakouts on the long side. Confirmation of the validity of the move will be given by a retest and hold of the convergence point that was previously broken, the resistance becoming support or vice versa, and a resumption in the direction of the breakout.

You can estimate the potential target of the breakout move by measuring the widest side of the triangle and adding it to or subtracting it from the level of the breakout point. Another way of calculating a possible target is to draw a parallel trendline to the pattern in the direction of the breakout that passes through the opposite point on the widest part of the triangle (the higher price if the breakout was to the upside, the lower price if the breakout was down). The distance to this trendline will give you the potential scope of the move.

Ascending

An ascending triangle is a bullish pattern that usually develops during an uptrend. It is a continuation pattern. These formations indicate a gradual accumulation. The shape is that of a right-angle triangle. There is a horizontal line at the top built off at least two equal highs; the higher lows go building up the ascending slope, which converges toward the horizontal line.

There has to be an ongoing trend for this pattern to be validated as a continuation signal. The highs that form the horizontal upper line should be quite near one from the other, with a reaction low between them. The ascending slope has to contain at least two reaction lows that are progressively higher. If any reaction low is equal to or lower than the previous one, the validity of the ascending triangle is canceled.

The volume goes on contracting as the pattern evolves and then expands as soon as the breakout occurs. This will confirm the pattern, and the breakout level should be retested for a more solid confirmation. The price projection to determine the scope of the move after the price has broken the resistance is calculated by measuring the widest distance of the triangle and adding it to the price level at the breakout.

The ascending triangle has already been showing a bullish tendency before a breakout occurs. The reaction lows are continually rising, even if the horizontal line is signaling a level of supply, and prices cannot move forward for a while. The continuous ascension of the lows indicates an increase in the buying pressure and qualifies this pattern as bullish.

Descending

Descending triangles usually are formed in a downtrend and are continuation patterns. On a few occasions, they can signify a reversal, but the most common behavior is bearish. They signal distribution after accumulation.

Inversely to ascending triangles, the pattern is composed of two or more equal lows that form a horizontal line at the bottom of the moves. The descending trendline has a series of two or more successively decreasing peaks that converge with the horizontal line. If one of the peaks in the downslope goes above the previous high, the pattern will lose its validity.

The volume, as in ascending triangles, goes on contracting as the pattern evolves. An expansion of volume would occur just before the breakout of the end point of the triangle. The broken support line then will be retested, turning into resistance, which will confirm the pattern. The projected target of the breakout move can be measured relative to the widest range of the pattern, which then will be subtracted from the level of support.

In a descending triangle, the horizontal line forms because there is a volume of demand that impedes the price from going past that level; volume accumulates, though, and the series of lower highs indicates that there is a selling pressure that sooner or later will break and drive the prices much lower.

RECTANGLES

The rectangle is a consolidation and continuation pattern. It signals a pause in the current trend and is formed from two equal or equivalent lows and two equal or equivalent highs that can be connected, making the top and bottom of a rectangle. There is congestion in prices, and a consolidation of the levels is reached

Bearish Rectangle

The rectangle can be compared with a symmetric triangle. Most commonly, this will be a continuation pattern, but it also could signal a top or bottom on a particular trend. The confirmation and validity of this pattern will occur when a breakout happens. As with previous formations, confirmation of the breakout is given when there has been a retest of the broken support or resistance.

Bullish Rectangles

The rectangle usually forms a very tight range contained in the four point boundaries. The volume is quite low, and the price tends to bounce alternatively between support and resistance. The increase in volume occurs near the breakout point and can be an indication of the direction that the prices will take after surpassing the support or resistance level.

The longer the duration of the pattern, the stronger the impulse the breakout will show. The level will be retested afterwards, providing a confirmation if it holds.

As in other similar patterns that lead to a breakout, the moment of the retest and bounce is a good opportunity to enter the trend, but waiting for this pullback and bounce after a break is a safer strategy. The profit target scope of the subsequent move can be measured relative to the height of the rectangle and subtracted from or added to the price level of the break-out point.

The trading range inside the rectangle represents the struggle and deci-sion making of bulls versus bears, which both seem to "protect" each other on their own side of the price levels. When the price approaches the support, buyers enter the picture again and drive the price higher; as soon as it reaches the resistance, sellers counteract and force the price to go lower. The struggle ends when one of the sides wins, and the breakout occurs. The pattern in itself is neutral and a point of conflict and decision making of the markets.

PRICE CHANNELS
Price channels are patterns that usually determine a continuation of a trend. They are delimited by an upper and lower trendline that serves as a bound-ary where prices are contained, the upper trendline being a resistance and the lower trendline being a support.

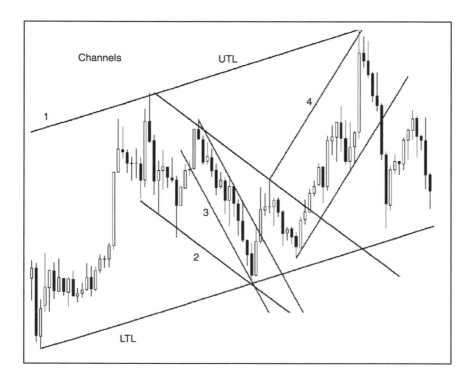

A price channel can be bullish or bearish depending on whether its slope is negative or positive, going down or up. The main trendline needs two points to be drawn; if it is bullish, those points will be two higher lows, and the trendline will be drawn in the bottom of the channel. If it is bearish, it will use the lower highs and will be drawn at the top of the channel. A parallel line from this trendline will be projected and aligned with the opposite highs or lows to get the whole channel. In the figure above, you can see four different channels evolving in different directions and at different angles. Number 1 is a bullish channel and contains number 2, which is bearish and represents the prices pulling back to the lower trendline; number 3 is a steeper bearish move inside number 2; and number 4 is a again a bullish leg going toward the upper trendline for continuation of the overall trend.

In a bullish price channel, as long as the prices are contained between the upper and lower trendline boundaries, the trend is in force. As soon as the prices fall through the lower trendline, the trend can be considered to be broken, and new lines should be drawn after the move to evaluate if the trend is continuing in the same global direction or if a reversal is taking place. In the same way, the prices evolving inside the limits of a bearish channel will confirm continuation of the downtrend until a break above the upper line indicates that there might be an acceleration of the bullish sentiment and thus a probable change in trend.

In both cases, you can have an early signal of those changes when the prices fail to reach the respective support or resistance in one of the inside swing moves. When using channeling swing trading strategies, traders usually look for a short position when the prices reach the upper trendline resistance and look to buy when the prices have reached the lower trendline support. In itself, the channel can't be taken as a sole reference; other technical analysis tools should be used to confirm that there is a continuation of the actual trend.

CUP WITH HANDLE

The cup-with-handle pattern was described by William O'Neil in 1988 in his book, *How to Make Money in Stocks*. It usually is an indication of a bullish continuation of the trend that signals a period of consolidation, which is then followed by a breakout.

This pattern consists of two parts: the cup, which will look like a bowl or a round bottom, and the handle, which is a small pullback on the right side of the pattern, a downtrending range that develops after the form of the cup has been completed. A breakout of this small range is needed to confirm resumption of the bullish trend.

Cup and Handle

The form of the cup ideally should be smooth and rounded, ensuring that this is indeed a consolidation pattern going through several periods and forming the support at the bottom. In a perfect shape, both highs on the sides of the cup would be equal, but this is not always the case; the pattern will be valid if a handle range is formed afterwards, independent of whether the highs of the cup match or not. The usual retracement marked by the depth of the cup is one-third or one-half the previous rising move. The handle is similar to a flag or pennant with a downward slope, although it can be shorter sometimes. It is a final consolidation that takes place before a strong breakout. The smaller this retracement is, the stronger the bullish sentiment of the formation. It is recommended that you wait for the break above the resistance line formed by the highs of the cup to confirm the validity of this pattern. Also, there should be a significant increase in volume when this breakout occurs.

The projected scope of the subsequent breakout move can be measured with respect to the distance in points from the bottom of the cup to the right high of the cup before the handle.

MEASURED MOVES: BULLISH AND BEARISH

A *measured move* consists of three definite parts and usually begins as a reversal pattern and ends as a continuation of the preceding reversal. A bullish measured move will consist of a reversal rise, a correction or consolidation of prices, and a continuation of the advancing move. A bearish measured move will consist of a reversal fall, a retracement or consolidation of prices, and a continuation of the descending move. Both moves cannot be identified properly until after the correction, retracement, or consolidation period has resumed. Thus these are categorized as continuation patterns. They are usually long term and form over several periods.

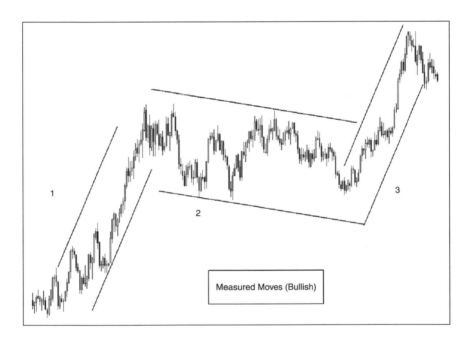

Measured Moves (Bullish)

First Part: Advance or Decline

The first move usually begins near the established lows (bullish) or highs (bearish) of the previous direction and extends for several periods. The initial trend change sometimes can be signaled by a reversal pattern or is established by the formation of new highs or lows or a break above resistance or below support. Usually the initial move is made of regular alternating moves that could form a price channel.

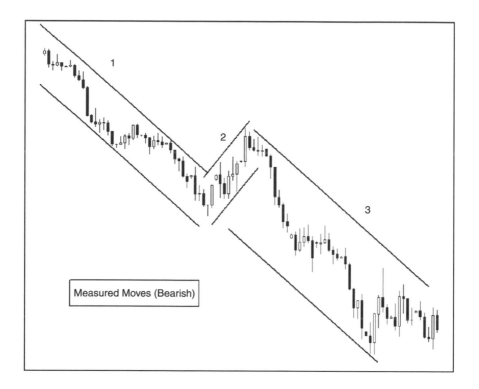

Measured Moves (Bearish)

Second Part: Consolidation/Correction

A retracement in the opposite direction of the first move takes place. You can find further patterns that will determine which kind of corrective move it is, for example, a rectangle or an ascending or descending triangle in the case of a consolidation, a flag with a downward slope, or a falling wedge. In the case of a retracement, you could expect a pullback of one- to two-thirds of the previous move. The bigger the move in the first phase, the bigger the correction move will be.

Third Part: Continuation

The scope of the continuation after the correction move can be calculated by applying the length of the first-phase move to the level that marks the end of the second phase. For example, in a bullish move, if the length of the first move was from a price level ending at 40 to a price level of 70 (30 points) and the subsequent consolidation or correction pulled back to the 50 level, the target of the third continuation phase would be 80 (adding the 30 points to the end level of the correction). In the case of a bearish move, if the first phase showed a fall from 70 to 40 (same 30 points) and the correction brought the price to 50, the target would be set at 20, which is the end point of the correction at 50 minus the 30 points of the first fall.

Volumes

The volume ideally increases at the beginning of the first phase, diminishes in the second phase, especially at the end, and rises again at the beginning of the third or continuation phase. Volume confirmation is more important in bullish than in bearish patterns.

Both bullish and bearish measured moves can contain a series of different patterns. You can find double bottoms or double tops at the start, price channels during the reversal consolidation or correction, ascending or descending triangles at the end of the consolidation or retracement, and again price channels in the continuation phase.

ELLIOTT WAVES

HISTORY

The Elliott wave theory was developed by Ralph Nelson Elliott in the late 1920s when he discovered the existence of a repetitive and cyclic behavior in the stock markets that formerly was considered to be mostly random and chaotic, a behavior that depends on the reactions of investors at a particular moment and thus is a result of mass psychology. Elliott studied the structure of those repetitive patterns that show up as waves within waves and can repeat themselves indefinitely, showing two specific characteristics, impulse and correction, and applied this to market prediction.

COUNTING WAVES

Elliott wave theory is interpreted as follows:

- Every action is followed by a reaction.
- Five impulsive waves move in the direction of the main trend and are followed by three corrective waves (a 5–3 move).
- A 5–3 move signals completion of a cycle.
- This 5 3 move then becomes two subdivisions of the next higher 5–3 wave.
- The underlying 5–3 pattern remains constant, independent of the time scale you are using.

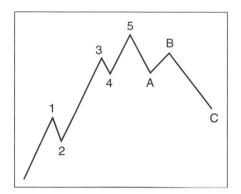

In the figure above, you can see that the three waves that go in the direction of the trend are impulses, so these waves also will have five waves within them. The waves against the trend are corrections and are made up of three waves.

Elliott wave theory assigns a series of categories to the waves from largest to smallest. These are grand supercycle, supercycle, cycle, primary, intermediate, minor, minute, minuette, and subminuette.

FIBONACCI

In mathematics, Fibonacci numbers are a sequence of numbers in which the first number is 0, the second number is 1, and each subsequent number is the result of the sum of the previous two numbers. The Fibonacci sequence of numbers is as follows: 0, 1, 1, 2, 3, 5, 8, 13, 21, 34, 55, 89, 144, etc. Each term in this sequence is simply the sum of the two preceding terms, and the sequence continues infinitely. Each subsequent number in this series has a common relationship with the others in that they all are approximately 1.618 times greater than the preceding number, which also corresponds to the golden ratio value.

The key Fibonacci ratio of 61.8 percent—also referred to as the *golden ratio* or the *golden mean*—is found by dividing one number in the series by the number that follows it. For example, $8/13 = 0.6153$, and $55/89 = 0.6179$. The 38.2 percent ratio is found by dividing one number in the series by the number that is found two places to the right; for example: $55/144 = 0.3819$. The 23.6 percent ratio is found by dividing one number in the series by the number that is three places to the right, for example, $8/34 = 0.2352$.

The sequence was named after Leonardo of Pisa, known as Fibonacci (a contraction of *filius Bonaccio,* "son of Bonaccio"), who introduced the concept to western European mathematics in the year 1202 in his book *Liber Abaci*. The sequence was already known, though, having been described earlier in Indian mathematics.

The different Fibonacci patterns, especially retracement, are used commonly by traders to identify the scope of a reversal or correction of prices after a continued leg or wave of a trend. These ratios have been shown to have an important recurrence in nature as well as in the financial markets. The direction of the current trend usually resumes to one of the ratios after the retracement.

In addition to the proper ratios based on the sequence, another retracement level to 50 percent of the move is usually added, although it is not a Fibonacci ratio in itself. The reason for this is that the most common tendency for a price is to make a correction to the mean point after a move and continue in the previous direction after this retracement to 50 percent has been completed.

RETRACEMENTS

It has been observed that currency pairs or stocks exhibit a recurrent behavior, pulling back or retracing a certain percentage of the last move before resuming the trend. These are the Fibonacci levels, which usually occur most often at three levels—38.2, 50, and 61.8 percent; 50 percent is not a Fibonacci number but represents the tendency of prices to go back to the mean and reverse after having retraced half the move.

This figure is a graphic representation of the reversal points for the AUS/USD currency pair in a downtrend. The pattern is reversed for currency pairs that are in an uptrend. The Fibonacci retracement tool can be found in practically all the charting packages.

To calculate this manually, first of all, you would have to plot the range between the last swing high and swing low as soon as the price starts to retrace and calculate the relative percentages of that range that are shown on the chart: 23.6, 38.2, 50, 61.8, and 76.4 percent are the most basic retracement levels; those are the most probable areas of support and resistance and a useful mark when setting a target profit point.

Fibonacci extensions are simply derived ratios that go beyond the standard 100 percent retracement range and can be used as a projection of possible targets outside that range on both sides. The most common projections are 127, 138.2, and 161.8 percent of the range and larger extensions to 261.8 and 423.6 percent for longer-term predictions.

EXPANSION

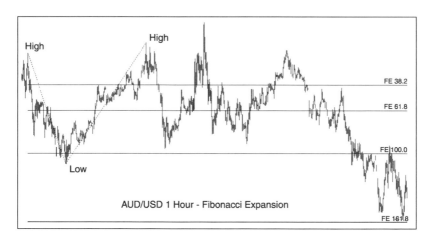

AUD/USD 1 Hour - Fibonacci Expansion

Fibonacci expansion is calculated by taking three swing points (two highs and one low or two lows and one high). It is built on two consecutive waves. It is similar to the retracement but is usually employed to indicate the end of the third wave. The height of the first wave is considered as a unit interval, and the resulting lines are equivalent to 61.8, 100, and 161.8 percent of that range. This tool is used mostly along with wave-based analysis such as Elliott waves or Wolfe waves.

CHANNELS

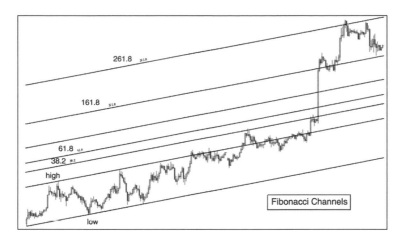

Fibonacci channels are a diagonally represented variation of the Fibonacci retracement pattern. They are used in the same way as horizontal price patterns—to evaluate possible areas of support and resistance. Both horizontal and diagonal representations can be used together or in combination with other support/resistance indicators to define those areas more accurately.

FANS

Fibonacci fans are formed with three diagonal lines using Fibonacci ratios to help identify major levels of support and resistance. They are created by drawing an imaginary trendline between the high and low and then dividing the vertical distance between those two points by the major Fibonacci ratios: 38.2, 50, and 61.8 percent. Each of these divisions will represents a point in the imaginary vertical line that measures the distance between the high and the low, and the lines indicate levels of support and resistance.

ARCS

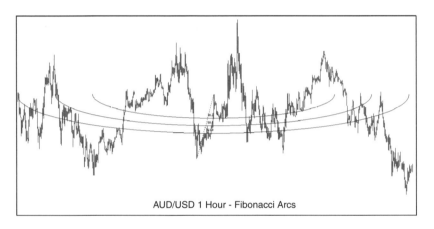

AUD/USD 1 Hour - Fibonacci Arcs

Fibonacci arcs consist of three curved lines with the same Fibonacci number proportions that will help anticipate ranging areas and important support and resistance levels. They are created by drawing an imaginary trendline between the high and low and then drawing the curves that will intersect this trendline at the major Fibonacci levels: 38.2, 50, and 61.8 percent. Trading decisions are made when the price crosses through those levels.

HARMONIC PRICE PATTERNS

Harmonic price patterns are specific series of impulsive and corrective waves (two impulsive and two corrective) whose calculations and relationships are based on Fibonacci levels and ratios and that have as a continuation a bigger impulsive wave. The first corrective wave from starting point to the top of the first impulsive wave is what determines the kind of pattern you should expect.

BUTTERFLY

In the butterfly pattern, the first corrective wave from A to B is a deep retracement to 0.786, or 78.6 percent, of the move from the starting point 0 to A. If this happens, the second corrective move from C to D would have to reach 1.272 percent retracement of the first impulse wave from 0 to A. In this pattern, the projections from point B to point C can vary, but the Fibonacci ratios relative to the first impulse wave from 0 to A are always formed at those precise levels.

The following figure shows a bullish butterfly pattern, where the first impulse wave from 0 to A is pointing upward. A bearish butterfly would have the same measurements but would be inverted, starting from a downward move, as shown in the model.

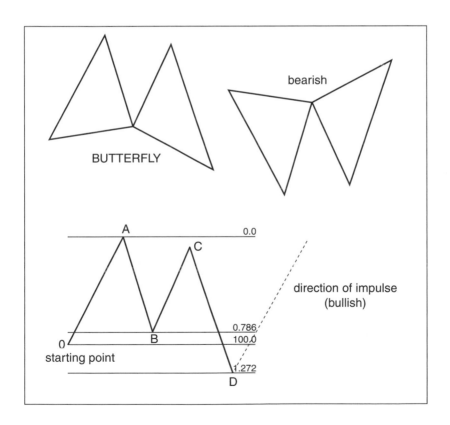

GARTLEY

This is an exact pattern where the first A-to-B corrective wave is always the 61.8 percent retracement of the move from 0 to A. The second corrective wave from C to D then should form at 0.786 of the move from 0 to A. Both corrective waves always will form precisely at those levels.

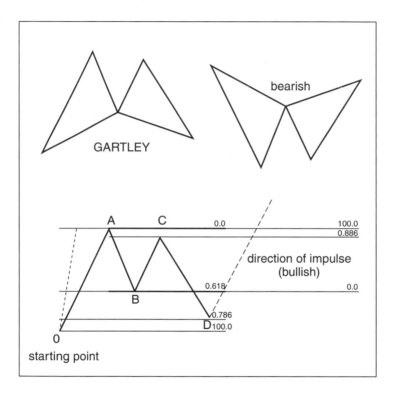

The figure image shows a bullish Gartley pattern, where the first impulse wave from 0 to A is pointing upward. A bearish Gartley would have the same measurements but would be inverted, starting from a downward move, as shown in the model.

BAT

In the bat pattern, the first corrective wave from A to B is a small correction, and it retraces most of the time to the 0.382 level (as a maximum to 0.50). If this happens, the second corrective wave from C to D should form at the 0.886 Fibonacci retracement of 0 to A.

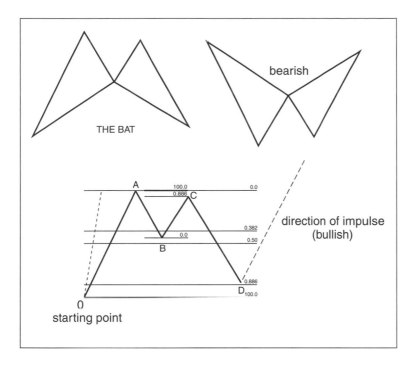

The figure image shows a bullish bat pattern, with a first impulse wave from starting point 0 to A pointing upward. If the first impulse wave were pointing downward, the same calculations for the retracements would apply, and the pattern would be inverted, as shown in the model.

CRAB

The crab pattern is not found very often, and it can be identified only when the complete five-wave structure has been finished. This happens because the main factor that allows us to identify this pattern is the second corrective wave from C to D, which is a very deep move, retracing up to 1.618 of the first wave from 0 to A. The first corrective wave from A to B can vary between 0.382 and 0.618, making its level completely subjective. What counts is the exact position of the last move for the pattern to be considered correct.

The figure above shows a bullish crab pattern, with a first impulse wave from starting point 0 to A pointing upward. If the first impulse wave were pointing downward, the same calculations for the retracements would apply, and the pattern would be inverted, as shown in the model.

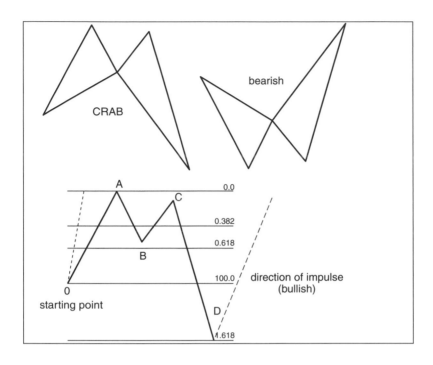

AB = CD

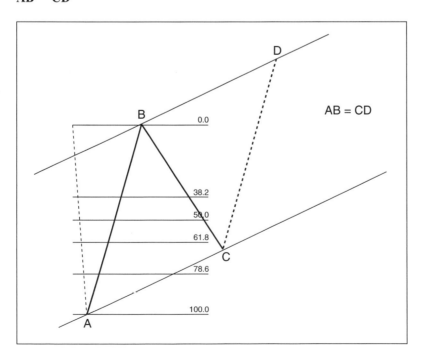

This is a pattern where both impulse waves are equal. It is quite common to find and easy to recognize, and it is one of the most powerful patterns in trading. The retracement wave between both legs can vary from 0.382 to 0.786, although in a strongly trending market it doesn't usually go much further than a 38.2 percent retracement.

Basic characteristics are as follows:

- Both AB and CD must be equal.
- The retracement cannot go further than the price of the starting point. This means that the price can't retrace more than 100 percent.
- Point D has to be higher than point B on a bullish move or lower on a bearish move for the pattern to be valid.

THREE DRIVES

This pattern consists of three consecutive impulse waves followed by a small correction. The noticeable aspect of this pattern is that each subsequent drive reaches either a 127.2 or a 161.8 percent Fibonacci retracement. In addition, each of the waves should form over equivalent time periods and be symmetric one to the other.

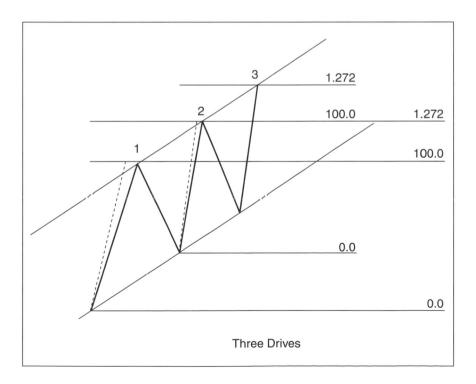

Three Drives

FRACTALS

BILL WILLIAMS AND CHAOS THEORY

The idea of fractals was discussed by Bill M. Williams, Ph.D., in his book, *Trading Chaos*. From his point of view, he defines an *up fractal* as a middle bar with two lower highs on each side of it and a *down fractal* as a middle bar with two higher lows on each side of it. Chaos traditionally is seen as a lack of structure or order, but Williams considers chaos to be a higher degree of order instead, where there is no relationship between cause and effect because the financial markets pertain to a nonlinear and thus nonpredictable situation.

Bill Williams goes against most of the theories of technical analysts in that he believes that the markets can't be predictable and that a past behavior can't determine a future behavior. He affirms that the only way to achieve a success in the financial markets is to understand and explore its five-dimensional structure, which consists of the following elements: the fractal or space phase; the driving-force or power phase; acceleration or deceleration, which would be the power phase; the zone, which is a combination of strength and power phase; and finally, the balance line.

FRACTALS

A *fractal* is an indicator developed by Bill Williams for his own trading system, and it allows you to detect the bottom or top of a move. Basic fractals are composed of five bars. They can be identified with the following rules:

- A pattern forms with a highest high in the middle and two lower highs on each side; this would be a bearish probable reversal point.
- A pattern forms with a lowest low in the middle and two higher lows on each side; this would be a bullish probable reversal point.

Fractals help to identify the underlying fluctuations in price waves and also allow larger trends to be broken down into simple and predictable reversal patterns. They can be used in three different ways:

1. *Catch the trending.* Depending on the series of fractals that are successively broken, you can identify whether the trend is bullish or bearish. More up fractals will be broken in an uptrend, and more down fractals will be broken in a downtrend. The more they are broken, the stronger the trend will be.

2. *Catch the range.* Fractals can help to identify a consolidation area and will set resistance and support points between which the price will move. If the price can't seem to break above or below the most recent

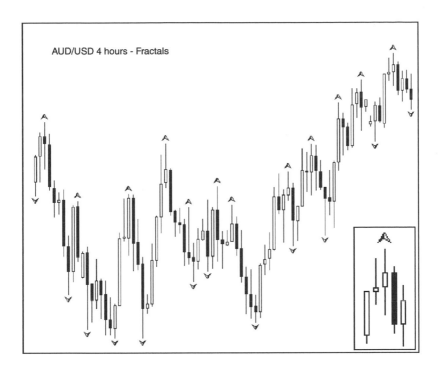

fractals, price is said to be consolidating and ranging or sideways. This also can help you to define a strategy for a potential breakout later on.

3. *Catch the break.* Finally, fractals simply can be used as breakout points, especially in longer time frames, for example, above 4 hours. The fractal points will be very helpful in drawing trendlines because they signal the bars or candles that have the highest high or lowest low of a series.

TRADING NAKED (ONLY PRICE ACTION)

Trading without any kind of technical indicators is familiarly described as *trading naked.* Naked traders only use price action, along with areas of support and resistance, pivot levels, swing highs and swing lows, tests of tops or bottoms, etc. Price action is how the money moves.

As you saw earlier, an up bar is a bar with a higher high and a higher low than the preceding bar. Up bars signal an uptrend. The close is higher than the open, and on the last bar of the trend, the close will be lower than the open because there will be more sellers than buyers on that last bar. A down bar is a bar that has a lower high and a lower low than the preceding bar. Down bars signal a downtrend. The close will be lower than the open, and on the last bar of the trend, the close will be higher than the open because there will be more buyers than sellers on that last bar.

Inside bars represent a market deliberation or indecision. The market is also denominated a narrow-range bar, in which its high is lower than the preceding bar and its low is higher than the preceding bar. An outside bar or engulfing bar has a higher high and a lower low than the preceding bar. When the open is in the bottom quarter or third of the bar and the close is in the top quarter or third of the bar, the engulfing bar is bullish engulfing, and the buyers are in control; conversely, when the open is in the top quarter or third of the bar and the close is in the bottom quarter or third, the engulfing bar is bearish engulfing, and the sellers are in control.

When the trend is going on, it will be continuously making higher highs and higher lows if it is an uptrend or lower highs and lower lows in the case of a downtrend. When the price stops making those higher/lower highs and lows, the trend is said to be *broken*. Then comes usually a period of consolidation or ranging, which thereafter resumes in the same direction, as a continuation of the previous trend, or either breaks out in the opposite direction in the case of a reversal. You can use multiple time frames to help you understand the behavior of prices and determine if they are trending or ranging.

It is perfectly possible that one time frame is trending in one direction and the other higher or lower time frame is trending in the opposite direction or is showing a consolidation pattern. There are infinite trends within trends. Price can be rising on a daily chart but meanwhile in a retracement or correction on a smaller time frame.

The best way to start to understand naked price action is to practice visually and observe the behavior patterns in several time frames simultaneously, determining the trend that is showing in each of them. For example, a 15-minute price action can be showing only two trends; meanwhile, the 5-minute price action is possibly showing five different trends for the same period. You can, of course, trade the smaller time-frame trends, but waiting for every time frame to align in the same direction as the larger time frame is signaling would be really trading with the trend.

Trading naked is the ultimate way to trade because in the end, everything can be narrowed down to the price. Any technical indicator or instrument is always directly related to price behavior and will only reflect what is already shown in the numbers.

12

SUPPORT AND RESISTANCE

Two of the most important subjects of FOREX technical analysis are support and resistance, which refer to the price levels at which there seems to be a barrier beyond which the price of a currency pair may not keep falling or rising. They are often viewed as quite complex because despite the obvious simplicity behind the concept, support and resistance can be determined in several ways, and it is not always easy to understand how they work or to master their use.

Support and resistance are key levels, mostly price areas or zones instead of a particular single price, where supply and demand meet and are of equal strength, neutralizing each other's forces. Supply is when traders are *selling* the base currency; demand is when a currency is being *bought.* Prices change when there is an imbalance between supply and demand, and one of the sides win. Prices rise when demand is higher and decrease when supply is greater. When both are at the same level, the market is said to be *moving sideways,* and there is a struggle between bulls and bears to take control.

SUPPORT

Support is the level where demand has acquired enough strength to stop the prices from decreasing further. As the price gets cheaper, more buyers are looking to hold the currency, and fewer sellers want to give it away. When the prices reach the support level, usually the demand and supply tend to get even or the number of buyers overcomes the number of sellers, and this will prevent the price from falling through the support level.

However, support levels sometimes are broken, which indicates that the selling pressure is still strong and that the bearish sentiment has taken over the bullish impulse. There is a renewal of the incentive to sell, and buyers stop wanting to acquire the currency. Since breakouts occur with a certain momentum, it is not until the next lower support level that buyers might come back into the picture, and the same struggle will present itself between bulls and bears. If the support holds, then there will be a bounce from the support, and the bullish sentiment will have won the battle.

Support levels are established under the current price, but since the support levels are not set at an exact price but rather mostly in an area of possible prices, volatility could cause prices to drop a little below a given support level without effectively breaking it. This is why it is preferable to establish support zones. A small dip will have no strength to indicate a breakout; usually a certain number of points and other confirmatory indicators are needed to really consider that a support level has been broken. The most common confirmation is a retest and bounce from the support level after it has been crossed. At that moment, the support becomes resistance.

RESISTANCE

Resistance is the level where selling pressure acquires enough strength to stop the price from a further increase. As the price goes up and keeps advancing toward resistance, more sellers will want to enter the market, and fewer buyers will be willing to buy. At the moment the price reaches the resistance level, as happens with support, both sides tend to get even, and sellers even may overcome the number of buyers, thus bouncing back and driving the prices lower.

When resistance does not hold, and a new buying surge pushes the market, the price will break above the resistance, signaling that the bullish sentiment has won the battle and bears are not interested in selling anymore. Buyers will be buying at higher prices until they reach a further resistance level, which will form after the initial momentum of the second move fades away.

Resistance levels are established above the current price, but in the same way that happens with support levels. You should consider resistance levels more like a zone, and small rallies or peaks through the level shouldn't be taken as a breakout signal unless the price really has increased by a fair number of points and there is further confirmation. This is commonly seen by means of a small pullback and retest of the recently broken resistance, where the price will bounce back up and confirm the bullish sentiment, making that resistance become a support.

TRENDLINES

A *trendline* is an ascending or descending price level that can be drawn between at least two lower highs in a downtrend or two higher lows in an uptrend. This level then is seen as a constant barrier that prevents the price from going higher or lower, forming a certain range that can be parallel or converging in the case of triangular formations.

The level formed by this trendline constitutes a support or a resistance and usually is a place where the prices will bounce back in the opposite direction. An upper resistance is formed every time the price action slows down and pulls back to the trendline in an uptrend and every time a bearish move runs out of steam and moves back to the lower highs trendline in a downtrend. This occurs because of profit-taking or market uncertainty after a prolonged move, creating a defined range between the trendlines and the series of tops or bottoms.

Traders usually will watch for the prices to reach the top or bottom levels of the range and buy or sell accordingly when other confirmatory conditions are met.

MOVING AVERAGES

Moving averages can be of help in identifying levels of support and resistance. In either of its forms, a moving average is a reflection of the dynamic price level that has the greater incidence. When the trend is going up, the price finds its support at the moving average. This indicator acts as a resistance when the trend is going down. Some values—or number of periods averaged—will work better than others and also depend on the relative time frames. Experimentation is needed to find which moving average is best suited to show the levels of support and resistance in each particular trading situation, but there are specific periods, such as the exponential moving average (EMA) or the simple moving average (SMA) 200 (which can signify 200 days, weeks, hours, or minutes with regard to the distinct time frames), that seem to work independently of the time variable. I personally like how the prices behave when near the SMA 34; I find this value quite appropriate to predict bounces and potential targets for taking profits or exiting a position.

OTHER INDICATORS

Many other indicators can be used to identify areas of support and resistance. One of them is the Fibonacci retracement tool, which was described in detail in Chapter 11.

Being able to determine future levels of support or resistance is an important way to improve FOREX trading returns by getting a more accurate view of the possible levels that can be reached and the most probable reaction of the prices when those levels are hit. In this way, targets and stops can be set in a more precise form, and a trader can avoid entering a position at places where the price is more likely to reverse.

Independent of the method you use to foresee the levels where price is going to encounter a pressure against its current direction, in all of them the significance of the support or resistance is the same: Those are the levels beyond which the price of the currency pair or financial asset that you are trading probably will not move in either direction.

ENTERING POSITIONS

The establishment of areas of support and resistance allows traders to choose a more precise entry point for their positions. The forces of supply and demand show clear patterns and can be predicted, provided that other indicators or patterns confirm the potential reversal or continuation of a trend.

When the market is alternating inside those extreme zones, there is certain stability between supply and demand. When the forces of supply overcome the forces of demand, or vice versa, there is a breakout of the range delineated by support and resistance, and other zones are reached that will act as such, and the broken levels will turn into their opposite.

There is an old adage that says, "Buy low; sell high." This means buy at the support level, and sell at the resistance level, provided that the conditions maintaining the prices inside a given range are still valid. Breakout entries would respond to the inverse—sell low; buy high—after the breakout point. How can you determine that a particular support or resistance is holding or if its weakness will lead to a breakout? You saw in Chapter 11 that many technical patterns can help to identify the potential weakness or strength of a certain move.

A rejection of the support or resistance level, followed by a retest and subsequent bounce back inside the channel, is a good indication to enter a position. Candlestick patterns of reversal and moving averages, as well as pivot lines and any oscillator that can show an oversold or overbought condition, will help in the decision. In the case of a breakout, a break of the trendline, followed by a retest of the trendline from above or below, and the subsequent bounce back with the former support becoming resistance or the former resistance turning into support is also a good confirmation for an entry point, with the help of the preceding indicators to ensure a safer decision.

Identifying main support and resistance levels is a key element leading to a successful technical analysis. When you are aware of their existence and location, it is much easier to forecast and be prepared when prices move near those levels. Look for extra signs of an increase in the buying or selling pressure and potential reversal and volume of transactions. When a support or resistance level has been broken, this signals that there has been a change in the relationship between supply and demand. A resistance breakout signals that the bulls are stronger than the bears, and a support break indicates that the bears have won the battle.

EXITING POSITIONS

Support and resistance levels provide excellent areas to set target profits or simply exit a position manually. You can either chose to trade a single position or split it into two or more parts, which you will be exiting progressively at every level based on a preset plan.

When setting a stop loss based on support and resistance, the stop level should be set a few points (usually 5 or 10 depending on the time frame that you will be using) below or above the most recent strong point of support or resistance. This can be determined through observation of the levels where the price has stalled most often or with the use of fractals, Fibonacci levels, pivots, and psychological levels.

A target profit will be set inversely, a few points below a strong projected resistance, pivot, or Fibonacci level or above a support that has proven to be holding. It is important not to forget the spread of the particular currency pair that you are trading and the side, or direction, on which your trades are placed because what is commonly defined as *actual price* is usually the bid price on most platforms. For example, on short positions, the price used to close will be the ask or offer price, so be sure to add or subtract the spread from any calculations.

When there is a strong expectation of a continued trend, positions can be split into several parts, and actions can be performed sequentially on each of them. For example, with this approach, a trader would exit one of the parts at the first perceived strong resistance or support level and set the stop losses on the remaining parts of the trade to breakeven (the entry price) or, better, to one positive point, thereafter exiting the next part at the next support or resistance level and trailing the stop losses or simply letting the free trades run to gather the most possible profits from the overall position.

PIVOT POINTS: DO THEY WORK?

"Big dogs" are a very important part of the market. Usually the settings used by the greater number of people will work the best because everybody will be reacting to those levels at the same time and place. However, I would recommend testing different approaches so that you can determine by yourself which settings work more accurately on your charts.

The key is support/resistance—former levels at which the price has been rejected many times—as well as channels and trendlines too. Also, pivots should be considered as zones more than a particular and exact price (especially because there are differences among most brokers on prices that can go as far as 10 to 12 pips).

I want to point out that this is my personal opinion: I check the pivots but personally prefer the psychological levels to work with short term in 1 minute increments also known as M1, which I consider to be small pivots in themselves.

Price goes in waves, not linearly. When price action is observed in a very small time frame, you can see that at every lower level, a "decision" must be made, a price is approved or rejected. Bulls or bears win the small battle, then go on to the next level or come back to the previous one, and later on "decide" to retest again until the level breaks or the opposite party wins and rejects the "proposed" price, just like a staircase. Then the key levels (previous bigger staircases on larger time frames) are made by the support or resistance levels that held through many attempts at being crossed.

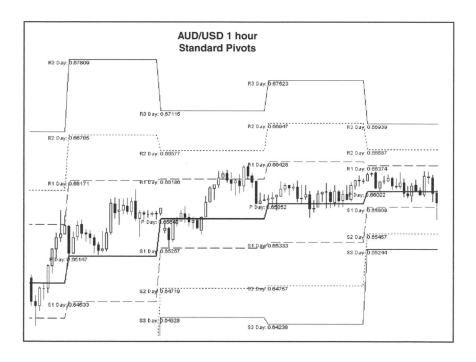

Pivots are, like Fibonacci lines, the result of a calculation made based on an analysis of historical data, and in a certain way and because of it, they can become a self-fulfilling prediction because everyone is watching the same prices and has the same information. Thus, indeed, the best pivots will be those that are used by the greater number of traders.

For me, it's more logical to start the day when the FOREX day "officially" starts in Sydney through the New York close (5 p.m. Eastern Time). In my opinion, this doesn't matter much because in the end, you won't have more than 24 hours in a daily candle.

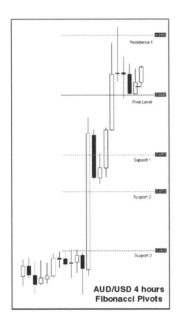

The pivot indicator is based on the high-low and close price of the daily candle (calculated with respect to every different set of settings and based on 24 sequential hourly candles), which will show differently on each platform according to its own time zone.

The "daily session" consists of the whole day (all the markets involved), and personally, I don't think that two hours difference can make much noise unless there's a huge move at the end of the day (New York close), and even then, I don't think it would matter because it would be compensated by the hours not taken from the preceding day.

Settings that start at Greenwich Mean Time (GMT) 00:00 (eight hours before the London session) are perhaps a more normalized time where more people calculate the pivots (you would have to know how many brokers start the day with GMT 00:00). Mine starts with the Sydney session two hours earlier because it seems more logical to me, since most markets open on Sunday at the Sydney open and close on Friday at the New York close. Other people may like to base the close/open of the daily candle on the New York Stock Exchange (NYSE) close at 4 p.m. Eastern Time. The more people who use the same setting, the more probabilities there will be for a pivot price to become predictable. This works exactly like the Fibonacci levels.

Since I see pivots more as a range level (or zone) than a particular exact price (and I prefer to take into account the psychological levels anyway), it doesn't bother me much if my pivot is 5 pips up or 5 pips down (because, anyway, prices between brokers differ sometimes by as much as 10 or more pips, and in some, there can be huge spikes that don't show on the others; this in respect to high highs and low lows). Therefore, it's really relative, and real support/resistances, which can be seen on the charts at the levels the price went and bounced back, in my opinion are more accurate.

Exactly the same is true for Fibonacci levels. It is impossible to calculate prices to the pip because of all the preceding. You can easily take a look at several sites that show the daily pivots, and there will be differences among them, too.

STANDARD		FIBONACCI	
R3	H + 2 (Pivot − L)	R3	Pivot + 1.000 * (H − L)
R2	Pivot + (H − L)	R2	Pivot + 0.618 * (H − L)
R1	(2 × Pivot) − L	R1	Pivot + 0.382 * (H − L)
Pivot	(H + L + C) / 3	Pivot	(H + L + C) / 3
S1	(2 x Pivot) − H	S1	Pivot − 0.382 * (H − L)
S2	Pivot − (H − L)	S2	Pivot − 0.618 * (H − L)
S3	L − 2(H − L)	S3	Pivot − 1.000 * (H − L)
CAMARILLA		WOODIE	
R4	R4 = C + RANGE * 1.1/2	R4	R3 + RANGE
R3	R3 = C + RANGE * 1.1/4	R3	R1 + RANGE
R2	R2 = C + RANGE * 1.1/6	R2	PP + RANGE
R1	R1 = C + RANGE * 1.1/12	R1	R1 = (2 * PP) − LOW
Pivot	(H + L + C) / 3	Pivot	(H + L + C) / 3
S1	R1 = C − RANGE * 1.1/12	S1	R1 = (2 * PP) − HIGH
S2	R2 = C − RANGE * 1.1/6	S2	PP − RANGE
S3	R3 = C − RANGE * 1.1/4	S3	S1 − RANGE
S4	R4 = C − RANGE * 1.1/2	S4	S3 − RANGE

DEMARK PIVOT POINTS

Tom DeMark, in calculating pivots projections, differentiates three situations:

1. Close > open:

   PHigh = [(H + H + L + C)/2] − L

   PLow = [(H + H + L + C)/2] − H

2. Close < open:

   PHigh = [(H + L + L + C)/2] − L

   PLow = [(H + L + L + C)/2] − H

3. Close = open:

   PHigh = [(H + L + C + C)/2] − L

   PLow = [(H + L + C + C)/2] − H

In intraday application with open (yesterday open), H (yesterday high), L (yesterday low), and close (yesterday close).

PSYCHOLOGICAL LEVELS

You might have noticed that you are constantly rounding off numbers in your daily activities. You tend to see round numbers as more perfect and whole and are invariably drawn to use them, especially numbers that end in zero. These round numbers also play an important role in FOREX trading.

If you take a look at previous support and resistance levels, you might discover a common characteristic that prices have with respect to certain prices: They can be seen as usually having difficulty moving past a round price, such as, for example, $100. Other strong levels are prices ending in 5, or *quarter prices,* such as 25 or 75. There is also a curious behavior that I have noticed that I can only associate with Fibonacci levels around prices ending on 66 and 33. All these are said to be *psychological levels.* Human beings also tend to be attracted to numbers that are factors of 10, a theory suggested by the fact that we have 10 fingers and toes for counting.

Hitting a major 00 mark is a quite common goal, and often it will be tested and tried until it is reached or crossed, only for the price to come back soon afterwards because the final milestone was reached, and the market continues toward its next new goal.

Supports and resistances are being created at those round-number levels through the accumulation of pending limit or stop orders. This also could be a reason why those levels are bounced off sometimes when they have been barely touched and, conversely, the price experiences a surge as soon as it has crossed the level for a few points. Limit orders will be placed a little below the higher round-number price or above the lower round-number price, whereas stop orders usually are placed beyond either level.

Most target prices or stop-loss orders are placed by market participants at round-number price levels because these are perceived to be a fair value and a more perfect price than nonround numbers. For example, the $100 mark will be more attractive to a trader than a price of $101.02 or $99.96. Such large numbers of orders act as a strong price barrier and, when triggered, will cause the price to bounce back. The levels are said to be psychological because there is no other logical, technical, or fundamental reason to explain the reaction of the market except for this simple attraction to round numbers.

Banks are known for implementing most orders around these levels, as can be seen from the relative volumes on the Interbank. Large pools of orders accumulate, and when the price level is reached, they are triggered, causing an avalanche in the contrarian direction, which is perceived on charts as a strong bounce.

This is very important information for traders, who then can base their strategies on this peculiarity of the markets and increase their profits by going with the flow.

round number levels

Round numbers can be better employed on smaller time frames. The first bounce from a round-number support or resistance is usually the strongest, and every time a round number is hit, a series of orders is executed. With every successive reach of the same level, the volume of orders decreases; if at any moment this volume is not strong enough to keep holding the support or resistance, the level will break.

Although successive moves from a support or resistance level also can yield handsome profits, it is better to try to take advantage of the first time the price hits the level and comes back because this is the moment when the volume is at its strongest peak for a rejection.

This penchant for round numbers is common to all trading markets but is especially dominant in the FOREX market. The principal reason behind this phenomenon is that, simply, most human beings are attracted to round numbers, and as long as trading is performed by human beings, the condition will recur.

USING MULTIPLE TIME FRAMES

When you look at multiple time frames, you can get a much better idea of what is happening with a currency pair. You should use at least two time frames, one to spot the trend and the other to pinpoint your entries at a better price. However, the best option is to use from three to four time frames, especially when you are swing trading, because the perspective will be much broader, and you will be able to understand how the market moves.

For example, in a usual swing trading situation, where the main chart is located in the daily time frame, you can use the weekly, daily, 1-hour, and 5-minute charts. Here is a short description of what you should look for in each of those time frames, and if you are trading intraday, you can translate the method to the series of smaller time frames.

Main Chart or Charting Workspace = Daily Chart
Buy and sell decisions are made here. You find the setups and signals given by your system to get to trading opportunities. You can see a general medium-term trend. However, you need to know what the longer-term trend is.

Overview of the General Trend = Weekly Chart
In this chart, you can step back and see what the longer-term trend looks like. You can find more data than in the daily chart earlier in time. You also can check the significant patterns to confirm that the decision made based on the daily trend is probably correct.

Looking Closer = 1-Hour Chart
You switch to a broader representation in detail of what is really going on during the day. You can see the smaller swings that occur that can't be seen in a single candle on the daily chart. For example, when you are buying consecutive pullbacks on the daily chart that have a series of consecutive lower highs, you will be able to see that the prices are showing a downtrend on the hourly chart. Thus you will be looking for a break of that trendline in this time frame and enter at the appropriate time.

The Magnifying Glass = 5-Minute Chart
The 5-minute chart is the smaller time frame, the one you will be using to time your entries. Your setup is perfect on the daily chart, and you have already checked the weekly chart to gauge the patterns and to be sure of the current main trend. You have drawn the trendline on the hourly chart and are waiting for a break. The decision to enter a long position is already made, and you will wait until the price pulls back to a support level on the smaller chart so as to enter at the best possible price.

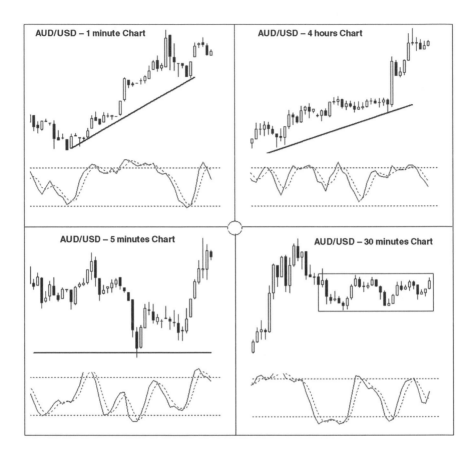

Every time frame has an effect on every other time frame, from the smaller ones to the bigger ones. Using smaller time frames for entries allows you to enter at better prices, thus giving you the opportunity to use much tighter stop losses than if you just traded off the main chart. Check every time frame, and spot the support and resistance levels and chart and candlesticks patterns. Finally, a good point of reference for general support and resistance is the SMA 200, which you should use in all time frames. I personally also add the SMA 34 because I have found that the prices always will bounce at least once from this particular moving average before resuming a move.

This type of multiple-chart analysis can improve your success as a swing trader. Your main goal is to identify the areas of support and resistance and to check if there is an alignment of your preferred setup on most of the time frames chosen. The more all the time frames are in alignment, the greater the opportunity for success. Try to look at two additional time frames along with your main chart. The lower time frame will be telling you what is happening in the present, and the higher time frame will show you what could happen in the future!

TREND IS YOUR FRIEND

The end of a trend is signaled when it stops making progressively higher (or lower) highs and higher (or lower) lows. A trend reverses its previous direction when the price begins making progressively lower (or higher) lows and lower (or higher) highs. However, you need to filter out any consolidation pattern (e.g., a flag in an uptrend may be making lower lows and lower highs, but its consequence is a further continuation almost three out of four times). For this, you can observe the momentum of the move or use moving averages or another indicator crossing to determine if there is a reversal of the trend or if it is only a pause before the strength of the trend resumes.

Very often, when the market looks the most bullish or bearish and everybody is jumping in, this is precisely the moment when professional FOREX traders will be loading their positions in the contrarian direction. Be very aware not to be late when entering a trend. At the same time, never trade against a trend (unless you are swing trading in a range or scalping in smaller time frames). When the trend is strong, apparent reversal patterns may have no meaning, and the reversal never happens, unless it is for just a few pips. In a strong market such as this, you trade breakouts—and that's it. Very often there isn't even a pullback to trade, and by the time a pullback happens, the move is already over. In a market such as this, the energy has to slow down before it can reverse.

C H A P T E R

13

AUTOMATED TRADING

EXPERT ADVISORS AND AUTOMATIC PROGRAMMING INTERFACES (APIs)

Trading systems are a series of rules that traders use to determine their entries and exits from a position. A well-designed trading system can help traders to attain consistent returns while limiting risk through its money-management specifications. In an ideal situation, traders should follow their system rules like robots, executing trades systematically and without emotion. However, the human condition makes this last part a little difficult, and this is why automated systems have started gaining in popularity.

I have always said the number one mistake investors make is that they let their emotions get in the way. To increase your winning percentage, you must trade emotion-free. A good system will help you to refine your ability to stick to your trading rules. The advent of program trading, which is nothing new, can maximize your opportunities. Program trading (robots) has really made headway with individual investors. With all the advances in personal computing, this is an area where I have spent considerable time and money on research and development. All my software, as well as new software yet to be released, incorporates some state-of-the-art programming language that allows all my customers to take advantage of the latest robots to trade for you.

The importance of an automated system is reflected in its wide array of uses in the financial markets. The FOREX market is not only the biggest market worldwide in terms of daily turnover but also because it involves the largest number of participants. Many of the biggest players in the FOREX market use a diversity of automated systems to help in their decision making and overall organization of the trading process.

Today, most of the order flow goes through a computerized communications network. This facilitates the use of computer-based automation. Automated trading systems are created simply by converting the rules of your trading system into code that can be interpreted by your computer and the software that is employed to interact on the financial markets. The computer runs those rules through your trading software, and the system itself will be looking for trades that comply with the coded rules. When the appropriate conditions are met, the system will place the trades automatically directly with your broker.

Many brokerage firms and platforms support automated trading systems. Such systems can be used in a totally automated manner or as semi-automatic variants, where the trader will be given a signal when conditions are met, and the trader will take the final decision of opening the trade. Some brokers require an authorization to be able to implement an automated system on your account.

These kinds of trading systems have many advantages, but they also have some negative aspects. The positive side is that all the emotion and stress are taken out of the picture. The hard work already has been done through the development and testing of the trading strategy, and thereafter, you only need to focus on its improvement and, of course, applying money-management rules. As long as market conditions do not change and the system has proven to be profitable in its development phase, it will not require additional work on your part. The negative aspects come from the fact that if the code is not defined and tested properly before using it in a real-money account, you could face losing trades. In addition, there are some combinations of rules that can't be translated to a code, especially when the system includes a discretionary approach, making it difficult to develop.

The following are the main areas to pay attention to if you decide to work with a trading robot: backtesting and performance and market phases (whether it is trending or ranging).

It is of an extreme importance to do a thorough backtesting of your system until you are sure that it performs well with historical data. Then trade it on a demo account to make sure that there will be no surprises along the way and that actual performance is equivalent to that which resulted from the backtesting. Very few strategies perform well in both phases of the markets because the conditions present in a ranging market are very different from those in a trending market. Be sure to use and implement the appropriate strategy for each of those situations, either in a single system or by developing and using two alternate automated systems.

Additionally, it is important that you keep things simple and that your code is well documented so as to be able to find out quickly when a portion of it is not performing or you need to change some of the conditions. Changes to code should be done one at a time so that you can more precisely pinpoint which changes improve the performance of the system and which ones set it back. Finally, make sure that you know what strategy operates behind your trading system. Sometimes the coded version can become so complex that it deviates from the original rules of the trading strategy.

ADVANCED ROBOTS: NEURAL NETWORKS IN THE FOREX

The first research on neural networks began back at the beginning of the nineteenth century, but only between the 1940s and 1950s, in the twentieth century, did the study of neural networks acquire its major strength, thanks to the Connectionist movement. This movement sustained the theory that the secret of learning processes and knowledge can be found in axioms or unquestionable truths; members of this movement affirmed that knowledge is independent of the structure that handles the symbols and that the representation of knowledge is done from the most basic stratum of intelligence—the brain, especially the neurons and the multiple interconnections between them.

This important interest in neural networks decreased in the 1970s because researchers such as Minsky and Papert in 1969 indicated that there were limitations in the learning processes of the architectures of neural networks that had been used until then. In their book, *Perceptrons,* they made a detailed analysis of the perceptron and considered that its extension to a multilayered structure was a totally sterile activity (the original perceptron, a neural network under research, possessed only one layer). The limitations of the perceptron were quite important, especially its failure to resolve many problems simultaneously. This caused a setback in the development of neural networks that lasted more than 10 years.

Advances in technology and in knowledge about the structure of the brain gave a new impetus to interest in neural networks that has allowed the development of a growing number of applications in several different fields and with diverse purposes. Artificial neural networks now are established as a technique of massive and parallel processing of information that emulates the essential characteristics of the neural structure of the biologic brain.

One of the fields in which these data-analysis methods have been introduced is the automated FOREX world. Neural networks consist of a large number of processing units that are linked together by weighted probabilities. They are a model that exhibits behavior that is similar to the working and learning of the human brain. This model "thinks and learns" based on the results of the previous actions.

Neural networks can be trained to interpret data and draw conclusions from them. They are able to take in multiple streams of data and give a single result as the outcome of their calculations. New forms of quantification of those data can be added to the series of factors that the neural network considers before it makes a decision, and the new forms will be processed along with the previous ones. This is why neural networks are being used increasingly in the FOREX to make price predictions.

The network is trained to adjust itself based on specific patterns that form between the time of the input data and the output it generates. This is quite time-consuming, but in the end, it will provide the neural network with the ability to predict a future outcome based on historical data. When it is presented with examples of pairs of input and output data, the network can "learn" the dependencies and apply those dependencies when presented with new data. Thereafter, the network can compare the new data with output it has generated previously and determine how far from or close to the real data its prediction was, go back and adjust the relationships among the various factors that determine the calculations, and keep on adjusting until it reaches the correct answer and the output is equivalent to the real event.

The training has to be performed with two different sets of data: the data specifically used for training and the data that will be used in testing. The neural network can continue to learn by continuously comparing the predictions it makes with the data that are being given to the system. The neural network also combines technical and fundamental data in its calculations; in this way, it can find additional patterns that might not have been included in earlier considerations and apply them to the prediction, coming up with very accurate results.

However, the output will be as good as the input data it is fed. The neural network is very good at correlations independent of the amount of data you are introducing in the process. It will be able to recognize patterns even among extremely different types of information, even if there is no existing relationship or particular pattern. Most important, the neural network can apply its intelligence without clouding it with emotions. However, this can become a weakness when unknown factors are introduced, such as, for example, when dealing with a volatile market, where it has no way of assigning emotional weight to events.

Many trading platforms actually include neural network theories and technology that will teach your particular system about the network and use its predictions and capacity to generate direct buy or sell orders based on those outputs. You can build your own neural network, but as in any of the different ways of applying a trading system, you first will have to thoroughly learn the process so that you can know exactly what you are doing and what you can expect. Know your system, its scope, and its basic tenets so that you can more likely attain the success you are looking for in your trading. Learn as much as you can. Automation can be a powerful impulse to the future growth of the FOREX market because it simplifies many processes and brings about many more positive outcomes than negative issues.

The use of an automated FOREX trading system allows traders to open positions in real time at any moment and from any place in the world. Especially in highly volatile markets, the delays are practically nonexistent, and thus most of the usual losses in manually operated systems that stem from delays in buying or selling in a fast-moving environment are avoided. In the same way, traders will be able to operate simultaneously in a wide range of currency markets at the same time because the automated system has no time limitations and can be set to work the whole 24 hours of the day.

Neural networks and artificial intelligence are the best method for economic modeling. Those robots adapt and are able to evolve and change based on market conditions and to train themselves based on a particular algorithm with a coded set of rules that will allow them to make the correct decisions. They will detect the most important input factors out of hundreds of factors that are used in the first phase of the network training setup. The selected factors then are employed to fine-tune forecasts on the training and test sets in order to maximize accuracy and profit. The results have proven that neural networks can be implemented very successfully to forecast the movements in the financial market.

P A R T

6

BUILDING YOUR PORTFOLIO

14

SECRETS TO FOREX DIVERSIFICATION

The ideal investment scenario is to have several alternatives so as not to put "all your eggs in one basket" and thus minimize the risks by broadening your portfolio's scope. The most common alternatives are marketable securities, which are very liquid assets that can be converted into cash quickly at a fair price. Their maturities usually represent less than one year, and the rate at which they can be bought or sold has little effect on their prices. Some examples of marketable securities include commercial paper, banker's acceptances, Treasury bills, and other money-market instruments.

Among them, and beyond trading FOREX currency pairs, you can invest in options, futures, exchange-traded funds, and contracts for difference, commodities, indices, and securities.

FOREX OPTIONS

An *option* is a contract through which the buyer, by means of paying a premium, acquires the right, though not the obligation, to buy or sell a particular asset at a given price—the *execution price*—on a certain date or before a future date, which is the *expiration time*. Options are negotiated in over the counter (OTC) and in organized markets. These are the financial products that offer the best possibilities of coverage and speculation, and they offer a high level of liquidity and low transaction costs.

For example, in the usual way, an investor who anticipates a rise in the price of wheat could buy the wheat directly and store it, waiting to sell it later to gain a profit if the price rises. Another way of benefiting from the price rise without having to mess with storage would be to buy a call option on the same amount of wheat for a three-month period. If three months later the price has risen, it will be good for both the first investor who bought directly and the one who bought the option. The difference is that the first investor would have to pay in full for the wheat bought; meanwhile, the option only requires the investor to pay a premium that represents a very small percentage of the actual price. If the first investor bought $500 worth of wheat, and the price increased to revalue his or her investment to $700, he or she will have made a profit of $200, which represents 40 percent of his or her initial investment. Conversely, the second investor used a small capital represented by the premium, which could be of $10, and realized a gain on the option of $200 (the difference between the previous price and the risen price), so the return on his or her investment would be of $190, that is, 1900 percent!

An important feature of options is that they are negotiable instruments in the market, and it is not necessary to materialize the transaction physically; you can buy an option for $10 and then sell it on the market for $200 with a profit of $190 while never having had the intention of really buying the asset.

Options are divided into calls and puts. A *call* is the right to buy a particular asset; you can buy a call (buy the rights) or sell a call (sell the rights). The buyer of a call has the right, but not the obligation, to buy the asset (underlying asset) at a certain price (execution price) on a certain date or prior to that date, which is the expiration time, in exchange for a premium that the investor pays to the seller of the call. A *put* is the right to sell an asset. You can buy or sell a put (the right to buy or sell). The buyer of a put has the right, but not the obligation, to buy the asset (the real asset) at a certain price (execution price) on a certain date or prior to that date, which is the expiration time, in exchange for a premium that the investor pays to the seller of the put. The right to buy or sell is acquired by the holder of the option. The person who sells the option is called the *writer.*

Underlying assets are the assets on which the option is negotiated. The *premium* is the cost of the option, that is, the price that gives the right to buy (call) or sell (put) the underlying asset of an option. In the preceding example, the premium would be represented by the $10.

When the holder executes the right to buy or sell, it is said that he or she *executes* the contract. The *execution price,* or *strike price,* is the price at which the right is granted to buy or sell (call or put) an option. The *expiry date* is the date on which the option contract expires.

There are three basic types of options: the *American option,* which can be executed at any moment until its expiry date; the *European option,* which can only be executed at the moment of its expiration; and the *Asian option,* whose price on the expiry date does not depend on the price of the underlying asset at that moment but on the average of its consecutive prices during a determined time period.

Options are commonly perceived as being a high-risk investment; however, this is not always true because certain positions in options bear much less risk than physical acquisition of the underlying asset. You could say that the maximum risk of option holders is the premium that has to be paid. The maximum risk of the writers or sellers is usually unlimited, and their maximum benefit is the option premium.

RISKS AND BENEFITS OF BUYING A CALL OR A PUT

A call option will be placed when the price of a particular underlying asset is perceived as rising. A put option will be acquired when the price of this asset is in decline. In both cases, the risk to the investor is limited to the full amount of the premium that has to be paid to perform the transaction, which represents only a small fraction of the cost of the underlying asset. However, if the prices don't evolve in the projected direction, the risk of loss is of all the premium paid.

Potential benefits are unlimited. In the case of a call, since the contract gives the holder the right to buy at a fixed price, this right will acquire a greater value as the price of the underlying asset increases. At the expiry date, the investor will get the amount determined by the difference between the execution price and the final price that has risen minus the premium paid. In the case of a put, the benefit will be equal to the fall in price minus the premium paid.

RISKS AND BENEFITS OF SELLING A CALL OR A PUT

When the price of the underlying asset is perceived as falling, selling a call is the strategy to use. Puts are sold when the price is perceived to be on the rise. The greatest benefit that can be obtained from selling both a call or a put is the amount of the premium that the seller receives for his or her option.

The greatest risk that can be incurred by selling a put is that the price falls instead of rising; the greatest loss is the amount to the execution price of the underlying asset minus the premium received. In the case of a call, the potential risk is unlimited because the price could rise indefinitely. This is why selling calls or puts is extremely risky if the investor does not have the underlying asset in his or her possession.

LEVERAGE

One of the most attractive characteristics of futures and options, and at the same time the most dangerous, is that they can be used as leverage effect. The *leverage effect* is the relationship between the invested capital and the result obtained from a given investment. The higher the leverage, the less capital is needed to obtain a particular result.

For example, say that an investor buys one call on company ABC shares with expiry in January 2009, paying a premium of $15 with an execution price of $100 (expressed as "1 ABC January 100 call"). At the moment, the shares of company ABC are quoted at $108. If on the expiry date the shares are quoted at $120, the investor will execute his or her buying option and will sell the shares on the market for $120. In this way, with an investment of $15 (the premium paid), the investor has obtained a profit of $20; the return he or she has gotten on the transaction is 133.33 percent. You can see that the return on options is much higher.

However, the leverage works both ways. If on the expiry date the shares of company ABC are quoted at $80, the investor would not execute his or her buying option because although he or she still has the right to buy shares at $100, he or she can buy them cheaper, at $80, in the market. In this case, the investor would lose 100 percent of the investment, that is, the $15 premium.

The leverage effect has to be treated with respect, and only experienced investors should speculate with options and futures because it is very easy to lose the whole investment and more.

To calculate the value of the premium of an option, the market usually employs the formula of Black and Scholes. Here is a simple example on how it is calculated: You have a share quoted at $100, and you could buy it in a year at $100. How much does this right cost? To answer this question, let us suppose that at the end of the year, the price of the share can only take one of two values: It either rises to $120 or it falls to $80. Now, you want to build a portfolio by buying 50 shares and selling 100 calls. How much would that cost? You would have to pay 50 shares × $100 = $5000; however, you will not need to pay all that money because for the options sold, you will receive $100 × the price of each option, which is still unknown. What you know is that if at the end of the year the shares rise in price, your option will be valued at $100 and if they fall in price, the option will have a value of 0. Thus the final value of your portfolio will be $4000 if the share price rises (50 shares × $120 per share − 100 calls × $20 per call) or $4000 if the share falls (50 shares × $80 − 100 calls × $0 per call). You can see that the value of your portfolio does not depend on the price of the share at that moment. That is, your portfolio is not at risk and thus offers a return similar to one-year Treasury bonds (the expiry date of the option).

If this nonrisk return is 5 percent, this implies that to get $4000 in a year, you will have to invest today 4000/1.05 = $3809.52; this is your portfolio's initial value. Since the 50 shares you have bought cost $5000, the amount you should have received on the 100 options you have sold would be 5000 − 3809.52 = $1190.48. For this reason, the price of each option at the moment of initiation should be $11.90. If the price of the option were lower or higher than $11.90, you could earn money by buying options and selling shares, or vice versa, which would bring the price to its theoretical value.

The Black and Scholes model uses an infinite number of subperiods and repeats the preceding procedure an infinite number of times to calculate the price of the option. In the example, the theoretical value of the option applying this formula is of $11.90, very near to the value calculated for a single period.

Some of the strategies used with options allow a more aggressive approach to the market:

Bull spread. Buying a call or a put with a particular execution price and selling another call or put with a higher execution price, where both options must have the same expiry date and a rise in the price of the underlying asset is expected.

Bear spread. Buying a call or a put with a given execution price and selling another call or put with a lower execution price (as in the bull spread, both options have the same expiry date). In this case, a decrease in the price of the underlying asset is expected.

Straddle buy. Buying a call and a put with the same execution price and expiry date. The expectation is for great volatility to the bullish as well as to the bearish side.

Strangle buy. Buying a call and a put with different execution prices and the same date of expiry. As with the straddle, the strangle expects great volatility in the financial markets, even higher than in the preceding case.

Butterfly. The buying and selling of options with three different execution prices: (1) buying a call or a put with a low execution price, (2) buying a call or a put with a high execution price, and (3) selling two calls or two puts with execution prices at about midway between the two preceding ones. The expectation is oriented to a stable market.

SPOT FOREX OPTIONS

Single-payment options trading (SPOT) options are a slightly different kind of FOREX option: The trader forecasts what is to happen in the FOREX market. If the trader is right in his or her predictions, the possible profit can be unlimited, and if the SPOT is unsuccessful, the trader loses only the premium.

SPOT FOREX options are more flexible to set and execute, but the premiums are higher than in traditional options. A basic example of how a SPOT option works would be that the trader states his or her prediction on the market: "EUR/USD will break through 1.4000 in 15 days." The investor gets a quote for the cost or premium associated with this option and will receive a payout if, effectively, the prediction happens. The option is automatically converted to cash when the trade is successful. If your prediction is incorrect, you lose only the premium.

There are three basic variants of SPOT options: double one-touch, one-touch, and double no-touch. A *double one-touch option* has two barrier levels; either one has to be breached before the expiration date for a profitable result. If none of them is crossed at expiration, the option loses its value. This type of option is usually employed on news releases because it is a nondirectional breakout prediction. If any of the barrier levels is broken, the payout will be made.

A *one-touch option* has a single barrier level. This makes the option a little less expensive than the double one-touch option. The same behavior applies; the level has to be surpassed before expiration for the option to be of value and yield a profit. This is a directional approach when you have good probabilities of forecasting that the market is going in a particular direction.

A *double no-touch option* is exactly the opposite of a double one-touch option. Here, you also have two barrier levels, but in this case neither one can be crossed before expiration. Otherwise, the option payout is not made. This option is usually employed when the trader forecasts that prices will remain in a range and that there will not be much volatility in the market.

Options are an excellent way to protect your existing positions by means of a hedge in order to limit the risk. Some traders even use them to replace stop losses.

FOREX FUTURES

A *future* is a standardized contract to buy or sell a specific asset at a fixed future date and at a price previously agreed on. There are two parties in a futures contract: the buyer and the seller. The buyer of the future has the obligation to buy on a determined date; meanwhile, the seller has the obligation to sell on that same date.

Futures contracts are negotiated in organized markets and thus are standardized instruments; for example, a futures contract on steel can involve 5 tons of the metal, or each contract can be set for 1 million dollars. For this reason, futures are only negotiated in multiples of contracts; that is, if you want to buy 50 tons of steel, you would have to buy 10 steel futures. These standards offer liquidity by increasing the number of potential buyers and sellers.

One *tick* is the minimum fluctuation allowed in the price of a futures contract. Since every futures contract has a fixed size, the minimum fluctuation will have a monetary value, which is the tick multiplied by the size of the contract; this is known as the *tick value*.

All kinds of people use futures; some of them, for example, farmers, use them to reduce risks; others look for a high rentability while assuming greater risks to achieve it. In the futures markets, the risk is transferred from the most conservative to the most aggressive traders.

Risk reduction is achieved by taking a termed position in the opposite direction of the real-time market's actual direction, trying to protect the investment against contrarian moves of the market. This is known as *coverage*. Arbitrage is achieved by buying or selling in two different markets (actual market price/futures), benefiting from the imperfections in each one of them. Speculators try to maximize their profits in the shortest time possible, thus assuming a very high risk in their investments.

In general terms, the prices of futures move in the same direction as the market of physical assets. The transaction in futures implies that both parties agree to buy and sell financial instruments or physical commodities that will be delivered in the future at a specific price. When you buy a futures contract, you agree to buy something that the seller has not yet produced. Physical goods are usually not exchanged nor delivered, unlike the transactions made between producers and consumers, but their prices allow traders to hedge their risks or speculate. The futures market is very risky and complex but also offers great liquidity.

Profits and losses are calculated on a daily basis. If the price of the commodity or financial instrument rises, the seller's account will be debited on the difference between the actual price and the value agreed on at the moment of establishment of the contract; the buyer's account will be credited with the equivalent amount. The buyer has profited because the price he or she is obligated to pay on the future is now less than the market price. These adjustments are made every day as the market moves and futures positions are settled. Thus gains and losses are deducted or credited to each party's account every day.

The futures market is a very important source of information about sentiment in the market and other indicators. It is extremely active and is the center of the global marketplace because transactions occur in the physical exchange of commodities and not only as pure financial speculation. Prices can be determined through estimation of tomorrow's levels of supply and demand based on today's transactions. Many factors intervene in the definition of prices, and a constant flow of information renders the overall operativity very transparent. On the other hand, risks are reduced because the prices of the futures were set previously, which allows planning for the quantities to be bought or sold. The result of a reduced risk is a higher stability in prices at the retail level because sellers will be less likely to push prices too far to make up for their losses.

FOREX EXCHANGE-TRADED FUNDS (ETFs)

ETFs allow small investors to perform transactions in the stock markets worldwide, for example, in countries such as China, India, Mexico, or Brazil, and profit from their strong economic potential, thanks to the present market globalization. These are funds that can be bought or sold on the market exactly as if they were stock shares. Their cost is much smaller than investing directly in the stock markets and without all the administrative obstacles that could arise if a trader were to transact directly on site.

The offer of ETFs is presently limited, and few entities commercialize them. They can be transacted through any financial intermediary such as online brokerage firms or other entities that offer investment services. This kind of instrument is very similar to an index and is the most attractive option to invest in foreign markets that are difficult access.

As with stocks, the prices of ETFs are constantly changing throughout the day based on supply and demand. The investor will be able to sell whenever he or she wants during the working hours of the specific market where the particular ETF is being quoted by giving the sell order to his or her financial intermediary.

The price paid to acquire a participation in an ETF depends on each broker. There are also other associated costs; for example, all those funds apply a management fee that ranges between 0.15 and 0.5 percent. This fee is lower than commissions taken by traditional funds, which hover around 1.2 percent. Since this product is quoted on the stock markets, there is also a brokerage commission to be taken into account.

ETFs are used to diversify a financial investment portfolio and at the same time hedge against the risks of other instruments already present in the portfolio. Currency ETFs are shares of a fund held by an ETF management firm, which buys and holds currencies to sell later on to the public. You can buy them in the same way you would buy stock shares. The value of the shares of an ETF is usually 100 times the current rate established for the currency that is being held. For example, if the current EUR/USD rate is 1.3320, the Euro ETF will be priced at \$133.20 (1.3320 × 100 = \$133.20).

Currency ETFs represent an opening to the FOREX market for investors formerly focused on stocks and an additional level for diversification of the portfolio; they also can be used effectively by shorter-term traders for quick profits. Most of these ETFs even have corresponding options available.

CONTRACTS FOR DIFFERENCE (CFDs)

CFDs are transactions performed on financial assets, stocks, and indices where the liquidation is realized by means of the difference between the buying price or ask and the selling price or bid without a real exchange and possession of the asset that is being negotiated. The prices of CFDs stem from the price of the underlying assets on the traditional stock or currency market. This means that the CFDs provide access to the same liquidity that is registered for the underlying asset.

CFDs are derivatives that allow investors to obtain the maximum return on trading capital. Unlike what happens with physical stocks or securities, the laws do not usually tax CFD contracts because the transaction doesn't involve a physical exchange of the document or underlying asset. Additionally, no administrative or custody costs are involved. CFDs are negotiated on margin. This is a more effective way to use the capital because only a small portion of it is blocked to guarantee the transaction. However, the exposure is for 100 percent of the position. This can increase the percentage of returns on capital.

The fact that all CFD transactions are always settled in cash is a much easier method, and investors get all the benefits and risks of owning a security without really owning it in its physical form.

COMMODITIES

Commodities are all those goods that constitute the essential raw materials of an economy and worldwide and represent an additional alternative of investment for various investors' profiles. Some of them are quite convenient to acquire and add to a trader's assets portfolio.

A commodity is any raw material that has gone through very little or insignificant transformation. In international financial markets, commodities are classified into the following basic groups: metals (gold, silver, copper), energy (oil, natural gas), food and supplies (sugar, cotton, cocoa, coffee), grains (corn, wheat, chickpeas, beans), and livestock (pigs, cattle).

This definition allows us to find a relevant characteristic of these types of goods. They are very homogeneous products, that is, very similar to each other. Take, for example, a well-known commodity—gold. You all know what gold is, what it is made of, and that its quality, if it is raw, should not have much variation independent of its location. For this reason, its price should not reflect any significant differences. This is so true that a single price exists for commodities at an international level. For example, if you see that today the price of gold is at $980 for 100 ounces, that would be the price at which any buyer or seller would be transacting. Some small differences may stem from transactions costs, intermediaries, and transportation, including insurance, but basically, the price would remain the same for everyone.

The first question you should ask prior to including commodities in your portfolio is if you think that a particular commodity is likely to rise in price in the future. Maybe it would be a good idea to incorporate this product into your trading portfolio because if you pay $5 today for a commodity and tomorrow its price is at $7.50, you will have made a 50 percent return. This return is a *capital gain.* However, some commodities involve heavy storage costs or even can be perishable, so it would be almost impossible to add them to an investment portfolio. If you physically buy cattle meat because you think that the price of this commodity will rise in the future, you have to take into consideration that this product will require refrigeration and special maintenance conditions so that it doesn't deteriorate. This will be very costly, and the product could perish and become totally stale if too much time has passed.

As an alternative, there are commodities that have less storage costs and are not perishable. The first ranked are precious metals, such as gold and silver. It is very common to observe these kinds of commodities in the favorite investment portfolios of either big or small investors. When the worldwide economy is expanding, that is, when it is expected that the real wealth will tend to increase on average in the whole world economy, this could be a good time to acquire commodities and hold them in a portfolio. The more industrialized countries are the biggest buyers of raw materials or commodities, which they use as supplies for the fabrication of products with a greater added value. If the world is getting richer, it is because it tends to demand a greater amount of elaborated products, and consequently, there will be a greater demand for supplies for the elaboration of those products. This logically causes the prices of commodities to rise, and if you had some of them in your trading portfolio, you would realize a capital gain.

Inversely, when the worldwide economy tends to slow down, the demand for commodities decreases because the forecast is that there will be a lesser demand for elaborated products. This would have as a consequence a decrease in the prices of those raw materials. When this happens, it is a good moment to sell.

The main commodities exchanges include the Chicago Board of Trade, the Kansas City Board of Trade, the New York Mercantile Exchange, the London Metal Exchange, and other foreign commodity exchanges.

INDICES (SECURITIES)

An *index* is an abstract number that represents the joint movement of several financial assets of which it is composed: stocks, bonds, currencies, commodities, and others. An index is a statistical measure of change. Applied to the financial markets, it would represent an imaginary portfolio of securities relative to a particular market or a portion of it.

Each one of the assets has a relative weight inside the index that is measured based on previously set parameters from before the index was created. At the moment when there is a change in the price of the asset, the index also will move, and its variation will be greater or lesser depending on the relative weight of the asset that has changed.

The most well-known indices that you normally follow in the world-wide market are the New York Stock Exchange (NYSE), the National Association of Securities Dealers Automated Quotations(NASDAQ), the Dow Jones, the Standard and Poor's 500, the Nikkei in Japan, the Financial Times 100 (FTSE) in great Britain, the CAC 40 in France, and the Dax in Germany, as well as assets such as bonds in the case of JP Morgan's Emerging Markets Bond Index EMBI or the Commodity Research Bureau CRB for commodities. The Standard & Poor's 500 Index is one of the world's best-known indices and is the most commonly used point of reference for the stock market, along with the Dow Jones.

You have already seen that the Dow Jones shows the joint evolution of 30 of the most representative companies on the market. The weight is usually determined by the volume of transactions, and the company that has performed with a higher volume during the last 6 months will have a greater influence on the index.

If a stock from one company represents a 10 percent weight of the index and another represents 20 percent, it is obvious that if each has experienced in a given month a 1 percent variation, this will not influence the index in the same proportion. This also explains why the index could be rising in a given period while several of the companies that compose it could see a decline in the value of their stocks.

An index is also used as a comparative measure for investments. For example, if an investor buys a particular stock, he or she can compare its performance with the index to see if it is going over or under the average.

One of the characteristics of the indices is that because they are a series of grouped assets, they represent an important diversification, and thus the risks are lowered. Usually an index reflects less volatility than the individual assets that compose it. You couldn't technically invest in an index because it represents the whole sum of the companies included, but indices traded through mutual funds and exchange-traded funds (EFTs) that are based on indexes allow people to invest in securities that represent ample market segments or even the complete market.

15

MY FAVORITE WAYS
TO TRADE

BREAKOUTS

RANGE BREAKOUT

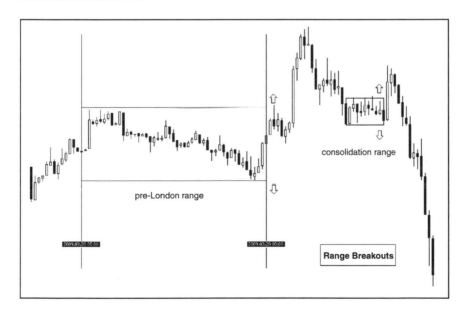

The range breakout setup is quite easy to spot. The markets have been trading in a sideways or consolidation pattern and usually in a tight range. I usually check the setup in a short time frame, such as the 5-minute chart, and if I see one in a higher time frame, such as, for example, the 1-hour chart, it most often will have an inside bar being formed.

There are two times during the trading day that I use to plan a range breakout: the Asian session or pre-Europe/pre-London range and the pre-U.S. session range. In the first case, I will place a horizontal line at the high of the range and another at the low of the range that has formed between 03:00 Greenwich Mean Time (GMT) and 07:00 GMT (the times on the chart above are GMT +2; this will depend on your own broker's server time). A few minutes before the time span ends, I place a straddle: two pending stop orders, a buy stop 5 pips plus spread above the high of the range and a sell stop at the low of the range. The stop loss of each position is placed at the entry price of the opposite position; on EUR/USD pairs, those ranges are usually 30 or 40 points on average. I place the stop loss at breakeven plus 1 point as soon as the price has gone 20 pips in my direction and delete the pending order that was not triggered. I keep on trailing the stops using parabolic stop and reverse (SAR) as a reference.

In the second case, the range I use is the time span between 5 a.m. Eastern Time (ET) and 8 a.m. ET, placing the straddle orders a few minutes before the U.S. market open. This strategy can be used any time a tight consolidation range is being formed.

A variation of this strategy is splitting the position into three parts (this would be three pending stop buy orders and three pending stop sell orders), taking profit on one of the orders as soon as 20 points have been reached and setting the stop loss to breakeven plus 1 point on the remaining two. Then I take profits on the second position when it reaches 40 points, leaving the third one with the above-mentioned trailing stops until it is finally stopped out.

Symmetric, ascending, and descending triangles also can be used for this strategy because they are also consolidation periods. In the case of an ascending or descending triangle, the breakout expectation usually will be in the previous direction of the trend.

Ascending and descending triangles are formed of both a diagonal support or resistance and a horizontal support or resistance. The level to watch for a directional breakout is the horizontal line. The ascending or descending triangle is a continuation pattern that usually will resume its direction after the consolidation pause.

It is also important to check other levels that are present, such as pivots and Fibonacci retracements, especially when deciding about the exact entry price. It is preferable to set the entry a few points above or below such levels to prevent possible bounces off a pivot line. As a rule, I would recommend trading only short positions if price is trading below the central pivot and only long positions if price is trading above the central pivot. Traders always should trade with the trend and never fight a trend.

A successful breakout also will depend on volumes. The higher the volume, the more significance the breakout will have. Volume depends on liquidity, and liquidity depends on the day and the markets that are open; it is also important to know when holidays occur and some of the markets are closed because when there are few participants, markets are usually choppy, lack a definite direction, and there is very little liquidity. The currency pairs that are most active also will depend on which markets are currently open.

The most active sessions are those where the biggest markets are active: London, the United States, and Japan. Usually the bigger liquidity shows in early hours of the session and decreases along the rest of the trading day. If you are trading the yen, the best session to employ is when Japanese markets open (at 7 p.m. ET). The euro and pound will be most active later on, when the Frankfurt and London markets start their activities. The London session is the most active for all the currencies involved in the FOREX market because it regroups the bigger volumes and liquidity. It is the most important FOREX market, followed by the United States and Japan, with 10 percent of the overall trading volume.

TREND BREAKOUT

I employ this strategy whenever there is a clear break of a consolidated trendline. I watch the price action, and as soon as the trendline has been broken, I wait for the broken level to be retested with a definite bounce back. When it is clear that the former support has become a resistance, I then open a position. In the figure above, that would be a short position in the next candle that follows the bounce from the retest. I place the stop loss a few points above the broken line. In both examples shown, you can see that the first one will yield fewer pips than the second one, but both trades end in positive. Since they are countertrend trades, especially the first one, which breaks the smaller trendline but is still contained in the greater lower trendline, stops should be very tight and placed at breakeven plus 1 point as soon as possible; in the first case, I exited the position when price action bounced from the lower trendline.

SUPPORT/RESISTANCE BREAKOUT

Support/Resistance Breakout

This strategy is similar to the range breakout but at a higher level and on higher time frames. Looking at daily and weekly time frames, I identify strong areas of support and resistance and set a pending order, buy and sell stop, a few points above and below the resistance and support levels.

If the range is wide, instead of a stop loss, I place a contrarian stop order that will be triggered if, instead of breaking out, the price action bounces back inside the range. The contrarian stop order is set after the first breakout order has been triggered, or if you have access on your platform to "If done" orders, it can be programmed to be placed at the moment the first order is effectively in the market.

PROGRESSIVE TIME-FRAME BREAKOUT

In the first figure, you can appreciate the weekly trendline, and a steeper daily trendline that has formed. After such a strong up move, prices most probably will turn back for a correction.

The parameters to use are the same as for a trend breakout: waiting for the price action to effectively break, retest, and bounce from the trendline with support or resistance changed into its opposite.

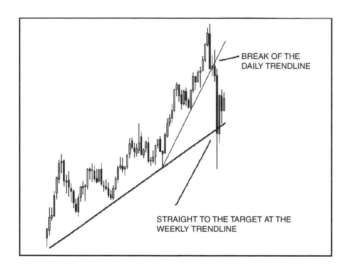

The difference here is that the higher-time-frame trendline will give you the possible target at which you can take profits. In the present example, I used weekly and daily charts, but this strategy can be implemented in any sequence of time frames: daily and 4 hours, 4 hours and 1 hour, 1 hour and 30 minutes, and even much smaller charts, always taking the higher time frame of both and its trendline as reference for the profit target.

CHANNELING

Using price channels as a reference for swing trading is similar to trading inside a range bound or sideways price action: You sell when prices are at the high of the range and buy when prices are at the low of the range. The only difference will be that, unlike the sideways market where the high and low levels are mostly the same throughout the whole range, you will have higher highs and lows in an uptrend and lower highs and lows in a downtrend.

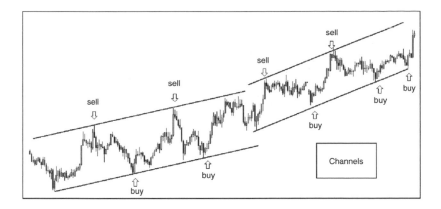

Depending on the time frame and style of trading, including risk management, that you decide to use, you can trade both sides of the swing or only the directional side, that is, buying longs, or "buying on dips," in an uptrend and selling shorts, or "selling rallies," in a down trend. If you trade both sides, stop losses should be much tighter on countertrend positions.

ANDREW'S PITCHFORK

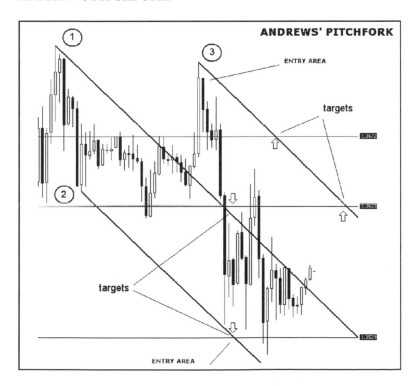

Andrew's pitchfork is a very useful tool that I employ to draw equidistant channels with a median line. It is constructed as follows: The first point is a previous high or low on the chart. This point is called the *pivot.* I then look for both a high and a low to the right of this first pivot point (points 2 and 3 on the chart above). The pitchfork indicator exists on almost all charting software, but you also can build it up by drawing parallel lines from all three points mentioned, in which the center or median line will be represented by the first pivot point. The other two lines serve as support and resistance of the price action.

This channel indicator allows you to predict the target levels of a swing entry inside the channel. When price touches and bounces from either support or resistance, the median line is the most probable target, and the opposite trendline would be the second probable target.

FIBONACCI CHANNELS

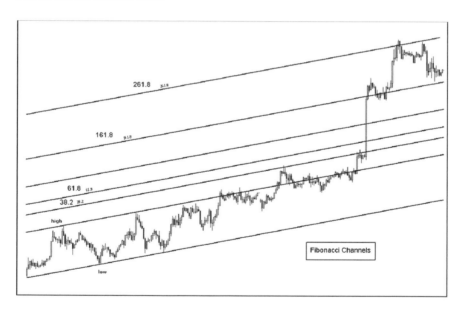

Fibonacci channels can be used alone or in conjunction with horizontal Fibonacci retracement and extension levels to identify probable areas that price can reach and thus set up the sequential targets for your trades or wait for the price action to reach one of those levels and fade the move by trading the bounce back.

HEDGING

TRUE HEDGING

A *hedge* is an attempt to profit from the arbitrage of two or more correlated currency pairs. Hedging has been erroneously related to opening a long and short position on the same currency pair, but this leads nowhere because it would end up as a neutral or zero-value position, and in addition, you would lose the price of the respective spreads on top.

A true hedge is realized by using different currency pairs, usually in the direction where the swap or overnight interest rate is positive for all or almost all the currency pairs involved. The total amount earned on overnight also will depend on each broker's swap rates, but they are mostly in the same range for a vast majority of firms.

Although negative correlation implies that when one pair is going up, the other one is going down—thus if you are long on both, one of them will end up as a losing position—there is always an arbitrage and difference in the number of points that the price has increased in the profitable position in relation to the points lost in the losing position.

PAIRS CORRELATIONS

A perfect hedge would imply a 100 percent inverse correlation between opposite pairs involved. However, this is not possible, although there are complementary currency pairs, such as EUR/USD and USD/CHF, that have a very high correlation index, nearing 96 percent most of the time.

BASKET OF CURRENCIES

This is a hedge that attempts to obtain a positive carry interest in the overall positions, which are closed at a certain point when the total balance of points is positive. You can use as many currency pairs as you want, but the hedge usually performs much better with only the four majors: EUR/USD, GBP/USD, USD/CHF, and USD/JPY.

Open a long position on all four currency pairs in the following proportion (stated here in lots):

  1 lot EUR/USD
  1 lot GBP/USD
  1.2 lots USD/CHF
  0.9 lot USD/JPY

The proportion is relative to the difference in the pip values of the currency pairs: $1 for EUR/USD and GBP/USD, $0.85 approximately for USD/CHF, and $1.08 approximately for USD/JPY (the pip value for pairs with USD as the quote currency do not vary, whereas there is a slight difference when USD is the base currency).

This is a medium- to long-term strategy. At a certain point, the overall basket of currencies will be showing a positive increase in equity, in addition to the swap interest accumulated throughout several days. All positions are closed at this time, and a new hedge is set up using the same parameters.

BASIC OSCILLATOR-BASED STRATEGY

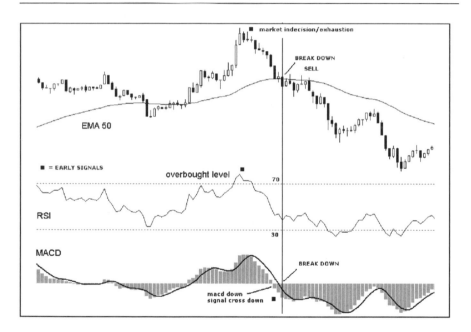

For this system, I use a break of the 50-period exponential moving average (50 EMA) with early signal and confirmation given from relative strength index (RSI) and moving average convergence-divergence (MACD) indicators. I plot a 50-period EMA on the chart, plus an RSI indicator with standard settings (RSI 14) and a MACD indicator also with standard settings (12, 26, and 9).

As you can see in the chart above, several early signals will alert you to the possible change in direction: You first have the RSI crossing above the overbought level, indicating that the current direction might be coming to an end; then you have a few candles indicating market indecision or exhaustion and a descent on the slope of the MACD. The price crosses down through the 50 EMA, and both the MACD and the signal MACD have crossed the zero line. I enter a short position on the next candle following the one that has closed below the 50 EMA.

All the elements have to be in alignment and coincide in the predicted direction to allow the decision on the entry to be made. If any of those elements is not present, I do not take the trade; rather, I wait for a much clearer opportunity.

This strategy is quite simple and can be used in any time frame. I personally use it intraday but on longer time frames, such as the 4-hour chart.

BASIC MOVING-AVERAGE CROSSES

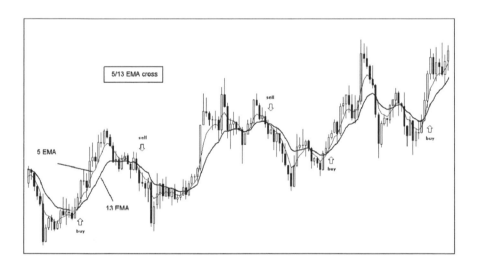

The 5/13 EMA cross is a very simple strategy that can be used for scalping in smaller time frames, such as 1 or 5 minutes. I just plot a 5-period and a 13-period EMA on a chart and wait for a cross of both to happen. When the 5 EMA crosses upward above the 13 EMA, I open a long position at the open of the next candle; when the 5 EMA crosses downward below the 13 EMA, I open a short position at the open of the next candle. This is a very short-term strategy that has to be tightly monitored because changes on those small time frames occur very fast.

TRADING GAPS

Market GAP after the week-end

A *gap* is a measurable difference in prices between the close of the preceding trading day and the open of the current day. Small gaps of a few points can occur throughout the week, but significant gaps usually are seen on Monday open after the weekend pause. As you can see in the figure picture, the price closed at 1.2861 and opened at 1.2792, 69 points lower, on the next trading session.

About 80 percent of gaps get filled during the day or at most during the trading week. This can give you a quite predictable pattern to place a trade in the opposite direction of the gap opening: If prices gap down, you buy; if prices gap up, you sell. Of course, it is not as simple as seeing the gap and jumping directly into a position. All the usual other factors have to be taken in consideration: pivots, patterns, and possible reversal signals. The first directional impulse of the gap tends to continue for a while, and sometimes prices can move a fair number of pips before turning back to fill the gap. I personally wait for prices to settle down and start a consolidation pattern or a clear reversal signal in candlesticks; then I open the corresponding position. In the case shown in the figure above, you can see a series of reversal candles and the start of a bullish impulse, which gives me the signal that the market can indeed start moving back to fill the gap. Only then will I open a long position. The stop loss would be set a few points below the lowest low of the recent down move, preferably also below a strong pivot line or established support.

DAILY HIGH-LOW

This is a quite simple and almost "set and forget" type of medium- to long-term trading strategy. It also uses a basket of currencies, which can range from four to six optimally.

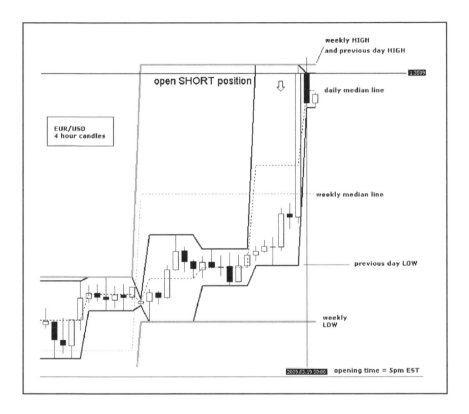

I personally use six of the majors—EUR/USD, GBP/USD, USD/JPY, USD/CHF, EUR/JPY, and AUD/USD—but you can choose any combination of pairs that suit you and more especially that have tested well in preliminary assessment conditions. The risk per pair shouldn't be higher than 2 percent of your equity balance for a total risk of between 8 percent of your account for four pairs and 12 percent for six pairs.

You will only need a few minutes daily before and during the New York close (5 p.m. ET or GMT 22:00) to monitor and adjust your trades. Here is a more detailed description of the overall steps: Open positions daily at 5 p.m. ET (just after the New York close). Use the weekly high/low and the daily high/low as references for the initial stop loss. Some pairs will require

wider stops, but as an average, you could consider around 100 pips for a
moderate stop. This means that your position size has to be defined accordingly. I personally use a fixed-percentage amount of the balance that represents a maximum risk of 2 percent per each pair based on a 100-pip stop
loss, which lowers the risk on pairs that will need much smaller stop levels.

Preparation of the trade and definition of the entry price: Draw a line
at the low and the high of the previous week and at the low and high of the
trading day that has just closed. Calculate the median line by adding both
high and low and dividing by 2. If the price is below the weekly *and* daily
median lines, be on the lookout for a long position; if the price is above
weekly and daily median lines, check if overall conditions can indicate a
short position. The entry will be mostly discretionary, but you usually can
assume that after a pronounced rise or decline there will be more chances
for a reversal or at least a good correction, so when prices are near the lows,
you should look for long opportunities, and the inverse applies when they
are nearing the highs: You would try to assess whether a short position has
a good possibility of success.

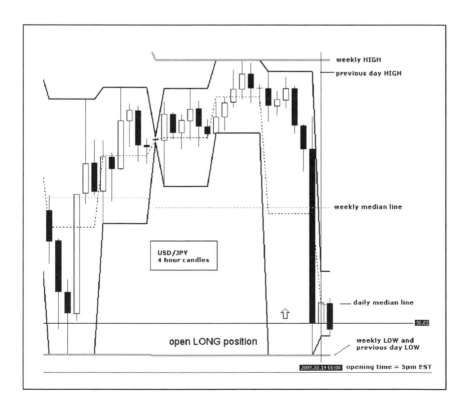

However, this is not a fixed, blind rule: You should check the overall trend from weekly to H4 down, and if there is a strong trend in development, you should stick with the overall trend. I place the market orders as soon as the new trading day begins, based in my trading plan and because this should be an ideal trading system for traders who do not have much time to sit and monitor the charts. However, depending on the positions of the prices with regard to the weekly and daily lows and highs and eventuality of pullbacks or corrections inside a given trend, a more precisely priced limit order could be set, allowing stops to be much tighter. In general, though, an average 100 pips distance is mostly what you will encounter.

Stop-loss price: the high of the previous day plus 10 pips for a short position; the low of the previous day minus 10 pips for a long position. Should the weekly high or low be very near the daily extremes, stops would have to be set at plus or minus 10 pips from those prices.

The trades usually can last for a week or more if a good trend is going on. This strategy, however, is not suited to sideways markets. It is definitely a trend-following system. The risk-reward ratio, if the system is followed to the letter with discipline and letting the market close your positions by itself instead of exiting earlier than needed, is higher than 1:3 or even than 1:4. The percentage of winning positions might be lower than 50 percent, though, but the winners could ride up to 600 or 700 points; meanwhile, the losing positions will not be more than 100 or 120 pips each.

Exit prices and daily adjustments: Every day at the same exact time, you check your positions and adjust the stop losses to the preceding daily high or low accordingly. If any of the pairs has been stopped out, reentry on that pair is done only and exclusively at 5 p.m. ET based on the preceding entry criteria. You keep on adjusting the stops every day as the market keeps moving in your direction, and the positions will be closed *only and exclusively* when they are finally stopped out by the market.

An addition to this system would be to include a new position in the same direction as the trend under the same rules as soon as the stop of the previous one is in the positive zone so that you can maintain the same risk-reward ratio and benefit from one or more free trades as the trend evolves. This would be considered position trading longer term. For example, when your previous position for the USD/JPY pair has its stops set at +20 at the moment of the daily adjustment, and only after determining the good probability of continuation of the current trend, you open a new position of USD/JPY, setting the corresponding stop loss at a 10-pip distance from the preceding day's high or low.

The figures above present an example with short and long entry levels on EUR/USD and USD/JPY. This is a quite simple and stress-free strategy that can yield handsome profits over time if you employ patience and discipline.

CONCLUSION

An Endless Quest for the Holy Grail

I have been teaching and trading the FOREX market for nine years. It has really been available to retail traders such as ourselves for only about 11 years. In addition, I have been a stock broker for more than 16 years. The one thing I always like to point out when I am talking to my many students is that there is no "Holy Grail" of trading. I often run into traders who think that they can buy FOREX trading software and use it like an ATM machine—just put in a pin number, and out pops the cash. It just doesn't work that way.

This is a real market. It is the largest financial market in the world, and you have to treat it as such. You can trade this market part time, or you can do it every day. In fact, you can make it your business—the business of trading.

The real "Holy Grail," if any, is inside—your brain, in conjunction with your psychological awareness and control and the cumulative experience and knowledge you have acquired and the alignment of your goals and your actions in harmony and perfection through a good amount of practice, then again practice, and then again more practice until knowledge transforms into intuitive wisdom.

Trading can be learned, of course, but the experience can't be transmitted. It has to be constructed by every individual through a personal effort of understanding and hard work. It will not happen overnight. Trading needs a similar dedication as any precision-driven career. Theory is good, but practice makes perfect and integrates all the knowledge you have acquired.

Another thing that is important to understand is that you will never, ever stop learning. Markets are changing every day, and the FOREX is a living organism that evolves in the same way as all its traders. Always remember that although it seems to be an anonymous entity, at the end of the day, the market is merely made up of investors, large and small, from all corners of the world, each with his or her own emotions, psychology, and predictable behaviors and reactions.

As I asked earlier, how long does a doctor, lawyer, engineer, or any other regulated professional have to go to school to learn his or her trade? Some of these individuals literally could be in school for 10 years just learning to be good at what they do, and that doesn't include any practical experience. Wow! That's a long time; to be a FOREX trader is no different. Okay, you don't have to go to school for 10 years, but you do have to put in your "seat time" on the computer.

You will only get out of this what you put into it. You will definitely have to invest in your education; you will have to seek out knowledge and someone who can help you learn to trade this market. I hope that after reading this book, you will easily decide that I am the person from whom you want to learn more.

You can go to *www.JamesDicks.com* to join my FOREX network for free, and you can access the many chat rooms and forums to learn from my other traders just like you, people who want to trade this amazing market and learn how to do it successfully.

The eagerness to learn at least one new thing every day is paramount. I keep having "Ah-ha" moments after all these years, and I hope they won't stop happening. But these consciousness-expanding experiences can't be transmitted either. Some of them will be considered common sense and obvious by many, whereas others will fail to grasp the true meaning. Finally, a few will have their own "Ah-ha" awareness through understanding of a particular situation.

Always remember that the essence of the market is the price, always the price, and only the price. Price action is the core of it all, and everything else revolves around it. The path is in the price. The market is always showing you where it will or will not go. You have to stop for a while and start listening to what the market is telling you. Most often the obvious things are the ones that are overlooked. The easiest path seems unbelievable, so we tend to complicate everything. Go back to the basics. Go back to the simple things.

In the FOREX and in life as well, this will be very useful to you. Keep it simple and straight (KISS)!

Learn to move on after losses. Don't dwell on missed trades or missed pips after you decide to close. There will be hundreds of opportunities in the future. Follow your plan, and follow your system. Practice every day, and experience will come with time, patience, and discipline. Don't look outside for what's already inside. Leave your ego behind; be humble and smart. You can't decide where the market will go, so learn to see where it wants to lead you, not the other way around. Exit bad trades, and hold onto good trades. Set yourself a goal, and stop trading when you have reached it. Be realistic about your annual percentage growth. Do not force yourself into overproduction. Don't open the doors to greed. Each FOREX trade is a new one with new conditions and perspectives. Do not dwell in the past. Choose the currency pairs that have proven to be profitable. Leave behind those you can't understand.

Finally, take a deep look inside yourself: There it is indeed—your own and personal "Holy Grail." The rest is history yet to be written, assuredly the history of your own path to the greatest of successes!

Keep checking *www.JamesDicks.com* for important FOREX information. We have FOREX conferences, and I personally hope to meet you soon.

Happy investing!

38 STEPS TO BECOMING A TRADER

BY ANONYMOUS TRADER

[As published in *Commodity Futures Trading Club News* and in Traders Organization's "Real Success Day Trading Course"]

1. We accumulate information—buying books, going to seminars, and researching.
2. We begin to trade with our "new" knowledge.
3. We consistently "donate" and then realize that we may need more knowledge or information.
4. We accumulate more information.
5. We switch the commodities we are currently following.
6. We go back into the market and trade with our "updated" knowledge.
7. We get "beat up" again and begin to lose some of our confidence. Fear starts setting in.
8. We start to listen to "outside news" and to other traders.
9. We go back into the market and continue to "donate."
10. We switch commodities again.
11. We search for more information.
12. We go back into the market and start to see a little progress.

13. We get "overconfident," and the market humbles us.
14. We start to understand that trading successfully is going to take more time and more knowledge than we anticipated.
    Most people will give up at this point, as they realize work is involved.
15. We get serious and start concentrating on learning a "real" methodology.
16. We trade our methodology with some success but realize that something is missing.
17. We begin to understand the need for having rules to apply our methodology.
18. We take a sabbatical from trading to develop and research our trading rules.
19. We start trading again, this time with rules, and find some success, but overall, we still hesitate when we execute.
20. We add, subtract, and modify rules as we see a need to be more proficient with our rules.
21. We feel we are very close to crossing that threshold of successful trading.
22. We start to take responsibility for our trading results as we understand that our success is in us, not the methodology.
23. We continue to trade and become more proficient with our methodology and our rules.
24. As we trade, we still have a tendency to violate our rules, and our results are still erratic.
25. We know we are close.
26. We go back and research our rules.
27. We build the confidence in our rules and go back into the market and trade.
28. Our trading results are getting better, but we are still hesitating in executing our rules.
29. We now see the importance of following our rules as we see the results of our trades when we don't follow the rules.
30. We begin to see that our lack of success is within us (a lack of discipline in following the rules because of some kind of fear), and we begin to work on knowing ourselves better.
31. We continue to trade, and the market teaches us more and more about ourselves.
32. We master our methodology and our trading rules.

33. We begin to consistently make money.

34. We get a little overconfident, and the market humbles us.

35. We continue to learn our lessons.

36. We stop thinking and allow our rules to trade for us (trading becomes boring but successful), and our trading account continues to grow as we increase our contract size.

37. We are making more money than we ever dreamed possible.

38. We go on with our lives and accomplish many of the goals we had always dreamed of.

DOW JONES INDUSTRIAL AVERAGE (DJIA)

COMPANIES INCLUDED IN THE DJIA

Company	Symbol
3M	MMM
Alcoa	AA
American Express	AXP
AT&T	T
Bank of America	BAC
Boeing	BA
Caterpillar	CAT
Chevron Corporation	CVX
Cisco Systems	CSCO
Coca-Cola	KO
DuPont	DD
ExxonMobil	XOM
General Electric	GE
Hewlett-Packard	HPQ
Home Depot	HD
Intel	INTC
IBM	IBM
Johnson & Johnson	JNJ
JPMorgan Chase	JPM
Kraft Foods	KFT
McDonald's	MCD
Merck	MRK
Microsoft	MSFT
Pfizer	PFE
Procter & Gamble	PG
Travelers	TRV
United Technologies Corporation	UTX
Verizon Communications	VZ
Walmart	WMT
Walt Disney	DIS

CANDLESTICK PATTERNS

BULLISH REVERSAL PATTERNS
High Reliability

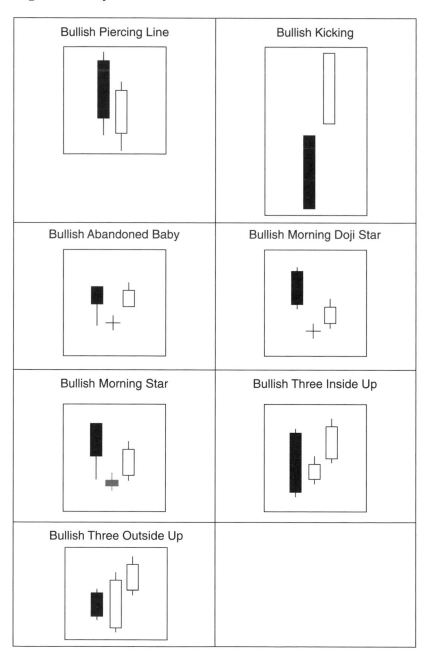

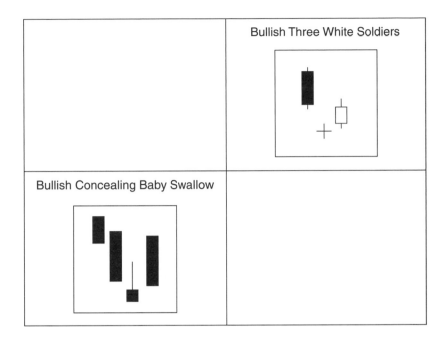

Medium Reliability

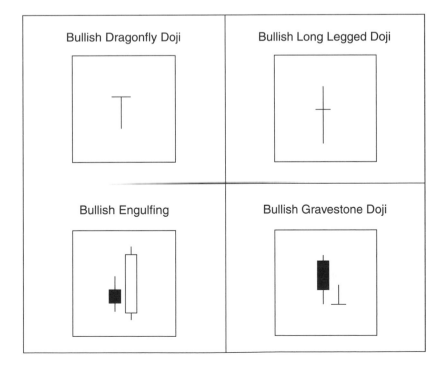

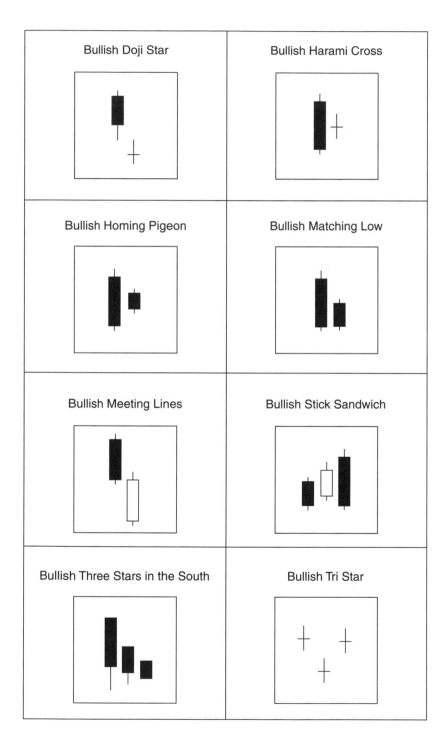

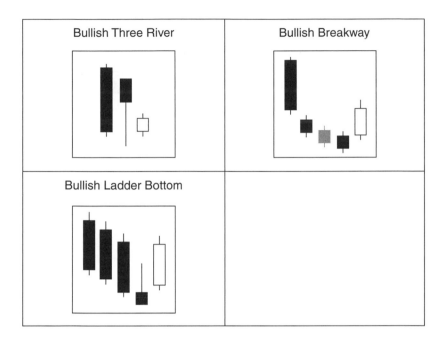

Low Reliability

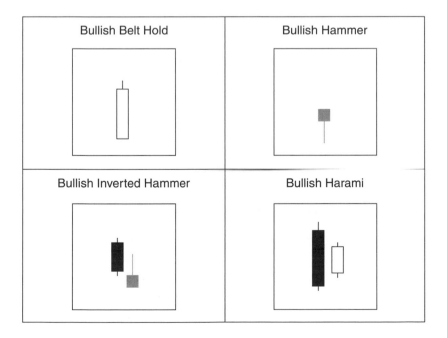

BULLISH CONTINUATION PATTERNS
High Reliability

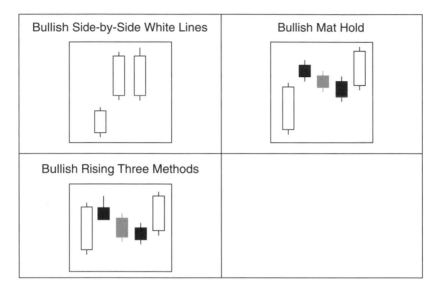

Medium Reliability

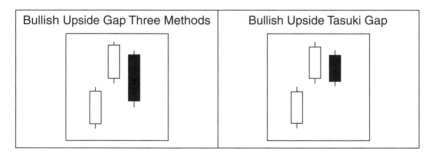

Low Reliability

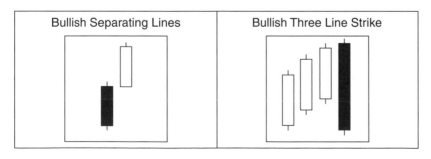

BULLISH REVERSAL/CONTINUATION PATTERNS
Low Reliability

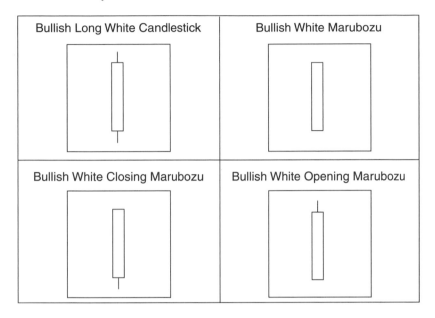

| Bullish Long White Candlestick | Bullish White Marubozu |
| Bullish White Closing Marubozu | Bullish White Opening Marubozu |

BEARISH REVERSAL PATTERNS
High Reliability

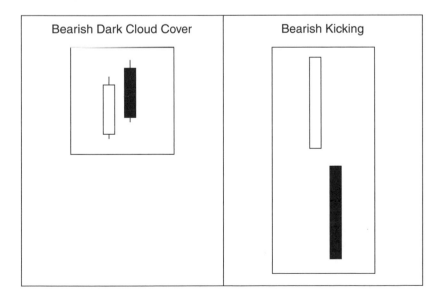

| Bearish Dark Cloud Cover | Bearish Kicking |

Bearish Abandoned Baby

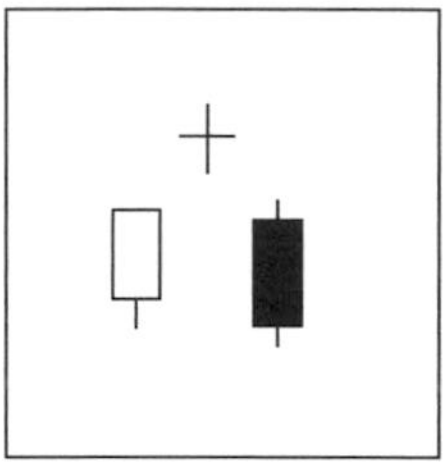

Bearish Evening Star

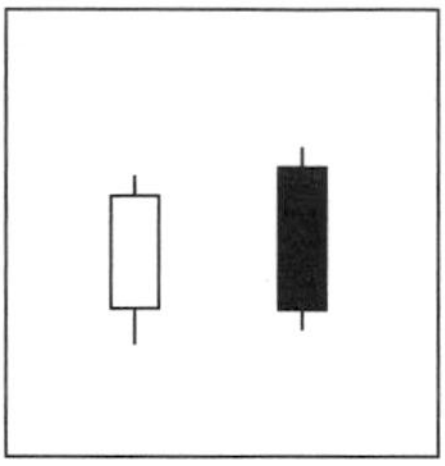

Bearish Evening Doji Star

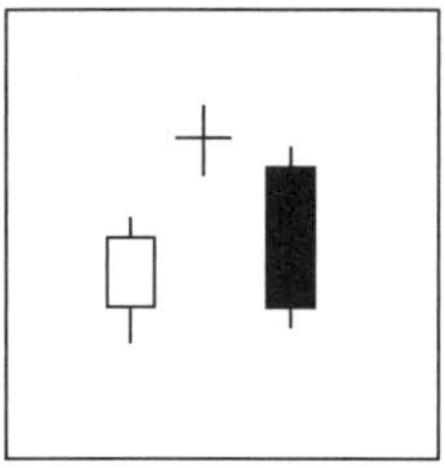

Bearish Three Black Crows

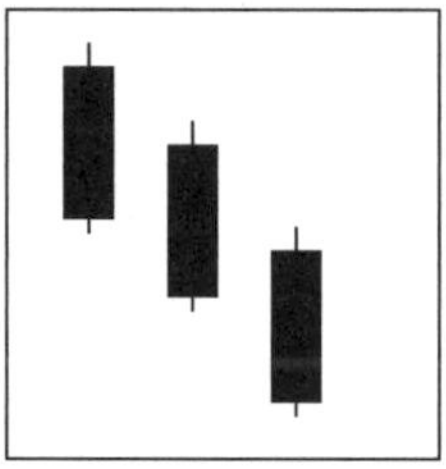

Bearish Three Inside Down

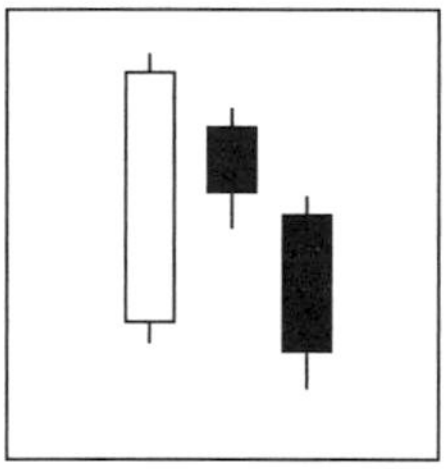

Bearish Three Outside Down

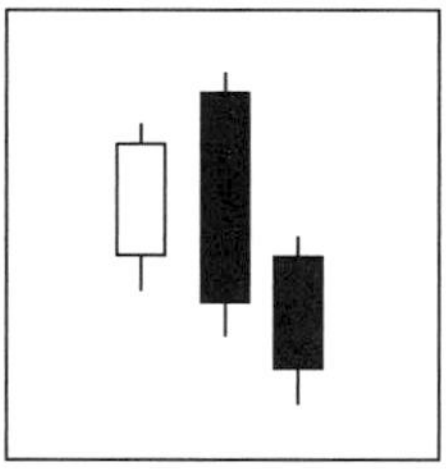

Bearish Upside Gap Two Crows

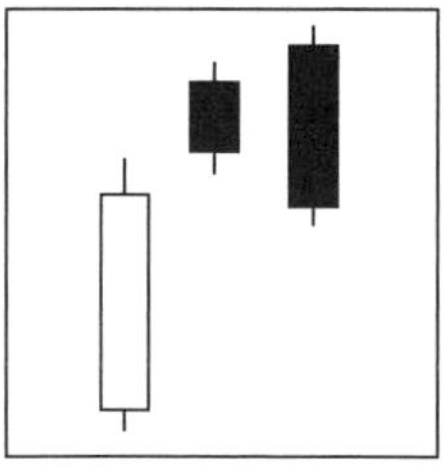

Medium Reliability

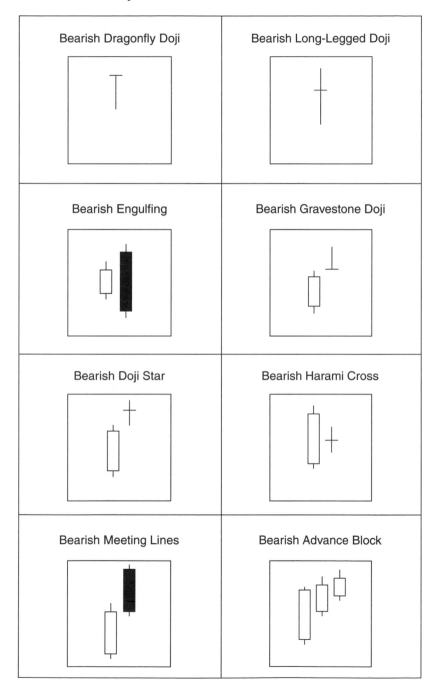

Bearish Dragonfly Doji	Bearish Long-Legged Doji
Bearish Engulfing	Bearish Gravestone Doji
Bearish Doji Star	Bearish Harami Cross
Bearish Meeting Lines	Bearish Advance Block

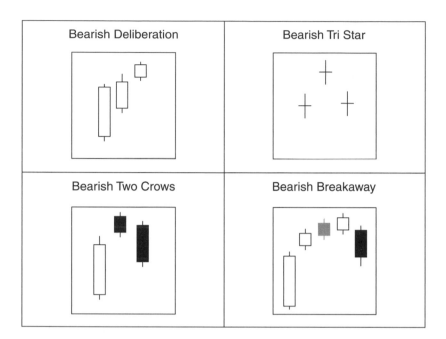

Low Reliability

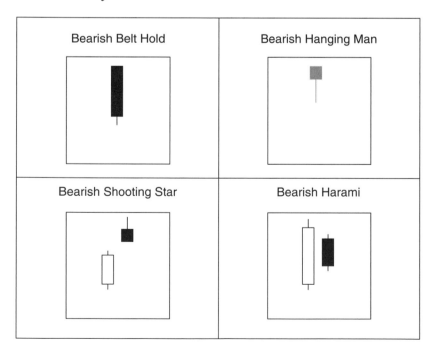

BEARISH CONTINUATION PATTERNS
High Reliability

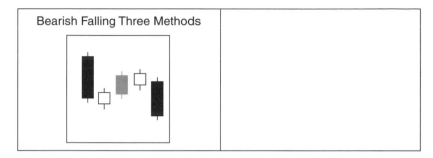

Medium Reliability

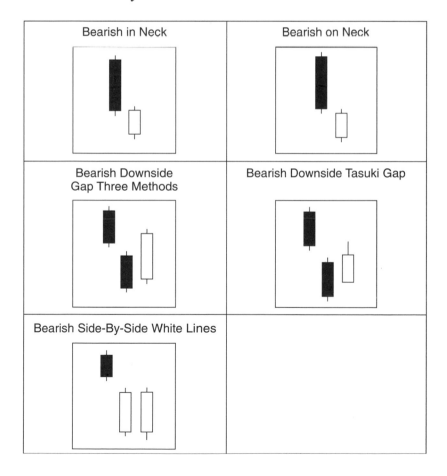

Low Reliability

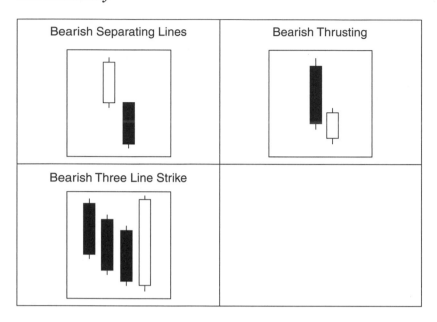

BEARISH REVERSAL/CONTINUATION PATTERNS
Low Reliability

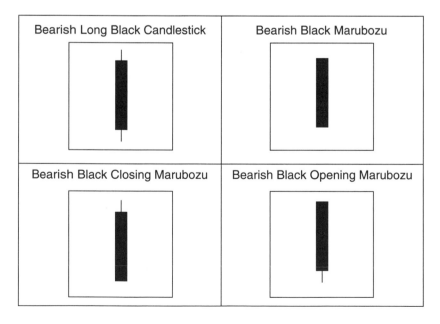

NEUTRAL REVERSAL PATTERNS
Medium Reliability

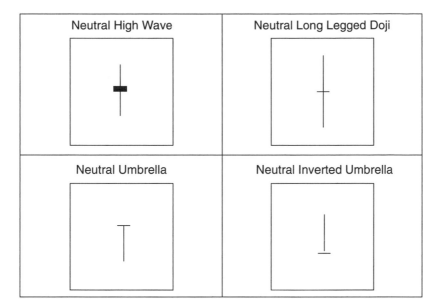

| Neutral High Wave | Neutral Long Legged Doji |
| Neutral Umbrella | Neutral Inverted Umbrella |

NEUTRAL REVERSAL/CONTINUATION PATTERNS
Low Reliability

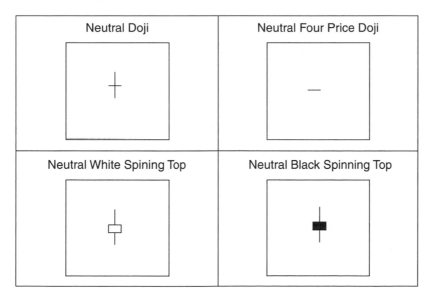

| Neutral Doji | Neutral Four Price Doji |
| Neutral White Spining Top | Neutral Black Spinning Top |

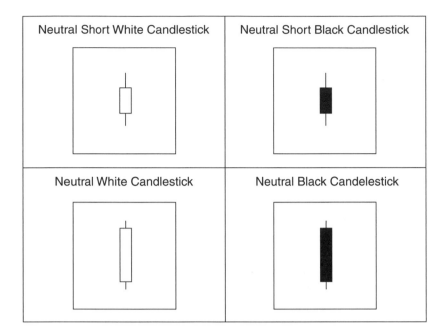

| Neutral Short White Candlestick | Neutral Short Black Candlestick |
| Neutral White Candlestick | Neutral Black Candelestick |

GLOSSARY

Ask (ask price, ask rate)   The price at which a currency pair or security is offered for sale; the quoted price at which an investor can buy a currency pair. This is also known as the *offer, ask price,* and *ask rate.*

Appreciation

An increase in value of an asset.

Arbitrage   Profiting from differences in the price of a single currency pair that is traded on more than one market.

Asset   An item having commercial or exchange value.

Bank rate   The percentage rate at which the central bank of a country lends money to the country's commercial banks.

Base currency   In FOREX trading, currencies are quoted in terms of a currency pair. The first currency in the pair is the base currency. The base currency is the currency against which exchange rates generally are quoted in a given country. Examples: In USD/JPY, the U.S. dollar is the base currency; in EUR/USD, the euro is the base currency.

Bear market   An extended period of general price decline in an individual security, an asset, or a market.

Bid   The price at which an investor can place an order to buy a currency pair; the quoted price where an investor can sell a currency pair. This is also known as the *bid price* and *bid rate.*

Bid/ask spread   The point difference between the bid and offer (ask) price.

Bretton Woods The site of a conference that in 1944 led to the establishment of the postwar foreign exchange system that remained intact until the early 1970s. The conference resulted in formation of the International Monetary Fund. The system fixed currencies in a fixed exchange-rate system with 1 percent fluctuations of the currency to gold or the dollar.

Broker An agent who executes orders to buy and sell currencies and related instruments either for a commission or on a spread. Brokers are agents working on commission and not principals or agents acting on their own account. In the FOREX market, brokers tend to act as intermediaries between banks, bringing buyers and sellers together for a commission paid by the initiator or by both parties. There are four or five major global brokers operating through subsidiaries, affiliates, and partners in many countries.

Bull market A market that is on a consistent upward trend.

Buy limit order An order to execute a transaction at a specified price (the limit) or lower.

Broker One of the market participants that acts as an intermediary between retail traders and larger commercial institutions.

Buy on margin The process of buying a currency pair where a client pays cash for part of the overall value of the position. The word *margin* refers to the portion the investor puts up rather than the portion that is borrowed.

Cable FOREX traders' slang word that describes the British pound/U.S. dollar exchange rate (GBP/USD).

Candlestick chart A chart that displays the daily trading price range (open, high, low, and close). A form of Japanese charting that has become popular in the West. A narrow line (shadow) shows the day's price range. A wider body marks the area between the open and the close. If the close is above the open, the body is white (not filled); if the close is below the open, the body is black (filled).

Carry (interest-rate carry) The income or cost associated with keeping a foreign exchange position overnight. This is derived when the currency pairs in the position have different interest rates for the same period of time.

Carry trade In the FOREX, holding a position with a positive overnight interest return in hope of gaining profits without closing the position just for the central bank's interest-rate difference.

Central bank A bank, administered by a national government, that regulates the behavior of financial institutions within its borders and carries out monetary policy.

CFD   A contract for difference, a special trading instrument that allows financial speculation on stocks, commodities, and other instruments without actually buying.

Chartist   A person who attempts to predict prices by analyzing past price movements as recorded on a chart.

Closing a position   The process of selling or buying a foreign exchange position resulting in the liquidation (squaring up) of the position.

Closing market rate   The rate at which a position can be closed based on the market price at end of the day.

Commission   The fee that a broker may charge clients for dealing on their behalf.

Confirmation   Written acknowledgment of a trade, listing important details such as the date, the size of the transaction, the price, the commission, and the amount of money involved.

Correspondent bank   The foreign bank's representative who regularly performs services for a bank that has no branch in the relevant center, for example, to facilitate the transfer of funds. In the United States, this often occurs domestically owing to interstate banking restrictions.

Counterpart   A participant in a financial transaction.

Cover   (1) To take out a forward foreign exchange contract. (2) To close out a short position by buying currency or securities that have been sold.

CPI   Consumer price index, which is the statistical measure of inflation based on changes in prices of a specified set of goods.

Cross-rate   The exchange rate between two currencies where neither of the currencies is USD.

Currency   Money issued by a government. Coins and paper money. It is a form of money used as a unit of exchange within a country.

Currency pair   The two currencies in a foreign exchange transaction. EUR/USD is an example of a currency pair.

Day order   A buy or sell order that will expire automatically at the end of the trading day on which it is entered.

Day trade   A trade opened and closed on the same trading day.

Day trader   A trader who buys and sells on the basis of small short-term price movements.

Day trading   Refers to a style or type of trading where trade positions are opened and closed during the same day.

Dealer   An individual or firm that buys and sells assets from its portfolio, acting as a principal or counterpart to a transaction.

Depreciation   A fall in the value of a currency owing to market forces.

Desk   Term referring to a group dealing with a specific currency or currencies.

Devaluation   The act by a government to reduce the external value of its currency.

Discretionary account   An account in which a customer permits a trading institution to act on the customer's behalf in buying and selling currency pairs. The institution has discretion as to the choice of currency pairs, prices, and timing, subject to any limitations specified in the agreement.

Expert advisor (EA)   An automated script that is used by the trading platform software to manage positions and orders automatically without (or with little) manual control.

ECB   (See *European central bank.*)

ECN broker   A type of FOREX brokerage firm that provides its clients direct access to other FOREX market participants. ECN brokers don't discourage scalping, don't trade against the client, don't charge spread (low spread is defined by current market prices), but charge commissions for every order.

Economic release (economic news release)   A scheduled announcement related to a particular fundamental indicator that includes the data of the previous release and the forecast value. At the moment of the release, revisions can be made to the previous release values, and these also count on the actual release.

Euro   The single currency of the European Economic and Monetary Union (EMU), introduced in January 1999. This is the amalgamation of the following currencies (after January 1, 2002, these currencies have been considered legacy currencies): German Deutsche marks, Italian lira, Austrian schilling, French franc, Belgium franc, Netherlands (Dutch) guilders, Finish markka, Portugese escudo, Greek drachma, Irish punt, Luxembourg franc, and Spanish peseta.

European central bank (ECB)   The central bank for the new European Monetary Union. The main regulatory body of the European Union financial system.

Execution   The process of completing an order or deal.

Fast market   Rapid movement in a market caused by strong interest by buyers and/or sellers. In such circumstances, price levels may be omitted, and bid and offer quotations may occur too rapidly to be fully reported.

Federal Deposit Insurance Corporation (FDIC)   The regulatory agency responsible for administering bank depository insurance in the United States.

Federal Reserve (Fed)   The central bank of the United States. The main regulatory body of the United States of America financial system, a division of which, the Federal Open Market Committee (FOMC), regulates, among other things, federal interest rates.

Federal Reserve System   The central banking system in the United States.

Fibonacci retracements   The levels with a high probability of trend break or bounce; calculated as 23.6, 32.8, 50, and 61.8 percent of the trend range.

Fill   The process of completing a customer's order to buy or sell a currency pair.

Fill price   The price at which a buy or sell order is executed.

Financial risk   The risk that a firm will be unable to meet its financial obligations.

Flat (square)   Term describing a trading book with no market exposure. A neutral state that occurs when all your positions are closed

FOMC   Federal Open Market Committee, the committee that sets money supply targets in the United States, which tend to be implemented through Fed fund interest rates, etc.

Foreign exchange   The purchase or sale of a currency against sale or purchase of another.

FOREX   Term commonly used when referring to the foreign exchange market.

FOREX club   Groups formed in the major financial centers to encourage educational and social contacts between foreign exchange dealers under the umbrella of Association Cambiste International.

Forward   A transaction that settles on a future date.

Fundamental analysis   Analysis of economic and political information with the objective of determining future movements in a financial market.

FX   Foreign exchange.

Good-til-canceled (GTC) order   A buy or sell order that remains open until it is filled or canceled.

Hedge   A transaction that reduces the risk on an existing investment position.

Initial margin   The deposit a customer needs to make before being allocated a trading limit.

Initial margin requirement   The minimum portion of a new security purchase that an investor must pay for in cash.

Kiwi   A FOREX slang name for the New Zealand currency, the New Zealand dollar.

Limit order   An order to execute a transaction at a specified price (the limit) or better. A limit order to buy would be at the limit or lower, and a limit order to sell would be at the limit or higher.

Liquidity   Refers to the relationship between transaction size and price movement. For example, a market is "liquid" if large transactions can occur with only minimal price changes.

Long position (or long)   In foreign exchange, when a currency pair is bought, it is understood that the primary currency in the pair is "long," and the secondary currency is "short."

Lot   The standard size of an order or trading position. One lot is equal to US$100,000 on currency pairs where the U.S. dollar is the base currency and its equivalent in dollars where the base currency is from another country. The amount is usually expressed in multiples of 100.

Maintenance   A set minimum margin that a customer must maintain in his or her margin account.

Margin   The amount of money needed to maintain a position.

Margin account   An account that allows leverage buying on credit and borrowing on currencies already in the account. Buying on credit and borrowing are subject to standards established by the firm carrying the account. Interest is charged on any borrowed funds and only for the period of time that the loan is outstanding.

Margin call   A call for additional funds in a margin account either because the value of equity in the account has fallen below a required minimum (also termed a *maintenance call*) or because additional currencies have been purchased (or sold short).

Market close   This refers to the time of day that a market closes. In the 24 hour-a-day FOREX market, there is no official market close. 5:00 p.m. Eastern Time is often referred to and understood as the market close because value dates for spot transactions change to the next new value date at that time.

Market maker   A person or firm that provides liquidity, making two-sided prices (bids and offers) in the market.

Market order   A customer order for immediate execution at the best price available when the order reaches the marketplace.

Market rate   The current quote of a currency pair.

Maturity   The date on which payment of a financial obligation is due.

Momentum   The tendency of a currency pair to continue movement in a single direction.

OCO order   One cancels the other order. A combination of two orders in which the execution of either one automatically cancels the other.

Offer   The price at which a currency pair or security is for sale; the quoted price at which an investor can buy a currency pair. This is also known as the *ask, ask price,* and *ask rate.*

Open order   Buy or sell order that remains in force until executed or canceled by the customer.

Open position   Any position (long or short) that is subject to market fluctuations and has not been closed out by a corresponding opposite transaction.

Order   A customer's instructions to buy or sell currencies at a certain rate.

Overbought   (See *Overbought/Oversold Indicator.*)

Overbought/Oversold indicator   A technical analysis tool that attempts to define when prices have moved too far and fast in either direction. This is usually calculated based on a moving average of the difference between the number of advancing and declining issues over a certain period of time. If the market is considered overbought, the technical analyst will sell, and if the market is considered oversold, he or she will buy.

Overnight position   Trader's long or short position in a currency at the end of a trading day.

Oversold   (See *Overbought/Oversold Indicator.*)

Pip   The smallest increment of change in a foreign currency price, either up or down. The last digit in the rate (e.g., for EUR/USD, 1 point = 0.0001).

Pipette   Fractional pip, 1/10 of a point. Additional decimal point quoted by some FOREX brokers, which provide a greater accuracy as to price movements. Examples: 1.27503 for EUR/USD or 110.052 for USD/JPY.

Pivot point   The primary support or resistance point that is calculated based on the previous period high, low, and close prices. It is usually calculated on daily rates, but other time frames also can be used.

Point   (See *Pip*.)

Price   The price at which an underlying currency can be bought or sold.

Price transparency   The ability of all market participants to "see" or deal at the same price.

Principal value   The original amount invested by a client.

Profit   Gain. Positive amount of money gained from closing a position.

Quote   A simultaneous bid and offer in a currency pair.

Quote currency   The second currency mentioned in a pair. The quote currency is the one that determines the exchange rate. Examples: In USD/JPY, the Japanese yen is the quote currency; in EUR/USD, the U.S. dollar is the quote currency.

Rate   Price at which a currency can be bought or sold against another currency.

Realized profit/loss   Gain or loss from already closed positions.

Resistance   Price level at which technical analysts note persistent selling of a currency. Price level for which the intensive selling can lead to the price increasing (uptrend).

Revaluation   Daily calculation of potential profits or losses on open positions based on the difference between the settlement price of the preceding trading day and the current trading day.

Risk (foreign exchange risk)   The risk that the exchange rate on a foreign currency will move against the position held by an investor such that the value of the investment is reduced.

Risk management   The employment of financial analysis and use of trading techniques to reduce and/or control exposure to financial risk.

Roll-over   The process of extending the settlement value date on an open position forward to the next valid value date.

Scalper   A trader who trades for small, short-term profits during the course of a trading session, rarely carrying a position overnight.

Scalping   The trading technique used by scalpers, taking small, short-term profits during the course of a trading session.

Sell limit order   An order to execute a transaction only at a specified price (the limit) or higher.

Selling short A situation where a currency has been sold with the intent of buying back the position at a lower price to make a profit.

Settled (closed) position Closed positions for which all needed transactions have been made.

Settlement The actual delivery of currencies made on the maturity date of a trade.

Short position (or short) In foreign exchange, when a currency pair is sold, the position is said to be short. It is understood that the primary currency in the pair is "short," and the secondary currency is "long."

Short squeeze The pressure on short sellers to cover their positions as a result of sharp price increases.

Slippage Execution of order for a price different from expected (ordered). Main reasons for slippage are a fast-moving market, low liquidity, and low broker's ability to execute orders at a certain moment.

Spot market Market where people buy and sell actual financial instruments (currencies) for two-day delivery.

Spot price The current market price of a currency that normally settles in two business days (one day for U.S. dollar and Canadian dollar).

Spread This point or pip difference between the bid and ask price of a currency pair.

Square (See *Flat (square).*)

Sterling Another term for the British currency, the British pound.

Stop (loss) order Order to buy or sell when a given price is reached or passed to liquidate part or all of an existing position.

Stop order (or stop) An order to buy or to sell a currency when the currency's price reaches or passes a specified level.

Support Price level for which intensive buying can lead to the price decreasing (downtrend).

Support levels A price at which a currency or the currency market will receive considerable buying pressure.

Swap A transaction that moves the maturity date of an open position to a future date.

Take-profit order A customer's instructions to buy or sell a currency pair that, when executed, will result in the reduction in the size of the existing position and show a profit on said position.

Technical analysis   Analysis based only on technical market data (quotes) with the help of various technical indicators.

Tick   The smallest possible change in a price, either up or down.

Transaction date   The date on which a trade occurs.

Trend   Direction of market that has been established with influence of different factors.

Turnover   The total volume of all executed transactions in a given time period.

Two-way price   A quote in the FOREX market that indicates a bid and an offer.

Unrealized (floating) profit/loss   A usually fluctuating profit or loss that derives from your nonclosed (active) positions.

Useable margin   Amount of money in an account that can be used for trading.

Used margin   Amount of money in an account that already has been used to hold positions open.

U.S. Dollar Index (USDX)   Measures the performance of the U.S. dollar against a basket of currencies: EUR, JPY, GBP, CAD, CHF, and SEK.

Value date   The maturity date of a currency for settlement, usually two business days (one day for Canada) after the trade has occurred.

Variation margin   Funds that are required to bring the equity in an account back up to the initial margin level, calculated on a day-to-day basis.

Volatility (VOL)   Statistical measure of the change in price of a financial currency pair over a given time period.

BIBLIOGRAPHY

RESEARCH MATERIALS

PremiereTrade: *http://PremiereTrade.com*
BabyPips: *http://babypips.com*
Bolsa Gráfica: *http://www.bolsagrafica.com/*
Candlesticker (Candlestick Patterns): *http://www.candlesticker.com*
Go Currency: *http://www.gocurrency.com*
Investopedia: *http://www.investopedia.com*
Stock Charts: *http://www.stockcharts.com*

LIST OF RECOMMENDED BOOKS

Booker, Rob. *Adventures of a Currency Trader: A Fable about Trading, Courage, and Doing the Right Thing,* Wiley, 2007.

Douglas, Mark. *The Disciplined Trader: Developing Winning Attitudes,* Prentice Hall Press, 1990.

Lefèvre, Edwin. *Reminiscences of a Stock Operator,* Wiley, 2004.

Livermore, Jesse L., Richard Smitten (Collaborator), Teresa Aligood (Editor). *How to Trade in Stocks : The Livermore Formula for Combining Time Element and Price,* rev ed. Traders Press, 2001.

Murphy, John J. *Technical Analysis of the Financial Markets: A Comprehensive Guide to Trading Methods and Applications (New York Institute of Finance),* Prentice Hall Press, 1999

Nison, Steve. *Beyond Candlesticks: New Japanese Charting Techniques Revealed,* Wiley, 1994.

Nison, Steve. *Japanese Candlestick Charting Techniques, Second Edition,* 2nd ed. Prentice Hall, Press 2001.

Schwager, Jack D.*Stock Market Wizards: Interviews with America's Top Stock Traders,* Marketplace Books, 2008.

Index

A

Abandoned baby pattern:
  bearish, 282*f*
  bullish, 276*f*
AB=CD patterns, 212*f,* 213
Abundance, 117
Account equity, 84
Account size, position and, 73
Accounts, trading (*see* Trading
  accounts)
Accumulation phase, in bullish trend,
  126
Actual price, 84, 222
Advance, in measured moves, 201
Advance block pattern, bearish, 283*f*
Advisors, 233–234
ADX (*see* Average directional
  movement index)
Affirmations, 113–117
Alliances, strategic, 117–118
American option, 243
Analysts, 9
Andrew's pitchfork (tool), 259*f,* 260
APIs (automatic programming
  interfaces), 233–235

Arcs, Fibonacci, 208, 208*f*
Ascending triangle patterns, 194*f,* 195
Asian option, 243
Ask price, 21
Assets, underlying, 242
ATR (*see* Average true range)
Attitude, toward losing, 68, 82,
  95–96, 101
Australian dollar "Aussie" (AUD),
  12–13
Auto sales, as economic indicator, 136
Automated trading, 44–45, 233–237
Automatic programming interfaces
  (APIs), 233–235
Avarice, 104
Average directional movement index
  (ADX), 163–164, 163*f*
Average true range (ATR), 31–32,
  168*f,* 169–169
Averages, in Dow theory, 125, 126
Averaging into a position, 52–53

B

Backtesting (automated trading
  systems), 234

Bad trades, 105–108
Balance of payments indicators, 127–128
Bank of Japan, 137–139
Banks, 49, 75, 124, 140–142
Bar charts, 155*f,* 156, 160–161, 161*f*
BARR pattern (*see* Bump-and-run reversal pattern)
Base currencies, xiv, 22
"Basket of currencies" hedge, 261–262
Bat patterns, 210–211, 211*f*
Bear spread strategy, 245
Bear traps, 173
Bearish deliberation pattern, 284*f*
Bearish divergence, 178, 179*f*
Bearish markets, 158, 170, 182, 182*f*
Bearish outside bars (BEOBs), 151
Bearish reversal patterns, 281*f*–284*f,* 286*f*
Bearish trends, phases of, 127
Bears power, 169–170
Beliefs, 98, 113–114
Belt hold pattern:
    bearish, 284*f*
    bullish, 279*f*
BEOBs (bearish outside bars), 151
Bid price, 21
Bid-ask spreads, 76–77, 81–82
Bids, 21
Binary contracts for difference (CFDs), 17
Black and Scholes formula, 244–245
Black candlestick pattern:
    bearish long black candlestick, 286*f*
    neutral, 288*f*
    neutral short black candlestick, 288*f*
Bodies (of candlesticks), 182–183
Bollinger, John, 164
Bollinger bands, 164–166, 165*f*

Box size (point and figure charts), 160
Brain, neural networks in, 235
Brainstorming groups, 118–119
Brazilian real (BRL), 19
Breakaway pattern:
    bearish, 284*f*
    bullish, 279*f*
Breakeven price, 63
Breakeven stops, 107
Breakouts, 215, 221, 231, 253–258
"Breathing," 31, 72
British pound (GBP), 13–14
Broken trends, 216
Brokers, 38–47
    features of, 41–45
    in FOREX market, 4–5, 7, 50
    regulation, reputation and size of, 39–40
    types of, 41–42, 45–47
Bulkowski, Thomas, 192
Bull spread strategy, 245
Bull traps, 173
Bullish divergence, 178, 178*f*
Bullish markets, 158, 170, 182, 182*f*
Bullish outside bars (BUOBs), 151
Bullish reversal patterns, 276*f*–279*f,* 281*f*
Bullish trends, phases of, 126–127
Bulls power, 169–170, 169*f*
Bump-and-run reversal (BARR) pattern, 191, 192*f*
Business inventories, as economic indicator, 132
Butterfly patterns, 209, 209*f*
Butterfly strategy, for options, 246
"Buy low; sell high.", 221
"Buy the rumor; sell the fact." in news trading, 144, 145
Buying opportunities, in Heiken-Ashi charts, 158

Buy/sell limit orders, 28
Buy/sell market orders, 27–28
Buy/sell orders, 71
Buy/sell stop loss orders, 28

C

C corporations, 111
"Cable," 13
Calls (call options), 242–244
Canadian dollar (CAD), 13
Candlestick charts, 156–157, 156*f,*
 160–161, 161*f*
Candlestick patterns, 276–288
 bearish, 281*f*–286*f*
 bullish, 276*f*–281*f*
 neutral, 287*f*–288*f*
 in technical analysis, 181–185
Capacity utilization, 131
Capital, risk, 82
Capital gains, 250
Capitalization, 82–83
Carry trades, 139–140
Caution, 73
CCI (*see* Commodity channel index)
Central Bank of Iraq, 19
Central banks, 49, 75, 124, 140–142
CFDs (*see* Contracts for difference)
CFTC (*see* Commodity Futures
 Trading Commission)
Channeling, 258–260, 259*f*
Channels:
 Fibonacci, 207, 207*f,* 260, 260*f*
 price, 198–199, 198*f,* 258–260,
 259*f*
Character (of traders), 61
Chartism, 16, 185
Charts, 73, 150–161
 bar, 155*f,* 156
 candlestick, 156–157, 156*f*
 Heiken-Ashi, 157–158, 157*f*

impulsive and corrective moves in,
 153 154
line, 154*f,* 155
pip range bar (candlestick),
 160–161, 161*f*
point and figure, 160, 160*f*
price action in, 150–153
Renko, 159, 159*f*
Chinese renminbi (RMB), 18
Chinese yuan (CNY), 18
Classic (regular) divergence, 177–179,
 178*f,* 179*f*
Close value (Heiken-Ashi charts),
 158
Closing positions, 24
Clouds (ichimoku kinko hyo),
 177, 177*f*
Coding, for automated trading,
 234, 235
Commerce, as basis of FOREX
 transactions, 74
Commercial banks, 49, 75
Commissions, 7, 9–10, 43
Commodities, 250–251
Commodity channel index (CCI),
 166–167, 166*f*
Commodity Futures Trading
 Commission (CFTC), 39, 86
Concealing baby swallow pattern,
 bullish, 277*f*
Confidence, 101–102 (*See also*
 Overconfidence)
Confidence and sentiments reports,
 128
Confirmation, in Dow theory, 126
Confusion, 100
Connectionist movement, 235
Consolidation, in measured moves,
 202
Consolidation patterns, 231, 254

Construction data, as economic indicator, 132–133
Consumer price index (CPI), 133
Consumer sentiment, as economic indicator, 136
Consumer spending indicators, 135
Consumption, in gross domestic product, 142
Consumption spending, 130
Continuation patterns, 154, 192–203
  bearish, 285*f*–286*f*
  bullish, 280*f*–281*f*
  cup-with-handle, 199–200, 200*f*
  flags and pennants, 192–193, 193*f*
  measured moves as, 201–203, 201*f*, 202*f*
  neutral, 287*f*–288*f*
  price channels, 198–199, 198*f*
  rectangles, 196–198, 196*f*, 197*f*
  triangles, 194–196, 194*f*
Contracts for difference (CFDs), 16–17, 249–250
Contrarian indicators, 145–146
Contrarian stop orders, 257
Control, 109
Corporations, trade, 111
Corrections (corrective moves), 145–146, 153–154, 202
Correlations, in currencies, 261
Counter currencies, xiv
Counter-trending, 166
Country risk, 86
Coverage, in futures, 247
CPI (consumer price index), 133
Crab patterns, 211, 212*f*
Credit risk, 86
Crossovers, in MACD oscillator, 173–174
Cross-rate currency pairs (crosses), 17–18, 26–27, 27*t*, 263

Crow patterns:
  bearish three black crows, 282*f*
  bearish three upside gap two crows, 282*f*
  bearish two crows, 284*f*
Crude oil, 17
Cup-with-handle pattern, 199–200, 200*f*
Currencies and currency pairs, xiv, 11–20
  brokers' access to, 44
  correlations between, 261
  and crude oil, 17
  and Dow Jones Industrial Average (DJIA), 16
  and gold contracts for difference, 16–17
  major, 143
  and U.S. Dollar Index, 15
Customer service (of brokers), 42

D

Daily charts, 229
Daily high-low trading strategy, 265–268, 265*f*, 266*f*
Danish krone (DKK), 19
Dark cloud cover pattern, bearish, 281*f*
Day trading, 51
DBHLC (double-high lower close) patterns, 151
Dealers, 110
Decline, in measured moves, 201
Deliberation pattern, bearish, 284*f*
Demand, 217
DeMark, Tom, 226
DeMark pivot points, 226
Demo (paper) trading, 38, 77–80, 234
Deposits, for brokers, 41
Descending triangle patterns, 194*f*, 195–196

-DI (negative directional indicator), 164

+DI (positive directional indicator), 164

Directional movement index (DMI), 164

Directional movement indicators (DMIs), 163

Discipline, 67–70, 103

Discouragement phase, in bearish trend, 127

Distraction, 103

Distribution phase, in bearish trend, 127

Distribution (speculation) phase, in bullish trend, 127

Divergences, 174, 177–179

Diversification, 241–252
  with commodities, 250–251
  with contracts for difference, 249–250
  with FOREX exchange-traded funds, 248–249
  with FOREX futures, 247–248
  with FOREX single-payment options trading, 246–247
  with indices, 251–252
  with options, 241–246

DJI (Dow Jones Index), 252

DJIA (*see* Dow Jones Industrial Average)

DJTA (Dow Jones Transport Average), 16

DMI (directional movement index), 164

DMIs (directional movement indicators), 163

Doji candlesticks, 184, 184*f*
  bearish doji star, 283*f*
  bearish dragonfly doji, 283*f*

bearish evening doji star, 282*f*
bearish gravestone doji, 283*f*
bearish long-legged doji, 283*f*
bullish doji star, 278*f*
bullish dragonfly doji, 277*f*
bullish gravestone doji, 277*f*
bullish long-legged doji, 277*f*
bullish morning doji star, 276*f*
dragonfly doji, 184
neutral doji, 287*f*
neutral four price doji, 287*f*
neutral long legged doji, 287*f*

Double bottoms pattern, 186–187, 186*f*

Double no-touch options, 246

Double one-touch options, 246

Double tops pattern, 186–187, 186*f*

Double-high lower close (DBHLC) patterns, 151

Dow, Charles H., 16, 149, 181

Dow Jones Index (DJI), 252

Dow Jones Industrial Average (DJIA), 16, 275

Dow Jones Transport Average (DJTA), 16

Dow theory, 125–127

Down bars, 216

Down candles (candlestick charts), 156

Down fractals, 214

Downtrends, 153

Dragonfly doji, 184

Drawdown, 67, 85, 85*t*

Durable goods orders, as economic indicator, 132

E

EBS (electronic broking service), 75

ECB (European Central Bank), 12

ECI (employment cost index), 135

ECNs (*see* Electronic communication networks)

Economic forecasts, 6, 74
Economic instability, 86
Economic modeling, 237
Economic news releases, 21, 66, 107, 123, 143–145
Economics, 123–146
  contrarian indicators in, 145–146
  Dow theory, 125–127
  and economic news releases, 123
  and FOREX currency carry trades, 139–140
  and fundamental analysis, 123–125
  gross domestic product, 142
  interventions in, 140–141
  Japan's monetary policy, 137–139
  and trading the news, 143–145
  U.S. economic indicators, 127–137
Economy growth, in fundamental analysis, 124
Efficiency, 68
Elder, Alexander, 169
Electronic broking service (EBS), 75
Electronic communication networks (ECNs), 45–47, 75–76
Electronic failures, 86–87
Electronic trading, tools for, 47, 71, 110
Elliott, Ralph Nelson, 203
Elliott waves, 203–204, 204*f*
EMA (*see* Exponential (exponentially weighted) moving average)
Emergency stops, 32
Emotions, 95–111
  and bad trades, 105–108
  controlling, 109
  effect of, on trading, 99–105
  of investors, 233
  of professional traders, 110–111
  and trader's ten commandments, 108–109

and trading psychology, 95–99
Employment cost index (ECI), 135
Employment indicators, 129, 134–135
Engulfing pattern:
  bearish, 283*f*
  bullish, 277*f*
Entering positions (entries), 62, 64, 66, 221, 266–267
Environment, for trading, 49–50
Envy, 104
Equity, account, 84
ESCB (European System of Central Banks), 12
ETFs (exchange-traded funds), 248–249
EUR/GBP currency pair, 26, 27*t*
Euro (EUR), 12
European Central Bank (ECB), 12
European option, 243
European System of Central Banks (ESCB), 12
European Union, 12
EUR/USD currency pair, 26, 27*t*
Evening star pattern, bearish, 282*f*
Excess trading, 105
Exchange-rate risk, 86
Exchange-traded funds (ETFs), 248–249
Execution (strike) price, 241–243
Exhaustion, 103
Exiting positions (exits), 62, 64, 66, 106–108, 221, 267
Exotic currency pairs, 18
Expansions, Fibonacci, 206, 206*f*
Expiration times (options), 241, 242
Expiry date (options), 243
Exponential (exponentially weighted) moving average (EMA), 162–163, 162*f*, 262, 262*f*, 263, 263*f*
Exports, 142

F

Factory orders, as economic indicator, 131
Falling wedges pattern, 189–190, 189*f*
Fans, Fibonacci, 207*f*, 208
FCMs (*see* Futures commission merchants)
Fear, 79, 105
"Fiber," 12
Fibonacci arcs, 208, 208*f*
Fibonacci channels, 207, 207*f*, 260, 260*f*
Fibonacci expansions, 206, 206*f*
Fibonacci fans, 207*f*, 208
Fibonacci patterns, 204–208
Fibonacci retracements, 205–206, 205*f*, 220
Filled candlesticks, 157
Fills, guarantees on, 41
Financial Services Authority (FSA), 39
5-minute charts, 229
Flagpoles, 192
Flags and pennants pattern, 192–193, 193*f*
Flat positions, 22
Flexibility, 108
Forecasts, 6, 74
Foreign exchange (FOREX) (FX) market, 3–10
  about, xiii–xiv
  futures market vs., 9–10, 10*t*
  history of, 3–6
  players in, 49–50
  stock market vs., xii, 7–9, 8*t*
  terminology, 21–34
FOREX exchange-traded funds (ETFs), 248–249
FOREX futures, 247–248
FOREX options, 241–246
FOREX quotes, 4

FOREX single-payment options trading (SPOT), 246–247
Forums, trading, 118–119
Four price doji pattern, neutral, 287*f*
Fractals, 214–215, 215*f*
FSA (Financial Services Authority), 39
Fundamental analysis, 5, 6, 35, 123–125
Fundamental phase, in bullish trend, 127
Future, predicting the, 71, 108
Futures, 9–10, 10*t*, 247–248
Futures commission merchants (FCMs), 24, 39 (*See also* Brokers)
FX market (*see* Foreign exchange market)

G

Gaps, 264
Gartley patterns, 210, 210*f*
GDI (gross domestic income), 142
GDP (*see* Gross domestic product)
GDP implicit deflator, 133–134
GDP per capita, 142
Generosity, 117
GFD (good for the day) orders, 29
Gluttony, 105
GNP (*see* Gross national product)
GNP implicit deflator, 133
Goals, 65, 69–70, 114–117
"Going long in the market," 22
"Going short," 22
Gold contracts for difference (CFDs), 16–17
Golden ratio (golden mean), 204
Good for the day (GFD) orders, 29
Good till canceled (GTC) orders, 29
Good trades, 106
Good until date/time orders, 29

Goods, durable vs. nondurable, 131, 132
Government spending, 130, 142
Gratitude, 115–116
Gravestone doji:
 bearish, 283*f*
 bullish, 277*f*
Greed, 79, 109
Gross domestic product (GDP), 128, 130, 142
Gross national product (GNP), 130, 131
Group mentality, 68
Growth, economy, 124
GTC (good till canceled) orders, 29
Guarantees, from brokers, 41

H
Hammer pattern:
 bullish, 279*f*
 bullish inverted, 279*f*
Hanging man pattern, bearish, 284*f*
Harami pattern:
 bearish, 284*f*
 bearish cross, 283*f*
 bullish, 279*f*
 bullish cross, 278*f*
Harmonic price patterns, 208–213
 bearish, 209–211, 209*f*–212*f*
 bullish, 209–211, 209*f*–212*f*
HDI (human development index), 142
Head-and-shoulders (H&S) pattern, 187–189, 187*f*, 188*f*
Hedges and hedging, 24, 40, 261–262
Heiken-Ashi charts, 157–158, 157*f*
HHs (*see* Higher highs)
Hidden divergence, 177 (*See also* Reverse divergence)
High value (Heiken-Ashi charts), 158

High wave pattern, neutral, 287*f*
Higher highs (HHs), 152*f*, 153
Higher lows (HLs), 152*f*, 153
HLC bars, 156
"Holy Grail" of traders, 269–271
Home offices, 49–50
Homing pigeon pattern, bullish, 278*f*
Homma, 181
Honesty (of brokers), 41
Housing figures, as economic indicators, 129
How to Make Money in Stocks (William O'Neil), 199
H&S pattern (*see* Head-and-shoulders pattern)
Human development index (HDI), 142

I
IBs (introducing brokers), 41–42
Ichimoku kinko hyo, 176–177, 177*f*
If done (IFD) orders, 29, 257
IMF (International Monetary Fund), 19
Imports, 142
Impulsive moves, 153, 154
In neck pattern, bearish, 285*f*
Income, personal, 137
Index(—ices), 251–252
Index of the Industrial Sector, 16
Index of the Transportation Sector, 16
Indicator(s):
 contrarian, 145–146
 fractals as, 214
 and price action, 150–151
 stock market as, 8–9
 stop and reverse, 32
 of support and resistance, 219–220
 U.S. economic, 127–137
 (*See also* Technical indicators)

Industrial capacity utilization, 131
Industrial production indicator, 131
Inefficiency, 103
Inflation, 124–125, 133
Information overload, 100
Inside bars, 152, 152*f,* 216
Interbank, xiv, 75
Interest rates, 34, 42–43, 125, 133, 137, 139, 140
Intermediaries, FOREX, 8
International financial markets, commodities in, 250
International Monetary Fund (IMF), 19
Interventions, in economics, 140–141
Intraday trading, 52
Introducing brokers (IBs), 41–42
Inventories, business, 132
Inverted head-and-shoulders pattern, 188–189, 188*f*
Investment, in gross domestic product, 142
Investment spending, 130
Investors, 110
Iraqi dinar, 19–20

J
James Dicks FOREX alerts, 90
James Dicks FOREX Network, 68, 117, 119
JamesDicks.com, xiv, 39, 44, 78, 117, 270, 271
Japan, 134, 137–139
Japanese yen (JPY), 14–15, 139–140

K
Kicking pattern:
  bearish, 281*f*
  bullish, 276*f*
"Kiwi," 15

L
Ladder bottom pattern, bullish, 279*f*
Lambert, Donald, 166
Leading indicators, 128, 136–137
Learning, 236, 269–270
Legal issues, 111
Leonardo of Pisa, 204–205
Leverage:
  brokers' levels of, 43–44
  in FOREX market, 4
  and options, 244–246
  in real-money trading, 87–89
  and trading on margin, 23
Leverage effect, 244
Liber Abaci (Leonardo of Pisa), 205
Liechtenstein, 14
Limit orders, 28
Limited-liability corporations (LLC), 111
Line charts, 154*f,* 155
Linearly weighted moving average (LWMA), 162*f,* 163
Liquidity, 9, 76, 255
LLC (limited-liability corporations), 111
LLs (*see* Lower lows)
Long black candlestick pattern, bearish, 286*f*
Long legged doji pattern, neutral, 287*f*
Long positions, 21–23, 170
Long white candlestick pattern, bullish, 281*f*
"Longing the market," 22
Long-term trading, 51, 107
"Loonie," 13
Losing and losses, 71, 73, 271
  attitude toward, 68, 82, 95–96, 101
  percentages to recover from, 85, 85*t*

Lots, 27, 27t
  micro, 27, 27t, 38, 91
  mini, 27, 27t, 38
  nano, 91
  standard, 27, 38
Low value (Heiken-Ashi charts), 158
Lower lows (LLs), 152f, 153
Lust, excess trading as, 105
LWMA (see Linearly weighted
      moving average)

M

MACD oscillator (see Moving average
      convergence-divergence oscillator)
Macroeconomics, 123–124
Major currencies, 143
Managing positions, 23
Margin, 88
Margin calls, 10, 43
Marginal trading, 5
Market and volatility indicators,
      168–173
Market corrections, 145–146
Market hours, 144
Market makers, 45–46, 75
Market orders, 28–29
Markets:
  bearish, 158, 170, 182, 182f
  bullish, 158, 170, 182, 182f
  commodities in, 250
  of FOREX, xiii
  sideways movement of, 217
  stalling, 161
  tendencies in, 126, 150
  traders' understanding of, 73–77
  in trading plans, 62
  trends in, 126–127
  unpredictability of, 73–74
Marubozu candlesticks, 182–183
  bearish black, 286f

  bearish black closing, 286f
  bearish black opening, 286f
  bullish white, 281f
  bullish white closing, 281f
  bullish white opening, 281f
MAs (see Moving averages)
Mat hold pattern, bullish, 280f
Matching low pattern, bullish, 278f
Maximum drawdown, 85, 85t
Maximum loss, 84
Measured moves, 201–203,
      201f, 202f
Meeting lines pattern:
  bearish, 283f
  bullish, 278f
Mentored trading communities, 119
Merchandise trade balance, as
      economic indicator, 134
Metals, as commodities, 250, 251
Mexican peso (MXN), 19
Micro accounts, 4–5, 27, 27t,
      37–39, 88
Micro lots, 27, 27t, 38, 91
"Million Dollar Portfolio Challenge"
      (television series), xiv
Mindsets, for trading, 113–119
Mini accounts, 4, 27, 27t,
      37–38, 88
Mini lots, 27, 27t, 38
Minor trends, 126
Minsky, M. L., 235
Mistakes, in trading, 96–99
Modeling, economic, 237
Momentum indicators, 170, 171f
Monetary policies, 129, 137–139
Money management, 79, 81–85, 109
Money supply, Japanese, 139
Monitors, computer, 47–48
Mood, 115
Morning star pattern, bullish, 276f

Moving average convergence-divergence (MACD) oscillator, 163, 173–174, 173*f*, 262, 262*f*, 263
Moving averages (MAs), 162–163, 162*f*, 219–220, 220*f*
"Moving sideways," 217
Moving-average crosses, 263
Multiple-chart analysis, 229–231, 230*f*

N

Nano accounts, 27, 27*t*
Nano lots, 91
National Futures Association (NFA), 39, 41, 86
Neck patterns:
  bearish in neck, 285*f*
  bearish on neck, 285*f*
Negative directional indicator (-DI), 164
Negative emotions, 99–101
Negative forces, 102–104
Negative thoughts, affirmations and, 114, 116
Net exports, 142
Net trade volume, 131
Networking, 117–119
Neural networks, 235–237
Neutral continuation patterns, 287*f*–288*f*
Neutral doji patterns, 287*f*
Neutral reversal patterns, 287*f*–288*f*
New Concepts in Technical Trading Systems (Welles Wilder), 168
New York Board of Trade, 15
New Zealand dollar (NZD), 15
News releases, economic, 21, 66, 107, 123, 143–145
News trading (trading the news), 54, 123, 143–145

NFA (*see* National Futures Association)
NFP (nonfarm payroll), 135
Nicollis, Vicente, 160
No slippage policies, 41
Nondurable goods, 131
Nonfarm payroll (NFP), 135
Norwegian krone (NOK), 19

O

OCO (one cancels the other) orders, 28–29
Offers, 21
Offshore brokers, 41
OHLC bars, 156
Oil, crude, 17
On neck pattern, bearish, 285*f*
One cancels the other (OCO) orders, 28–29
1-hour charts, 229
O'Neil, William, 199
One-touch options, 246
OPEC (Organization of the Petroleum Exporting Countries), 17
Open positions, 21–23
Open value (Heiken-Ashi charts), 158
Options, 241 246
Orders, 7, 22, 27–29 (*See also* Position[s])
Organization of the Petroleum Exporting Countries (OPEC), 17
Oscillator-based trading strategies, 262–263, 262*f*
Oscillators, 169, 173–176
Output reports, for U.S., 128
Outside bars, 151, 152*f*, 216
Overconfidence, 73, 89, 91
Overleveraging, 91
Overnight interest, 34 (*See also* Swaps)
Overtrading, 89–91

P

PAL (premiere advisor language), 45
Panic phase, in bearish trend, 127
Paper (demo) trading, 38, 77–80, 234
Papert, S. A., 235
Parabolic stop and reverse (PSAR), 167–168, 167*f*
Patience, 72
Payment currencies, xiv
PB patterns (*see* Pin bar patterns)
People's Bank of China, 18
Perceptrons (M. L. Minsky and S. A. Papert), 235
Performance, 67, 71, 72
Personal income, as economic indicator, 137
Personality (of traders), 61
Phase of accumulation, in bullish trend, 126
Phase of discouragement, in bearish trend, 127
Phase of distribution, in bearish trend, 127
Phase of distribution or speculation, in bullish trend, 127
Phase of panic, in bearish trend, 127
Phase of tendency or fundamental, in bullish trend, 127
Piercing line pattern, bullish, 276*f*
Pin bar (PB) patterns, 151, 151*f*
Pinocchio patterns, 151
Pip range bar (candlestick) charts, 160–161, 161*f*
Pip value, 84
Pips (points), 24–27, 72, 92, 144–145
Pivot points, 222–226, 223*f,* 224*f,* 225*t,* 260
Point and figure charts, 160, 160*f*
Points, 24 (*See also* Pips)
Political instability, 86

Position(s), 22
and account size, 73
closing of, 24
entering, 62, 64, 66, 221, 266–267
exiting, 62, 64, 66, 106–108, 221, 267
flat, 22
long, 21–23, 170
managing of, 23
open, 21–23
scaling out of, 73, 91
short, 21
sizes of, 62
splitting of, 222, 254
(*See also* Orders)
Position trading, 52–53
Positive directional indicator (+DI), 164
Positive emotions, 99–100
Power failures, 86–87
PPI (producer price index), 133
Prejudices, 108
Premiere advisor language (PAL), 45
Premiums (options), 242, 244–245
Preparations for trading, 37–58
choosing brokers, 38–47
defining players in FOREX, 49–50
selecting a trading strategy, 50–54
tools for trading, 47–49
and trader's levels of development, 55–58
trading accounts, 37–38
Price(s):
actual, 84, 222
ask, 21
bid, 21
breakeven, 63
execution (strike), 241–243

in FOREX market, 10, 76–77
quarter, 226
round-number, 226–228, 228*f*
Price action, 73, 150–161, 270
Price channels, 198–199, 198*f*, 258–260, 259*f*
Price development, in fundamental analysis, 124–125
Price line (line charts), 155
Price patterns, harmonic, 208–213
Price-action patterns, 151–153
Prices, salary, and wages figures, for U.S., 128–129
Pride, 104
Primary tendencies, in markets, 150
Primary trends, 126
Producer price index (PPI), 133
Professional traders, emotions of, 110–111
Profits, 22, 69, 71
Program trading, 233
Progressive time-frame breakouts, 257*f*, 258
PSAR (*see* Parabolic stop and reverse)
Psychology, trading and, 95–99, 145, 226–228
Puts (put options), 242–244

Q

Quarter prices, 226
Quote currencies, xiv, 22
Quotes, 4, 41

R

Range breakouts, 253*f*, 254–255
Real-money trading, 81–92
accounts for, 37–38
leverage in, 87–89
managing risk in, 86–87
and money management, 81–85

overleveraging, 91
overtrading in, 89–91
and paper trading, 38
trader expectations in, 92
Recession of 1990s, 136
Reciprocity, 117
Rectangle patterns, 196–198, 196*f*, 197*f*
Regular divergence, 177 (*See also* Classic divergence)
Regulations, for brokers, 39–40
Relative strength index (RSI), 175–176, 176*f*, 262, 262*f*
Renko charts, 159, 159*f*
Reputations (of brokers), 40
Resistance, 218–219 (*See also* Support and resistance)
Responsibility, in trading plans, 68
Retail brokers, 45 (*See also* Market makers)
Retail sales, as economic indicator, 135–136
Retracements, Fibonacci, 205–206, 205*f*, 220
Reversal patterns, 186–192
bearish, 281*f*–284*f*, 286*f*
bullish, 276*f*–279*f*, 281*f*
neutral, 287*f*–288*f*
Reversals, 145–146, 231
Reverse (hidden) divergence, 177–179, 178*f*, 179*f*
Rising wedges pattern, 189–190, 189*f*
Risk, 10, 72, 86–88, 108
Risk capital, 82
Risk management:
calculator for, 83–85, 83*t*
in demo trading, 79
for futures, 247
in trading plans, 62, 64, 65
Risk percentage, 84
Risk/reward ratio, 84

Rollover interest, 34 (*See also* Swaps)
Rounding bottom patterns, 190, 191*f*
Rounding top patterns, 190
Round-number prices, 226–228, 228*f*
RSI (*see* Relative strength index)
Rumors, 8–9

S
SAR indicators (*see* Stop and reverse
    indicators)
Saucers, in reversal patterns, 190
Scaling out of positions, 73, 91
Scalping, 39, 51–52, 90, 158, 168
Scams, 86
Secondary tendencies, in markets, 150
Secondary trends, 126
Self-destruction, 102–103
Separating lines pattern:
    bearish, 286*f*
    bullish, 280*f*
Shadows, 183, 183*f*
Shooting star pattern, bearish, 284*f*
Short black candlestick pattern,
    neutral, 288*f*
Short positions, 21, 23
Short selling, 7–8
Short white candlestick pattern,
    neutral, 288*f*
"Shorting the market," 22
Short-term trading, 51, 108
Side-by-side white lines pattern:
    bearish, 285*f*
    bullish, 280*f*
Sideways movement, 217
Simple moving average (SMA), 162,
    162*f*, 164
Simplicity, in trading, 109
Singapore dollar (SGD), 19
Single-payment options trading
    (SPOT), 246–247

Slippage, 28, 76–77
Sloth, 105
SMA (*see* Simple moving average)
Software, for trading, 39 (*See also*
    Trading platforms)
South African rand (ZAR), 19
Speculation, 8, 141
Speculation phase, in bullish trend,
    127
Spending, 128–130
Spinning top pattern:
    neutral black, 287*f*
    neutral white, 287*f*
Spinning tops, 183, 183*f*
Splitting of positions, 222, 254
SPOT (single-payment options
    trading), 246–247
Spreads, 21, 33–34, 43, 76–77
Stalling markets, 161
Standard & Poor's 500 Index, 252
Standard accounts, 38, 88
Standard lots, 27, 38
Standard of living, 142
Star patterns:
    bearish doji star, 283*f*
    bearish evening doji star, 282*f*
    bearish evening star, 282*f*
    bearish shooting star, 284*f*
    bearish tri star, 284*f*
    bullish doji star, 278*f*
    bullish morning doji star, 276*f*
    bullish morning star, 276*f*
    bullish three stars in the south, 278*f*
    bullish tri star, 278*f*
Stick sandwich pattern, bullish, 278*f*
Stochastic oscillators, 174–175, 175*f*
Stocks and stock market, xii, 7–9, 8*t*,
    125, 251–252
Stop and reverse (SAR) indicators, 32,
    167–168, 167*f*

"Stop hunting," 33
Stop loss, 84, 106–107, 222, 265–267
Stop-loss orders, 28, 84–85
Stops, 32–33
    breakeven, 107
    calculator for setting, 83–85, 83t
    contrarian, 257
    emergency, 32
    in trading plans, 62, 66
    trailing, 106
Straddle buy strategy, 245
Straddle trading, 54, 166
Strangle buy strategy, 245
Strategic alliances, 117–118
Stress, 100, 102
Strike (execution) price, 241–243
Subconscious mind, affirmations and, 114–115
Sub-S corporations, 111
Supply, 217
Support, 217–218 (*See also* Support and resistance)
Support and resistance, 217–231
    about, 217–219
    and Bollinger bands, 165
    and entering positions, 221
    and exiting positions, 221
    and fractals, 214, 215
    and identifying trends, 231
    indicators of, 219–220
    and pivot points, 222–226
    psychological levels of, 226–228
    in Renko charts, 159
    in stop-loss strategies, 107
    stops based on, 32
    in technical analysis, 150
    time frames for, 228–231
Support and resistance breakouts, 256–257, 256f, 257f

Swaps (overnight or rollover interest), 34, 42–43
Swedish krona (SEK), 18
Swing trading, 53–54
Swings, 53
Swiss franc "Swissie" (CHF), 14
Symmetric triangle patterns, 194, 194f
System failures, 86–87

T

Take-profit levels, 33
Tankan Index, 138–139
Targets (take-profit levels), 33, 66, 83–85, 83t, 106–107, 222
Tasuki gap pattern:
    bearish downside, 285f
    bullish upside, 280f
Taxes, 110–111
Technical analysis, 6, 35, 149–150
Technical indicators, 149–179
    charts with price action, 150–161
    divergences, 177–179
    ichimoku kinko hyo as, 176–177, 177f
    market and volatility indicators, 168–173
    oscillators as, 173–176
    and technical analysis, 149–150
    trend indicators, 162–168
Technical patterns, 181–216
    candlesticks, 181–185
    in chartism, 185
    continuation patterns, 192–203
    Elliott waves, 203–204
    Fibonacci, 204–208
    fractals as, 214–215
    harmonic price patterns, 208–213
    reversal patterns, 186–192
    for trading naked, 215–216

Ten commandments, trader's, 108–109
Tendencies, in markets, 150
Tendency (fundamental) phase, in
    bullish trend, 127
Tertiary tendencies, in markets, 150
Tertiary (minor) trends, 126
"38 Steps to Becoming a Trader,"
    273–275
Thoughts, negative, 114, 116
Three drives patterns, 213, 213*f*
Three inside down pattern, bearish, 282*f*
Three inside up pattern, bullish, 276*f*
Three line strike pattern:
    bearish, 286*f*
    bullish, 280*f*
Three methods pattern:
    bearish downside gap, 285*f*
    bearish falling, 285*f*
    bullish rising, 280*f*
    bullish upside gap, 280*f*
Three outside down pattern, bearish,
    282*f*
Three outside up pattern, bullish, 276*f*
Three river pattern, bullish, 279*f*
Three stars in the south pattern,
    bullish, 278*f*
Three white soldiers pattern, bullish,
    277*f*
Thrusting pattern, bearish, 286*f*
Tick value (futures), 247
Ticks (futures), 247
Time frames:
    for breakouts, 257–258
    defined, 29–32
    for support and resistance, 228–231,
        230*f*
    in trading plans, 63
    and trends, 153
Timed orders, 29
Trade balance, 125, 134

Trade corporations, 111
Trade size, 84
Traders, 61–80
    capital sins of, 104–105
    definition of, for tax purposes,
        110–111
    demo trading by, 77–80
    emotions of, 110–111
    expectations of, 92
    "Holy Grail" of, 269–271
    levels of development of, 55–58
    personality and character elements
        of, 61
    rules and discipline of, 67–73
    trading plans of, 62–67
    understanding of markets by, 73–77
Trader's ten commandments, 108–109
Trades:
    bad, 105–108
    carry, 139–140
    good, 106
    records of, 64–65, 67
    winning, 106
Trading:
    conditions for, 72
    effect of emotions on, 99–105
    excess, 105
    of interventions, 141
    learning about, 269–270
    marginal, 5
    and psychology, 95–99, 145,
        226–228
    tools for, 47–49, 71, 110
    with trends, 108
    (*See also* Preparations for trading)
Trading accounts, 37–38
    micro, 4–5, 27, 27*t*, 37–39, 88
    mini, 4, 27, 27*t*, 37–38, 88
    nano, 27, 27*t*
    standard, 38, 88

Trading Chaos (Bill M. Williams), 214
Trading communities, mentored, 119
Trading forums, 118–119
Trading naked, 215–216
Trading on margin, 23
Trading plans, 62–67, 97, 109
Trading platforms, 39, 44, 77–78
Trading psychology, 95–99
Trading strategies, 253–268
  breakouts in, 253–258
  channeling, 258–260
  daily high-low, 265–268
  gaps in, 264
  hedging, 261–262
  moving-average crosses in, 263
  oscillator-based, 262–263
  rules for, 70–73
  selecting, 50–54
  in trading plans, 63, 64
Trading the news (news trading), 54,
  123, 143–145
Trailing stops, 32–33, 106
Training, 103–104, 236
Trend breakouts, 255*f,* 256
Trend indicators, 162–168
Trendlines, 219, 221
Trends:
  broken, 216
  in FOREX, 149
  in Heiken-Ashi charts, 158
  holding to, 69–70
  identifying, 231
  of markets (in Dow theory),
    126–127
  phases of, 126–127
  staying with, 71
  in technical analysis, 149–150
  and time frames, 153
  trading with, 108
  on weekly charts, 229

Tri star pattern:
  bearish, 284*f*
  bullish, 278*f*
Triangle patterns, 194–196, 194*f*
Triple bottoms pattern, 187
Triple tops pattern, 187
True hedging, 261
True leverage, 87

U
Umbrella pattern:
  neutral, 287*f*
  neutral inverted, 287*f*
Underlying assets (of options), 242
Unemployment, 125, 134
United Kingdom, 13–14, 39–40
United States, 24, 39, 127–137
Unpredictability of markets, 73–74
Up bars, 215–216
Up candles (candlestick charts), 156
Up fractals, 214
Uptrends, 153
U.S. dollar (USD), 11, 17, 25–26, 143
U.S. Dollar Index (USDX), 15
USD/CHF currency pair, 25, 27*t*
USD/JPY currency pair, 25, 27*t*
USDX (U.S. Dollar Index), 15
Utilization of capacity, 131

V
Values (of traders), 114–115
Void candlesticks, 157
Volatility, 72, 86, 143, 158, 165,
  168–169
Volume, 126, 203, 255
Volume indicators, 171–173, 171*f*

W
Wedges, in reversal patterns, 189–190,
  189*f*

Weekly charts, 229
White candlestick pattern:
   bullish long white candlestick,
      281f
   neutral, 288f
   neutral short white candlestick,
      288f
Wilder, J. Welles, 167
Wilder, Welles, 168
Williams, Bill M., 214
Winning trades, 106

Wrath, 104–105
Writers (of options), 242

X
XpressFX.com, 42, 43

Y
Yen carry trade, 139–140

Z
Zero interest rates, 138

About the Author

James Dicks is president and CEO of a group of financial companies, including PremierTrade, LLC. He founded FOREX Made Easy, the largest introducer of spot retail FOREX customers in the United States. Dicks is from Orlando, Florida. For more information, visit www.JamesDicks.com.